WHO'S YOUR PADDY?

NATION OF NEWCOMERS: IMMIGRANT HISTORY AS AMERICAN HISTORY
General Editors: Matthew Jacobson and Werner Sollors

Who's Your Paddy?

*Racial Expectations and the Struggle
for Irish American Identity*

Jennifer Nugent Duffy

NEW YORK UNIVERSITY PRESS

New York and London

NEW YORK UNIVERSITY PRESS
New York and London
www.nyupress.org

References to Internet websites (URLs) were accurate at the time of writing.
Neither the author nor New York University Press is responsible for URLs that
may have expired or changed since the manuscript was prepared.

CIP tk
New York University Press books are printed on acid-free paper,
and their binding materials are chosen for strength and durability.
We strive to use environmentally responsible suppliers and materials
to the greatest extent possible in publishing our books.

Manufactured in the United States of America

10 9 8 7 6 5 4 3 2 1

Also available as an ebook

CONTENTS

ACKNOWLEDGMENTS

I wish to thank many people who helped me develop this project over several years. First and foremost, I thank Adam Green, whose unwavering encouragement and patience gave me the confidence to embark on this journey. Lisa Duggan, Faye Ginsburg, Arlene Davila, and Andrew Ross were incredibly generous with their time and suggestions. David Slocum extended so many wonderful opportunities in New York University's Graduate School of Arts and Science and the Center for Teaching Excellence. In these endeavors I had the good fortune to work with Barbara Abad, who provided great professional guidance. I owe my biggest thanks to where it all began. I must acknowledge Anne Gevlin, who first inspired me to become a history teacher, and extend a special thanks to Mark Naison for nurturing my intellectual curiosity about Irish bars and providing steadfast support throughout my career.

My wonderful colleagues at NYU read several drafts of this project at different stages, including Michael Palm, Leigh Claire Le Berge, Dawn Peterson, Diego Benegas Loyo, Ipek Celik, John Patrick Leary, Maggie Clinton, Naomi Schiller, and Sarah Nash. I am particularly grateful to Madala Hilaire, who provided administrative support and friendship. At Western Connecticut State University, Wynn Gadcar-Wilcox, Joshua Rosenthal, Burton Peretti, Marcy May, Kevin Gutzman, Eden Knudsen, Edward Hagan, and Margaret Murray (my sister from another borough!) offered many valuable comments and suggestions. Steve Ward shed new light on neoliberalism. Leslie Lindenauer, Kate Allocco, and Michael Nolan have shared great camaraderie and humor. This project also was supported by a Reassigned Time for Research Grant and encouragement from the School of Arts and Sciences, particularly Linda Vaden-Goad and Abbey Zink. At Haas Library, Jennifer O'Brien and Brian Stevens were incredibly resourceful. I also thank the staffs of the Tamiment Library, the Westchester County Historical Society, and the Yonkers Riverfront Library, especially John Favareau for his help with local sources.

It was a great pleasure to work with Eric Zinner and the staff of NYU Press, including Ciara McLaughlin and Alicia Nadkarni. Suggestions from the anonymous reviewers truly made this a better book, and I wish to thank Rachel Ida Buff for her generous comments and collegiality. I am quite honored that *Who's Your Paddy?* is part of Nation of Newcomers, a series that I respect and admire. I am especially beholden to Matthew Frye Jacobson for his tremendous interest and support.

My family and friends always believed in me, especially when I had doubts, and never once asked, "So when are you going to finish?" Many thanks to Seamus, Nora, Jimmy, and Sean Nugent, the Boyles (and the Boylettes), and the Dundalk Duffys. Karen Lizzo and Carly Yezzi extended many wonderful Friday afternoon reprieves. Thanks also to Allison Watson, my longest and dearest friend.

I may never find the right words to thank my partner, Niall Duffy, whose unfailing love and great humor sustained this work.

Finally, I am forever indebted to the many people who shared their time and offered generous answers to my never-ending questions about being Irish in Yonkers.

Who's Your Paddy?

Irish Immigrant Generations in Greater New York

"I was never racist until I came to this country," I was told by John, an Irish immigrant newcomer to Yonkers, New York, in the early spring of 1996. This nineteen-square-mile city of 200,000, which shares southern and eastern borders with the Bronx in New York City, gained national notoriety in the 1980s when its home-owning white ethnic majority resisted the desegregation of public schools and housing. Shortly thereafter, young and largely undocumented Irish immigrants began arriving in this racially tense locale in increasing numbers. The parallel movement of Irish bars onto McLean Avenue in southeast Yonkers met resistance from the neighborhood's homeowners, who claimed that an increased bar presence, like the presence of public housing, would cause property values to plummet. Though they lost their bitter battle against federally integrated neighborhoods, longtime residents were successful in their fight against bars, as the city council ratified a moratorium on future bar construction in 1996. A noticeably heightened police presence was dispatched to quell potential bar-related trouble. Conflicts between Yonkers police officers and Irish bar patrons ensued, prompting allegations of police brutality, which in one case resulted in a federal indictment against two police officers for violating the civil rights of three Irish immigrants in their custody. During the trial, defense attorneys called attention to the common Irish ancestry of both parties to dispel allegations made in the Irish American press that the incident was motivated by ethnic bias.[1]

At the time of the Yonkers bar moratorium, I was a master's student, and this local Irish bar conflict provided the basis for research on social movements in the United States. Over the course of that spring, I interviewed an array of people associated with this controversy, including homeowners, police officers, local politicians, and Irish immigrant bar owners, as well as their patrons. When I interviewed John, we initially discussed the harassment of Irish immigrant bar patrons by the Yonkers police, but our conversation turned to other topics, including the challenges posed by undocumented immigrant life in the United States. When I asked John to reflect on the most striking difference between living in the Republic of Ireland and the United States, he cited not wages, food, or weather but his newfound distain for "niggers," a word, he assured me, that he never used before coming to America. One bar proprietor angered by the increased Yonkers police presence also mentioned race when discussing this local controversy. He defended his right to operate a bar by declaring, "We don't collect welfare; the Irish built this country." His reference to welfare recipients (publicly imagined as nonwhite) stressed Irish racial fitness, but to no avail. While my research focused on the parallels between this conflict and the city's desegregation controversy a decade earlier, I was intrigued by these references to race. Only later did I begin to locate these race-conscious sentiments within a larger sociohistorical process within the United States.

This book examines how Irish immigrants have been, and continue to be, socialized around race and become race-conscious subjects in the United States. While I am not the first to consider the relationship between race and immigrant incorporation within the larger U.S. collective, this study traces how Irish race consciousness evolved over the nineteenth century and how this historical transformation resonates in contemporary American life. The sentiments of these immigrants suggest that disparaging people of color is a crucial component of this race consciousness, but it is by no means the sole element. In the context of nineteenth-century British colonialism and U.S. racial slavery, racial boundaries were determined by respectable households organized around a specific race, class, and gender order. In other words, they were racially homogeneous, middle-class households anchored in heterosexual marriages between hardworking male wage earners and family-rearing wives. Furthermore, these households espoused the Protestant faith. Households organized in this particular manner demonstrated racial competence but also loyalty to the white race.

The working-class, Catholic Irish (as well as many others) fell short of these standards, or what I call "racial expectations." Caricatures of the apelike, drunk, dirty, lazy, and potentially violent "Paddy," both in Great Britain and in the United States, epitomized the racialization of the Irish as a separate, inferior race. The challenges posed by a heterogeneous population within the United States, however, permitted the Irish to respond to this "racial hazing" over time, by claiming adherence to the same standards of order, hard work, family, faith, and loyalty that been used to assess their own racial fitness: they affixed white racial expectations to being "Irish." Learning to stress their racial aptitude in this particular manner is how the Irish became race-conscious subjects in the United States. Some might use "stereotyping" to describe how dominant groups mark and marginalize those who are different, but this term evokes an imposed outcome and fails to communicate how groups like the Irish responded to their racialization. Instead, I prefer "racial hazing," as this phrase better conveys the concept of race as an uneven *process*.

Scholars typically understand race and ethnicity as socially constructed categories, yet most people see ethnic and racial membership in terms of inherited traits. Sociologist Mary C. Waters, however, has argued that whites have greater freedom than people of color to choose their ethnic identity.[2] In this study, when I refer to race, I do so through the lens of my subjects, whereby membership in a white race endows certain biological and superior traits. At the same time, I understand Irish ethnicity as largely a chosen identity. When I discuss race as a process, I signify how the Irish began to define and defend their membership in a supposedly advanced, white race, but in ethnic terms. In other words, when they chose to publicly define and defend themselves as Irish, they did so with racial traits that were understood specifically as white, and exceptional. Therefore, in this study, when I discuss Irishness and whiteness, I understand these representations of ethnicity and race as interconnected and inseparable social categories.

Irish adaptation of white racial expectations was not merely a reactionary measure but also a benchmark for Irish American identity. As a result of this transformation, the Irish in the United States were then *expected* to be orderly—that is middle-class, married heterosexuals with families and distant from those perceived as racially inept. They were supposed to be hardworking and loyal as well as religious devotees, typically of the Catholic faith. Indeed, many are well acquainted with these supposedly Irish traits. Irishness and the Catholic faith often are understood as one and the same identity, and popular representations of the "fighting Irish" speak to Irish loyalty, often by way of military service to the United States. It is precisely because these traits are so thoroughly associated with the Irish in popular discourse that I am interested particularly in other, less contemplated components, such as race, class, and gender. I also wish to stress how these purportedly Irish traits are neither random nor inevitable, but together correspond specifically to Irish encounters with race and empire in the nineteenth century, both how they were seen and how they came to see themselves over time.

That the Irish continue to stress their racial fitness in the United States by way of these traits is how I have come to understand Irishness as a race-based *tradition*. "Good Paddies" uphold this tradition, while "bad Paddies" undermine it. Some may object to my use of the term "Paddy," as in my delineation between good Paddies and bad Paddies, as I distinguish between those who do or do not meet the racial expectations for being Irish. The Irish Paddy racial caricature was used to marginalize the Irish both in nineteenth-century U.S. society and under British colonial rule well until the twentieth century. As a result, many are offended by any invocation of Paddy, particularly Irish Americans around St. Patrick's Day.[3] But the experience of racialization epitomized by the Irish Paddy resonates in contemporary Irish American life in many interesting and unexpected ways. Therefore, the term is quite useful in my analysis. At the same time, I do not want to suggest that bad Paddies who challenge Irishness as a race-based tradition are somehow more genuine or legitimate than good Paddies who uphold this convention. Instead, I use these terms to underscore how Irish marginalization under both British and U.S. regimes fostered a social identity that historically marginalized, and continues to marginalize, other people, even seemingly Irish ones.

The city of Yonkers, New York, is an ideal setting in which to explore the complexities of Irishness as a race-based tradition because different cohorts of Irish Americans reside here. "Irish American," however, is a rather broad term that could refer to anyone in the United States of Irish ancestry. So as to better grasp the textures among the Yonkers Irish, I think of them as belonging to distinct groups: *assimilated Irish ethnics*, those whose ancestors arrived in Yonkers in the middle to late nineteenth century; *Irish white flighters*, those who left Ireland during the 1950s and early 1960s and made the "white flight" from the Bronx and Upper Manhattan to Yonkers in the 1970s; and *Irish newcomers*, the "new" Irish who left Ireland in the 1980s and made their way to Yonkers beginning in the early 1990s, and the "newer" Irish who continued to arrive from Ireland, migrating directly to Yonkers albeit in smaller numbers. This latest generation of Irish immigrants has settled largely in southeast Yonkers; as a result, this section of the city has been called "Little Ireland."[4]

Without the same access to legal residency, well-paying unionized work, and homeownership, class sets largely undocumented Irish newcomers apart from their predecessors and shapes how they encounter Irishness as a race-based tradition in the United States. Because of their precarious legal status, they are not and cannot be as invested in good Paddy values of hard work, loyalty, and family espoused by assimilated Irish ethnics and Irish white flighters. Instead, they tend to engage in behaviors such as hard drinking, work absenteeism, and casual sexual encounters. There are, however, consequences to these bad Paddy digressions. Once a thriving industrial city, Yonkers witnessed not only the loss of major manufacturing and middle-class residents in the decades following World War II but also the deliberate segregation of African American and Latino residents in public housing constructed solely on the city's southwest side.[5] The city's long history of contentious class and increasingly race politics ensured that the arrival of working-class Irish immigrants would not go unnoticed. Their departure from assimilated Irish ethnics and Irish white flighters, moreover, would be accentuated and managed by neoliberal policies more broadly.

By "neoliberalism" I refer to economic policies at the national and local level that channel public resources away from social services like schools, public housing, and welfare in the name of promoting economic growth and government efficiency. Though neoliberal polices have evolved over several decades, they take shape in cities by way of tax subsidies for private corporations and consumers to promote development in economically depressed and often crime-plagued areas and are usually accompanied by aggressive or "zero tolerance" policing to assure potential developers and consumers that their investments are safe.[6] This study is in line with the growing literature on how neoliberal urban redevelopment models, though shrouded in promises of growth, actually accentuate existing inequality.[7] While widening disparities in wealth, this neoliberal shift also has weakened civic commitment to collective well-being and responsibility. As an example, these policies have clearly sharpened disparities among the Yonkers Irish. They have promoted the racial hazing of undocumented Irish newcomers by their Irish contemporaries, the disparate treatment of good Paddies and bad Paddies under local redevelopment initiatives in the city of Yonkers, and the adoption of a race-conscious and arguably racist lobbying agenda in the national debate over immigration reform. Attention to these different outcomes offers neoliberalism as more than mere policy but as a condition of everyday life, which is all the more punctuated in a setting like Yonkers. Critical examinations of neoliberal urban redevelopment models typically focus on larger cities such as New York or Los Angeles, but attention to a midsize city such as Yonkers allows us to better understand how citizens more acutely bear the consequences of these policies. And while many former industrial cities would like to replicate the purported success of redevelopment strategies in larger cities, they are more likely to consider Yonkers, a city they more likely resemble. Because the costs are heightened and the city's redevelopment plan is more likely to be replicated elsewhere, a critical examination of Yonkers is all the more pressing.

How, then, does this neoliberal context shape how Irish immigrant newcomers encounter Irishness as a race-based tradition? Because many are not, and cannot be, invested in hard work, family, or loyalty to the United States, do they learn to stress their racial fitness by becoming enthusiastic guardians of America's racial order? Because diverse peoples—Native Americans, African slaves, and heterogeneous Europeans—were present at its inception, the United States adapted a more flexible criterion for white racial fitness that could include Irish Catholics. At the same time, white racial homogeneity became all the more closely safeguarded in the United States, resulting in a "bipolar racial order" whereby a "national ideology," anthropologist Aihwa Ong explains, "projects worthy citizens as inherently white." Not only the Irish but all newcomers to the United States must navigate this specific construction of racial difference.[8] The global flows of goods, media images, people, and ideologies, in addition to Ireland's own troubled history with social difference, would make it difficult to suggest that recent Irish immigrants arrive in the United States unfamiliar with racial difference or racism. In this neoliberal context of heightened policing, staggering wealth disparities, and subsequent downturns in housing, employment, and capital markets, in both the Republic of Ireland and the United States, Irish newcomers learn to disparage racial ineptitude and blackness specifically, in ways they perceive to be novel.

This study also is interested in how the good Paddy Irish model reaches beyond the Yonkers Irish. Neoliberal policies are advanced through an ideology of "color blindness" and promise to erase existing inequality along lines of race and ethnicity. Under neoliberalism's guise, any consumer who espouses market-oriented values and choices such as efficiency and private investment can accumulate wealth. In reality, these policies keep white structures of power intact, and therein resides their appeal.[9] While purportedly color-blind, the language of neoliberalism is color-coded. In this current climate, demonized "welfare recipients" and "illegal aliens," for example, serve as a proxy for Black and Latino, while Irishness serves as a stand-in for white racial fitness. Everyday practices, local Yonkers policy, and national immigration agendas perpetuate the good Paddy model for Irishness. In stressing Irish racial fitness, working-class communities of color appear more racially inept and in need of zero tolerance policing as well as the so-called progress promised by unfettered privatization and a dismantled welfare state. The good Paddy Irish model, therefore, serves this larger "racial project."[10]

Attention to race is particularly pressing given the election of President Barack Obama as evidence of a "color-blind" or "postracial" American society. This racial ideology, as it often is used politically by the Right, attributes race-based structural inequalities to individual irresponsibility and cultural deficiencies and has been used to dismantle race-based practices such as affirmative action. According to this rhetoric, race is socially and politically divisive in the United States solely because of race-conscious agitation emanating from communities of color. While many "color-blind realists," as they have been called, wish race simply would go away, my project challenges this larger trend, calling attention instead to the ways many whites inhabit a race-conscious identity on an everyday basis.[11] More important, my study aims to expand how we understand race itself, both its articulation and its range, by illustrating how the Yonkers Irish grapple with race in an uneven and differentiated fashion.

At the same time, my work intervenes in scholarly debates about the Irish in the United States. Scholars traditionally understand the Irish, and European immigrants more generally, within the context of nineteenth-century migration from Europe and rely primarily on "ethnicization," a model tracing the restructuring of ethnic symbols, boundaries, and affiliations over time, whereby renegotiated ethnic boundaries are incorporated into equally dynamic shifts in what it means to be American.[12] Labor historians David Roediger and Noel Ignatiev radically challenged this paradigm in their consideration of race and the incorporation of European immigrants in the United States. Specifically, Ignatiev has examined how the Irish "became white," that is, how apelike caricatures of the Irish and comparisons with African Americans in popular culture dissipated by the turn of the century; Roediger has traced how working-class Irish men increasingly articulated a specifically white identity as they engaged in progressively racist behavior. By looking to immigrants specifically, these studies underscored the social construction of race, how racial ideologies are not innate but learned, and how racial identities and associations are not fixed but instead change over time. While these approaches to race were particularly insightful, inspiring a new field of inquiry that increasingly has been called "whiteness studies," they also raised important questions.[13] Favorable treatment of the Irish under U.S. immigration law prompted some to ask whether the Irish were ever seen really as "nonwhite," and the approach of European immigration scholars more generally prompts uncertainty about the ethnic identity of the men in Roediger's and Ignatiev's studies. Did "Irish" play a supporting role to their new-found "white" identity? Or did their newfound racial identity supplant and replace their Irish identity? And while their work adds new depth to our understanding of working-class Irish men in the nineteenth century, what about their female counterparts? How did they encounter race and articulate a race-conscious identity in the United States?

Developments in postcolonial studies, and the work of feminist scholars in particular, can begin to answer these questions. Ann Laura Stoler and Anne McClintock have shown how full white racial membership, as it was defined within the larger context of nineteenth-century nation-building, was determined by domestic standards, or "respectable" households.[14] When we locate racial boundaries here, in the race-, class-, and gender-coded values of order, family, hard work, faith, and loyalty to the United States, we can begin to understand how the working-class Catholic Irish, though treated favorably under U.S. immigration law, also were subject to racial hazing by way of apelike caricatures. Though they had the skin color necessary for naturalization, they were lacking in other racial standards, namely, class and religion. When we think of racial boundaries in terms of domesticity, rather than solely in terms of skin color, or access to race-based structures of power, we can better consider the malleability of race and how the Irish could utilize these standards to articulate their ethnic identity in the United States. In other words, these domestic standards allow us to better consider the ways in which racial and ethnic identities converge, how ethnicity is informed by larger racial meanings, and how race consciousness involves more than racist sentiment and behavior. At the same time, the very domestic nature of these standards brings Irish women, who typically toiled in respectable American homes, into the scope of analysis. These domestic racial standards, which address the shortcomings in previous whiteness scholarship, also present their own challenges in regard to the Irish.

While the domestic standards that governed racial boundaries were imagined specifically in terms of "black" and "white," I am quite hesitant to use "blackness" or "quasi-black" or "nonwhite" to describe how the Irish fell short of white racial expectations. These terms are confusing, given the typically fair complexion of the Irish, but they are equally troublesome, as they have the potential to obscure the treatment accorded those with darker skin under empire. Referring to the

Irish in these terms flattens distinctions between the Irish and African experiences, for example, under both British and American regimes. Discussing racial boundaries solely within a white/black binary also hides the complexities of racial exchanges, how the "others" created by these standards also were quite literally schooled in and attempted to adapt these same racial standards imagined specifically as white. Racial others, after all, needed racial potential to be incorporated within larger imperial agendas. As a result of these concerns, I discuss racial boundaries with terms such as "racial aptitude" and "racial incompetence."

While examinations of the Irish in U.S. immigration history typically focus on ethnicity, rather than race, the same cannot be said of cultural studies. Recent studies of contemporary Irish American identity stress the ways in which Irishness is inseparable from white racialness. Within the interdisciplinary work of Diane Negra, Catherine Eagan, and Lauren Onkey, Irishness is not only transnational but profoundly dynamic, intersecting with other social categories of race, class, and gender. This study, therefore, seeks to reconcile their insights into Irish American identity with historical examinations of Irish immigrant generations in the United States. And in doing so, I heed Eithne Luibheid's call for scholarship on the Irish that explores the relationship between race and migration across time and space.[15]

At the same time, my work falls into the "second wave" of whiteness scholarship, a field that has been attentive particularly to how class shapes the powers and privileges associated with white skin. These studies have demonstrated how poor whites have been marginalized historically in U.S. society and American popular culture. More important, scholars such as John Hartigan Jr. have captured the ways in which intragroup relations shape the boundaries of whiteness.[16] Related to my hesitation to use terms such as "nonwhite" to describe the Irish, I equally am weary of a trend in this field. Such focused attention to class marginalization is positioned to conflate the experiences of "white trash" and working-class communities of color and suggest that class subordination supplants racial privilege. While class surely limits the racial privilege enjoyed by undocumented Irish newcomers, my study is deliberately attentive to how it does not render it obsolete.

To successfully uncover how the race-conscious good Paddy Irish model evolved historically and how it resonates in contemporary Irish

American life, my study equally is a methodological departure from previous studies of the Irish. This project juxtaposes both historical and ethnographic analysis. Such an approach underscores the long trajectory of racial socialization as a process unbound by the nineteenth century. Because of the long history of Irish migration to the United States, no other group is as uniquely positioned to demonstrate the continuity between race and Americanization over time. Furthermore, an interdisciplinary methodology better reveals the complexity of this process. When they are examined only historically, Irish immigrants move in a linear trajectory, becoming more assimilated and progressively racist over time. Ethnography, however, better conveys the instability of race and how Irish immigrants contemplate and challenge race-conscious identity in the United States. At the same time, my use of qualitative, rather than quantitative, methods to study race is deliberate. While few whites express racist sentiments publicly, in surveys or opinion polls, for example, recent scholarship reveals how their sentiments diverge considerably in private, in everyday stories and interviews, especially among other whites. As a result, in a society that claims to be color-blind and postracial, the "richness of data," according to sociologist Krysten Myers, "can best be achieved through qualitative methods."[17]

Therefore, in addition to archival research, this study is supported by more than two years of ethnographic fieldwork, both participant observation in various sites associated with the Yonkers Irish and extended taped interviews. I made regular visits to an array of places associated with the Irish in Yonkers: the Yonkers St. Patrick's Day parade and dinner; St. Patrick's Day celebrations in local public schools, Catholic parishes, and Irish bars and restaurants; meetings of various Irish cultural organizations, as well as their sponsored events, including golf outings, picnics, and dinner dances; fund-raisers sponsored by or organized in support of a member of the Yonkers Irish community; other Irish businesses such as delis, butchers, and gift shops; Irish football matches played by adults and children (both male and female); educational programs sponsored by various Irish ethnic organizations, including Irish step-dancing and music classes for children, Irish history, music, and Gaelic classes for adults, homeless outreach, yoga, and special group gatherings targeted at "moms and tots" or senior citizens. Additionally, I attended weekly meetings and events sponsored by the Irish Lobby for

Immigration Reform. My informants were recruited largely from contacts made in these sites.[18] My fieldwork additionally was sustained by reading national Irish American newspapers sold in Yonkers, especially the *Irish Echo* and the *Irish Voice*.

I was able to access these sites largely because of my personal ties to different cohorts of Yonkers Irish. My parents are Irish white flighters who emigrated from Ireland in the 1960s and moved to Yonkers in the late 1970s. As a child, I visited Ireland regularly and was enrolled both in Irish step-dancing and traditional Irish music lessons for many years. My experience with Irish newcomers began in the 1980s when several of my Irish cousins arrived undocumented in New York. Through these contacts, I socialized in Irish immigrant bars in the Bronx and Yonkers in the 1990s and made friends with many Irish newcomers. My contact with the city's assimilated Irish ethnics, whose ties to the city of Yonkers reach back to the nineteenth century, stems from bartending for more than a decade in my family's bar in northwest Yonkers. Through my interactions with these Irish groups, I became aware of the many distinct notions of "Irish" that coexisted within the same city. Despite introducing myself as a graduate student conducting research on the Irish in Yonkers, I was often referred to as "Seamus and Nora's daughter" or "that bartender from Nugent's," or was told by many Irish newcomers that they recognized me from the neighborhood. Because of that familiarity, I believe people were willing to talk about being Irish in Yonkers. To protect the identity of my informants, I have created pseudonyms and composites of both people and events. Given the political momentum at both local and national levels to criminalize undocumented immigrants, I feel it is necessary to protect not only my informants—many of whom are or were undocumented—but also other people, including the assimilated Irish ethnics and Irish white flighters, with whom they may come in contact.[19]

This study begins with the history of Yonkers. Chapter 1 traces the city's unfettered industrial growth in the nineteenth century and concomitant loss of manufacturing in the decades following World War II. I also examine the ugly desegregation controversy waged during the 1980s, in the name of protecting property value, that nearly emptied the city's coffers. This chapter considers how Yonkers's long-standing competition with New York City for new business and investment has been waged at the cost of accentuating class and race inequality. Chapter 2 examines the histories of assimilated Irish ethnics, Irish white flighters, and Irish newcomers in Yonkers. This chapter is attentive to the conditions in both Ireland and the United States surrounding each generation of migrants and traces the evolution of the good Paddy model for Irishness as well as the bad Paddy detraction from it. Chapter 3 examines the contentious politics that occurred when the equally contentious historical trajectories of the Irish and the city of Yonkers collided. I look specifically to Irish bar politics, to the mass-produced "Guinness" pub and its good Paddy appeal, imagined as part of a larger $3.1 billion agreement to lure new investment in southwest Yonkers, and the policing of bad Paddy Irish immigrant bars in southeast Yonkers beginning in the 1990s. In tracing the separate treatment of Irish bars, and by extension Irish people, this chapter shows how neoliberal policies of aggressive privatization and policing accentuate disparities among the Yonkers Irish.

Everyday interactions between the Yonkers Irish are the focus of chapter 4. This chapter considers how Irish racial expectations get communicated in an array of cultural practices associated with Yonkers's assimilated Irish ethnics and Irish white flighters. These displays, which reinforce the good Paddy construction of the Irish as orderly, hardworking, family-oriented, and loyal, legitimatize neoliberal polices in Yonkers that will displace working-class and working-poor communities of color. At the same time, this chapter considers how the larger neoliberal order that is governed by zero tolerance policing encourages the racial hazing of undocumented Irish newcomers. Chapter 5 then turns to Irish newcomers in Yonkers, both new and newer Irish immigrants and how they interact with the good Paddy Irish model. By underscoring their voices, this chapter illustrates how a precarious legal status encourages indifference to the benchmarks for Irishness in the United States, but also certitude regarding America's bipolar racial order.

Chapter 6 follows the Irish Lobby for Immigration Reform (ILIR), which organized in December 2005 to "legalize the Irish." I maintain that calls for a zero tolerance approach to immigration at both the national and the state level encouraged this organization to adopt a race-conscious and racist lobbying agenda, and to work undocumented Irish immigrants into good Paddies. Race politics surrounding immigration both in the United States and in the Republic of Ireland,

Map I.1. Map of Yonkers, NY. Map data (c) 2013 Google.

however, stalled efforts to change the legal status of the undocumented Irish. And with severe downturns in both nations' economies—the former beginning in 2007 and the latter in 2008—their legal status remains ever the more precarious.

Ultimately, my analysis of the Yonkers Irish shows that there is more to being Irish American than the ubiquitous green beer and shamrocks around St. Patrick's Day. Attention to how one must be a particular kind of Irish person speaks to the conditions required of being "Irish" but also of being "American." Hard work, loyalty, religious faith, and heterosexual family are the standards by which the racial fitness for all groups is assessed. Since its inception, the United States has imagined itself as a white nation. As a result, communities of color are always suspect and must perform a hyperadherence to these standards.[20] The Irish encounter these standards differently, but they encounter them, nonetheless, and thus this study speaks more broadly to the conditions that establish belonging and alienage in the United States.

1

From City of Hills to City of Vision

The History of Yonkers, New York

> No place feels quite like Yonkers, rough-hewn and jagged,
> a working-class bridge between the towers of Manhattan to
> the south, and the pampered hills of Westchester County
> to the north. . . . In sum, there is a defiant nostalgia here,
> the hallmark of a place that used to be something else, and
> that, too, is apt. During an era that no one still living actually
> remembers, but everyone seems to yearn for, Yonkers was a
> great city.
>
> Lisa Belkin, *New York Timwes* , 1991

In 1969, after two weeks of public hearings, a New York State Commission of Investigation discovered a private carting deal with Mafia leaders that cost the city of Yonkers approximately $1 million a year. When asked for his reaction, the Yonkers Chamber of Commerce president shrugged off the charges by stating, "All cities have their scandals." In his report, Paul J. Curran, the commission's chairman, admonished the city for being plagued with "intimidation, servility, favoritism, mismanagement, inefficiency and waste."[1] This incident might very well be the basis for the familiar Yonkers epithet, "a city of hills where nothing is on the level." Though this characterization clearly is meant to disparage Yonkers, the city's hilly geography is a suitable metaphor for understanding its complicated history.

Advancements in steamboat and railroad technology and the subsequent growth in business and population marked Yonkers's ascent from small agricultural community to the "City of Gracious Living" by the end of the nineteenth century. Despite an influx of new residents and housing spurts in suburban tracts of north and east Yonkers during the 1920s and 1950s, the staggering loss of industry and jobs in the decades after World War II deeply wounded the city. These trends, coupled with a bitter battle during the 1980s over the desegregation of its public schools and housing, sent the Yonkers into a downward spiral from which it has only begun to recover. In 2004, the city unveiled one of the largest redevelopment programs in the New York metropolitan area, a $3.1 billion agreement in projected improvements that include a minor-league baseball stadium, retail and office space, and luxury waterfront housing. These projects, coupled with the new appellation "City of Vision," suggest that Yonkers is not only on the mend but also on the rise.[2]

Heeding the call of "new suburban" historians such as Kevin Kruse and Thomas Sugrue, this chapter is attentive to Yonkers's relationship with other communities in Westchester County, as well as its long-standing competition for new business and investment with neighboring New York City. These exchanges have been waged at the cost of accentuating class and increasingly racial inequality.[3] To this end, this chapter narrates several episodes of economic pursuit that shaped the city's history: unfettered industrial growth in the nineteenth century and the concomitant loss of manufacturing in the decades after World War II, federal and local housing policy, as well as the ugly desegregation controversy waged during the 1980s, in the name of protecting property value, that nearly emptied the city's coffers. Together these periods reveal a long history of indifference in Yonkers to members of its working class. The city of Yonkers is hardly alone in its quest for economic development, but because it is smaller than New York City, and less politically powerful than its wealthier and influential suburban neighbors in Westchester County, the costs borne by its residents are more acute. As I relate events that accentuate inequality, I place the Yonkers Irish within that contentious history (although each cohort will be discussed at greater length in the chapters that follow). At the same time, I seek to contextualize the marked arrival of working-class Irish immigrants in Yonkers during the early 1990s as the city's plans for redevelopment began to accelerate.

Becoming the City of Gracious Living

In 1609, when his *Half Moon* sailed along the river that later would be named after him, Henry Hudson stopped at the site of what is now southwest Yonkers and encountered a Native American settlement of

Rechgawawanck Indians. The area was called "Nappeckamack," or "trap fishing place," because of the plentiful fishing offered by the nearby Nepperhan (later Saw Mill) River. The bay provided fresh water and a safe dock for canoes, and the village itself was located on high ground, making the vicinity safe from attacks launched from the nearby Hudson River.[4] After receiving a grant from the Dutch West India Company, a young lawyer named Adriaen Van Der Donck purchased the land from Chief Tacharew in 1646. Shortly thereafter, he built a plantation and sawmill on the banks of the Nepperhan. Despite an untimely death in 1655, the area still bears his name. Called "de jonkheer," or young gentleman, "De Jonkheer's Landt" evolved into what we now call Yonkers.[5]

Frederick Philipse, who purchased much of Van Der Donck's land in 1672, is thought to be the real founder of Yonkers. His sprawling estate, which became the Manor of Philipsborough by royal charter in 1693, remained in his family for more than a hundred years. Philipse's home, Manor Hall, was built in 1682 and still stands. The U.S. government later confiscated surrounding property because his descendants had been loyal to the British during the American Revolution. Much of the land was sold to former tenants, who made a livelihood from the local farming of apples, peaches, and cucumbers, the latter earning Yonkers the nickname of "pickle port."[6] In addition, abundant waterpower offered by the confluence of the Hudson and Saw Mill Rivers made possible the cultivation of rye, wheat, corn, and oats. At the same time that fresh produce was being shipped out of Yonkers, many people passed through the small community by way of the stagecoach that began to travel between New York City and Albany in 1785. Here letters and mail were dropped off, horses were changed, and weary travelers found refreshment at the Indian Queen, where vegetables from the keeper's garden supplied the food for simple, wholesome meals. Despite being an important rest stop, this village of little more than 1,100 remained primarily a community of small shops, mills, taverns, and farms into the early decades of the nineteenth century.[7]

Steamboats and railroads changed Yonkers in the years that followed as reliable transportation facilitated the growth of New York City's periphery. One contemporary noted in 1855 that suburban enclaves were "springing up like mushrooms . . . in Yonkers and other places on the Hudson River."[8] Five steamboat liners were stopping daily in Yonkers en route from New York to Albany by 1840. The completion of the Hudson River Railroad in 1849 brought trains into Yonkers three times a day. As a result, the village of Yonkers grew from 1,365 in 1810 to 11,484 by 1860.[9] The increased connectivity with surrounding areas, coupled with the availability of waterpower, brought a new cohort of industrialists to Yonkers who sought an alternative to growing land and labor costs in nearby New York City. Some in Yonkers not only welcomed, but felt entitled to, this development. One local booster declared, "We are reasserting our right, as the natural suburb of NYC, and as the most beautiful residential property of the world, to a large share of the outgrowth of the city."[10] Yonkers soon became home to the refining of sugar and the manufacture of silk and furniture. The city's better-known industrial wares included Alexander Smith's carpets, Elisha Graves Otis's elevators, Habirshaw's cable and wire, and John T. Waring's hats.

The small farming village of 1,300 grew into a city of 47,931, employing 8,615 people in 387 industries over the course of a century.[11] Yonkers's promise of a "better" business climate than neighboring New York City, which meant little or no government interference and a largely unorganized labor force, spurred part of this change. This environment may have been better for industrialists, but laissez-faire did not benefit all Yonkers residents, especially its working class. The Saw Mill River, previously dammed to produce mill ponds and harness maximum waterpower, had become so polluted by the turn of the century that Mayor James Weller first ordered the destruction of their ponds. The water was redirected to an underground flume beginning in 1892.[12] Those who labored in the factories and mills often lived in substandard cold-water tenements in and around Getty Square.

With some of the oldest housing stock in the city, southwest Yonkers had its neighborhood charm. The proximity of homes and the abundance of small stores and pedestrian traffic in Getty Square created a close-knit feel, prompting many residents to refer to this area as "the village."[13] The sound of clanging trolleys in the distance added to the hum of busy streets filled with shoppers stopping to chat with neighbors and friends while children fished off the nearby piers. Notable in this working-class landscape was the presence of bars, where men could fill their pails with beer on their way to and from work in the city's many factories. Or perhaps they might sit a spell in the aptly named local

Figure 1.1. The Moquette mills at Smith Carpet, 1904. Courtesy of Yonkers
Riverfront Library, Local History Collection.

watering hole, the Port of Missing Men. That Yonkers residents liked
to drink was much to the chagrin of local resident William Anderson,
state superintendent of the Anti-Saloon League. Yonkers voted overwhelmingly against Prohibition during a statewide referendum in 1926,
and a discovery four years later revealed the city's willingness to defy
federal law. The Public Works Department found a four-inch hose that
ran underground from a brewery that was supposed to be concocting
"near beer" to a garage. Real beer actually had been traveling through
the hose en route to distributors. New York University's H. H. Sheldon
commented that the public construction of such a line would have been
an outstanding engineering feat, but its successful creation in secret was
nothing short of extraordinary.[14]

Racial and ethnic divides, nonetheless, punctuated working-class life
in the city. More than half of Yonkers's residents in 1900 were foreign-
born or the children of immigrants. Beginning in the middle of the
nineteenth century, first the Irish and later Italians, Poles, Hungarians,
and Slavs toiled in the factories and mills. A small African American

community labored in lesser-paying foundry work or service-oriented jobs.[15] An equally segmented housing market paralleled Yonkers's stratified labor market as the city's ethnic and racial groups lived in their own enclaves in and around Getty Square. Despite these constraints, minorities pioneered many firsts for the city. In 1905, John Alexander Morgan was the first African American physician to practice in Yonkers, and in 1925, Thomas Brooks became the city's first African American police officer. Eastern European Jews, who left New York City's Lower East Side for slightly larger, albeit cold-water, tenements, established Yonkers's first permanent synagogue in 1887. Together these feats were firsts not only for Yonkers but for Westchester County at large.[16]

Yonkers's wealthy industrialists, however, enjoyed greater economic and geographic mobility. They could afford to avail themselves of streetcar transportation and escape the increasing congestion and pollution of "the Square." The Victorian homes and mansions that began to dot North Broadway housed the Smith, Otis, and Waring families. Northwest Yonkers, which contained successive heights of streets with Hudson River views, soon could boast of being home to mayors and state representatives, as well as William Gibbs McAdoo, former U.S. senator and secretary of the Treasury, and Samuel J. Tilden, Democratic candidate for the U.S. presidency in 1876. And in 1888, the city hosted the first round of golf played in the United States.[17] The movement of the city's elite from the southwest to the northwest quadrant marked the first wave of suburbanization in Yonkers. Not only did the city try to entice businesses seeking less expensive land and labor costs, but Yonkers also sought New York City's wealthier residents, who were escaping the same problems associated with industrialization and urbanization that plagued Getty Square. A series of articles in the *New York Times* during the spring of 1894 touted Yonkers's infrastructure, its "high standing" schools, nineteen railway stations, and "ample" supply of "pure water" but also its music hall, twenty-one churches, and an array of clubs that identified it as a "cosmopolitan" city. Two types of New Yorkers, the series maintained, could appreciate Yonkers, "Queen City of the Hudson": the Wall Street man who enjoyed the "panoramic" commute to New York City, and the factory operator, drawn by conservative government, good police protection, and low taxes. The extension of the New York City subway system to bordering Woodlawn Heights in the

Figure 1.2. Getty Square, Yonkers, New York, 1925. Courtesy of the Westchester County Archives.

Bronx after World War I, and the opening of the Bronx River Parkway in 1923, accelerated the suburbanization of Yonkers, especially in the city's southeast region.[18]

An array of local boosters including politicians, newspaper editors, leading families, and real estate developers launched a campaign of civic promotion at the end of the nineteenth century. With the appellation "City of Gracious Living," they sought to lure a wealthier demographic to Yonkers. Park Hill exemplified the type of development desired by the city. A community planned by the American Real Estate Company, Park Hill boasted of "fresh air, extra room for children and shady lawns," of having "no foreign element," and restrictions against saloons, shops, trolleys, and manufacturing establishments.[19] The first homes were built in the early 1890s, although prospective residents could purchase lots and hire their own architects or charge the American Real Estate Company to oversee construction. In addition, the company could provide financing for any of these options. Early Park Hill residents had their own country club and could enjoy outdoor sports such as billiards and horseback riding. They did not, however, get to use the hotel, which a fire destroyed one month before its opening.[20] Though Park Hill specifically lured many American-born upper-class residents from neighboring New York City, Yonkers more generally also attracted the upwardly mobile.

After World War I, working-class southern migrants and West Indian immigrants first settled Runyon Heights, which became one of the first middle-class Black suburbs in the metropolitan region. Perhaps capitalizing on the restraints Blacks faced in the housing market, both locally and in New York City, real estate advertisements in the *Amsterdam News* boasted of nearby churches, public schools, and a short trolley ride to subway trains. Because much of the better-paying manufacturing work in Yonkers was closed to people of color, Runyon Heights became a trolley suburb of commuters to New York City. One woman recalled, "Yonkers just wasn't hiring black people, so you had to work in New York."[21] Runyon Heights, nevertheless, was an exception, as most working-class residents, both Black and white, lived within walking distance of local industry in the southwest. Residents of new suburban enclaves in northwest and southeast Yonkers usually were native-born middle-class whites. If anything, the city's efforts to attract investment, whether in the form of new industry or wealthy residents, served to accentuate the class divides that already existed. Despite local boosterism, Yonkers was, according to the Works Progress Administration's *Guide to the Empire State*, "on the east bank of the Hudson . . . a jumble of factories, mills and warehouses surrounded by the drab homes of workers [and] in attractive residential districts of eastern Yonkers [residents] have little to do with the industrial section to the west."[22]

Postwar Challenges

On the heels of industrial and early suburban growth in the late nineteenth century and early twentieth century, the Great Depression brought hard times to Yonkers. On average, 40,000 Yonkers residents received government aid each year, and 63 percent of the total population received assistance at some point during that troubled era.[23] New

Figure 1.3. View of the Palisades from Lake Avenue water tower, 1904. Courtesy of Yonkers Riverfront Library, Local History Collection.

industrial work opportunities opened for women and people of color during World War II as defense contracts issued to the city gave southwest Yonkers a badly needed economic jolt. Both Smith and Otis operated twenty-four hours a day on war orders, although Smith Carpet hired Black workers only after losing a government contract for refusing to do so. Workers at Habirshaw Cable and Wire secretly manufactured a sixty-five-mile-long hollow cable that secretly pumped 1 million gallons of gasoline daily from Great Britain to France.[24] Economic growth during World War II, however, was relatively short-lived in the city. Federal legislation meant to strengthen the U.S. economy drained southwest Yonkers of its industry and its middle class and institutionalized the vestiges of segregation that had been in place for many years.

Staggering unemployment during the Great Depression strengthened the militancy of workers in the decades to follow. The 1935 Wagner Act legalized collective bargaining as a protected right in the United States, the reverberations of which were felt in smaller manufacturing cities like Yonkers. Workers at Smith Carpet, one of city's largest employers, no longer were satisfied with the company union. They launched a series of strikes demanding Smith's recognition of the United Textiles Workers Union in the years following World War II. In response, Smith left Yonkers in 1954 for Greenville, Mississippi, where the ninety-year mainstay found newer facilities, lower taxes, and less expensive and less troublesome labor costs. These same considerations brought industry to Yonkers many decades earlier.[25] But unlike the nineteenth century, where advancements in technology and transportation enabled the movement of industry by way of steamboat seventeen miles north from Manhattan to Yonkers, airplanes and automobiles in the decades after World War II allowed for a greater mobility of capital. Yonkers, like many other industrial cities in the Northeast, largely lost its manufacturing base to the American South or abroad and restructured into a service economy. With little to fill the void left by the closing of Smith, the loss of manufacturing sent southwest Yonkers into a tailspin.

In 1950, approximately 6 percent of the city's 153,000 people had been collecting unemployment; with Smith closing, nearly 6,000 more joined them.[26] More than half of Smith's employees were older than fifty, and nearly a quarter of those were over the age of sixty. Finding new employment was difficult, particularly for these older workers who had skills that were not easily transferable to other industries. Persistent unemployment quickened the movement of people from southwest Yonkers who sought work elsewhere. Already struggling businesses eventually closed. The decline was so significant that some observers remarked that one southwest neighborhood looked like a "haunted town" after the loss of its residents and retail.[27]

Furthermore, the relocation of Smith sparked the movement of other industries that now sought greater concessions from employees and the city in exchange for remaining in Yonkers. Otis Elevator, a sizable employer of 1,300, issued its first threat to leave in 1955 despite posting record sales and profits. Reflecting the anger of residents, Harry Taubin lamented in a letter to the *Herald Statesman* that "no one has had the courage to say a word against the threats that Otis is making and has made to the city and its people: If you don't do as we ask, we will not play ball, we will move."[28] Nonetheless, Yonkers eventually offered a $13.9 million package of federal, state, and local funds, cleared nine acres (which displaced sixty businesses and several hundred families), and sold the site to Otis for one-tenth of its value. Otis paid $539,000 and promised to spend $852,000 on improvements and an additional $10 million to construct a new plant, which opened in 1976, the same year the company was taken over by United Technologies.[29] Six short years later, Otis, whose elevators carried millions of people to the tops of the Woolworth, Empire State, and World Trade Center buildings in New York City, announced its plans to leave Yonkers. Despite launching a lawsuit for breach of contract, the city was not able to keep the elevator manufacturer or many other industries in southwest Yonkers.

Advancements in transportation and federal subsidies for highway construction helped move manufacturing out of southwest Yonkers, but these trends also relocated industry within the city. With the loss of its manufacturing base, Yonkers restructured into an economy anchored by service, particularly retail. This transformation did not take place in Getty Square, which was plagued by narrow, car-choked streets, old housing stock, and aging manufacturing infrastructure. With the newly constructed New York State Thruway, which cut through the center of the city and transported 25 million cars per year, new economic growth took place on undeveloped tracts of east Yonkers. Strip malls began to dot Central Avenue in northeast Yonkers, while southeast Yonkers became home to the Cross County Shopping Center, one of the largest shopping malls in the United States at its opening in May 1954 to 15,000 enthusiastic onlookers.[30] Still, the jobs these developments created typically were nonunionized and paid less than the manufacturing jobs they replaced. Indeed, 1954 was a watershed year for the city of Yonkers, as Herbert Salisbury maintained in a series of articles for the *New York Times* over the following spring. That year witnessed the loss of Smith Carpet, its oldest and largest industry in the west, the opening of new retail in the east, and the construction of a highway that added physical dimension to the once imagined but nonetheless real boundary between "old" west Yonkers and "new" east Yonkers. This divide would only intensify in coming years.[31]

Other federal programs such as the Federal Housing Authority (FHA) additionally worked to channel economic development from southwest to north and east Yonkers in the decades after World War II. The FHA created by the Federal Housing Act of 1934 was one of President Franklin

Figure 1.4. Protestors at Smith Carpet, 1954. Courtesy of Westchester County
Historical Society.

D. Roosevelt's most ambitious New Deal programs. Urban historian Kenneth T. Jackson writes that "no agency of the United States government has had a more pervasive and powerful impact on the American people over the past half-century." By insuring long-term mortgage payments made by lenders, lowering down-payment requirements, and extending the amortization of mortgages, the FHA put homeownership within the reach of many working-class Americans. Between 1934 and 1972, the percentage of American families living in owner-occupied dwellings rose from 44 percent to 63 percent.[32] This shift was felt in Yonkers particularly in the city's northwest quadrant and on its east side. Between 1940 and 1950, the population of Yonkers increased by 7 percent, but population on the east side rose by 23 percent. The pace of growth was even more pronounced in later years. The northern sector saw a population increase of 64 percent and the construction of 3,500 upscale single-family homes between 1950 and 1958. In the first quarter of 1958, Yonkers ranked fourth in the nation and second to New York City in the state with its percentage increase in building permits, hovering slightly over

115 percent.[33] In contrast, the city's population as a whole rose by only 14 percent, while the southwest quadrant lost residents.

The FHA simultaneously institutionalized bias in favor of extending loans to all-white neighborhoods and "red-lining," or denying loans to Black and mixed-race areas assumed to be in decline.[34] Working-class white ethnics were able to leave Getty Square and its environs and purchase newly constructed Cape Cods, colonials, and split-level ranches in the city's northwest and east side, while large sections of southwest Yonkers and its increasingly nonwhite residents were neglected. African American and Latino workers were moving into southwest Yonkers in greater numbers and were starting to make inroads just as the manufacturing industry was beginning to disappear. Historically, African Americans represented a small minority in Yonkers, but their numbers grew in the postwar years, as part of a larger migration of 1.5 million people dislodged by the wide-scale mechanization of agriculture in the American South. Puerto Ricans largely were newcomers to Yonkers, and like their African American counterparts, they too arrived as displaced agricultural workers.[35] Although New York City received larger numbers of these postwar migrants, their presence nonetheless was felt in Yonkers. A southwest neighborhood that was 73.6 percent native-born white, 25 percent foreign-born white, and 2 percent "Negro" in 1940 was, by 1980, 49 percent white, 31 percent Black, and 17 percent "Spanish." This neighborhood not only was more racially diverse than in years past but also was poorer; 24 percent of its families lived below the poverty level.[36]

With the hemorrhaging of well-paying manufacturing jobs that had once sustained European migrants and generations of their descendants, welfare rolls expanded in Yonkers, especially Aid to Dependent Children (ADC). Local welfare offices were ill equipped to meet both the growing need for assistance and the increasing numbers of Spanish speakers. For the latter, the city relied largely on a local parish priest to assist with translation.[37] Welfare caseloads in Yonkers increased, not only because of greater need but also because of better access to public assistance. Prior to the 1960s many barriers prevented women, and Black women especially, from receiving full assistance under ADC. State governments administered this program, and many mandated "suitable home" policies. To this end, unwed mothers or wives of the incarcerated could be denied benefits, while those who received assistance could be subjected to home inspections for male guests. Caseworkers conducted these checks without warrants, and not uncommonly in the middle of the night. Furthermore, women could be asked questions about their sexual history; children also could be asked about their mother's relationship with men. Many states also had "employable mother" rules that prevented mothers with dependent children from refusing work if it was available. In the South, many Black women were steered to the employment office during cotton season. In addition, independent caseworkers had extraordinary discretion over the allocation of benefits. They could (and often did) withhold smaller grants for clothing and household furniture and terminate benefits without explanation or an appeal from the denied applicant.[38] In response to these policies and practices, a national welfare rights movement developed in the United States, which also touched ground in Yonkers. In 1967, the local Welfare Mothers Association waged a thirty-hour sit-in for better treatment by caseworkers and a clear breakdown of benefits mothers were entitled to by law.[39] As a result of such tactics in cities across the United States, ADC liberalized its policies, and the numbers of recipients increased both nationally and locally.

With deindustrialization and increased unemployment, poverty, and crime, Getty Square, the geographic anchor of Yonkers industry and its working class, now was mocked colloquially as "Ghetto Square."[40] Streets and homes in the vicinity increasingly were unsafe. By the mid-1960s, the "Flats," a Getty Square neighborhood of 9,000, witnessed 200 major crimes per year. At the same time, housing deteriorated, as many structures in Getty Square and its environs had been built nearly a century earlier. Housing conditions on Ravine Avenue were poor enough to merit a state hearing in 1968, as tenants in one three-story building paid twice the market rate for units with cracked walls, peeling paint, water streaks, sealed windows, and broken light fixtures.[41] Because these neighborhoods contained increasing numbers of Black and Latino residents, they were assumed to be in decline and thus were denied loans for badly needed improvements. The larger political and economic structures that shaped the conditions of Getty Square, however, typically were overshadowed by cultural explanations, legitimatized by then assistant secretary of labor Daniel Patrick Moynihan's *Report on the Negro Family* (1975). The purpose of this report was to argue for massive federal spending to create jobs for Black men, and end poverty, as well as what Moynihan called the "tangle of pathology" in female-headed households. The report's provocative language was intended to propel the administration into action, and it did influence President Johnson's War on Poverty, particularly its attempt to improve housing, education, welfare, and health; the job creation program, however, never materialized. Though the expression "culture of poverty" often is attributed to Moynihan, its origins lie with Oscar Lewis, who first used the phrase to describe poor Mexican families and later Puerto Rican households in New York City. Moynihan's report, nonetheless, had a "chilling" effect on public debate and social science research. Liberals tended to avoid addressing problems in poor Black communities, leaving conservatives to explain them in terms of dysfunctional "cultural" values and an overly generous welfare state. At the same time, *Report on the Negro Family* gave academic credence to images of poor Black families readily available in postwar America.[42]

As a result, residents of Yonkers had a new moniker for Getty Square but also a new "cultural" language for its residents. The conditions of Ghetto Square only worsened in coming years. This was at a time when there was little or no Black or Latino representation in elected office, the ranks of the police and fire departments, the board of education, and the administration of the city's public schools.[43] Yonkers and New York City, its larger bordering competitor, both lost their manufacturing base during this era. The latter, because of its status as a banking center and an array of economic-driven measures at both the state and the national level, restructured into a service economy anchored by finance and supporting industries such as accounting, public relations, and higher education.[44] The development of retail and the expansion of homeownership in Yonkers was not enough to recoup the loss of manufacturing. Sales at the Cross County Shopping Center, which was expected to generate $300,000 a year in tax revenue for the city, paled in comparison to the nearly $14 million in purchases lost with the demise of downtown Yonkers.[45] In the absence of a significant tax base, Yonkers decreased funding for its public schools and police and fire departments. In addition, the city financed years of deficits through the sale of municipal bonds during the 1970s and embarked on a plan to redevelop its waterfront into a residential and retail enclave. But as the nation faced growing inflation and an oil crisis, several remaining businesses closed in Getty Square, and in 1975 the city twice averted default when New York State employed emergency powers and put the city's finances under state control.[46]

While the economic horizon looked especially grim in southwest Yonkers, many found in north and east Yonkers a suburban retreat from parts of Upper Manhattan and the Bronx. New York City lost approximately 1 million of its white residents between 1950 and 1970. As one of the few cities in New York State to increase its population during the 1960s, Yonkers replaced Syracuse as the state's fourth-largest city by 1970.[47] Arriving in the city's post–World War II phase of suburbanization were upwardly mobile white ethnics and white immigrants—Irish, Jews, and Italians—fleeing the same forces of deindustrialization and changing racial demographics in New York City that had transformed Getty Square, but with what might be considered a greater ferocity. Although crime rose in deindustrializing cities across the United States, in New York City the murder rate rose 123 percent between 1955 and 1965, and another 137 percent between 1966 and 1973.[48] Subways and buses were covered, quite literally, in graffiti, and the city witnessed a string of riots and civil service strikes across the 1960s. The Bronx was particularly devastated in the decades to follow, losing 300 companies and one-fifth of its housing stock to unscrupulous landlords cashing in on abandoned or dilapidated buildings and low-premium fire insurance. Entire neighborhoods were leveled to make room for the Cross Bronx Expressway and Triboro Bridge, and thirteen years after the riot of 1977, a twenty-block area along Tremont Avenue still had not recovered from the damage. Largely renters, white ethnics did not have deep economic ties to their neighborhoods and moved.[49] Some relocated several times within the borough, leaving the South Bronx neighborhoods of Castle Hill and Mott Haven for the Central Bronx neighborhoods of Fordham and Kingsbridge; others moved directly to Yonkers, drawn like earlier generations by suburban tracts of east Yonkers and the easy commute to New York City.

The familiar pattern of flight among white ethnics from New York City and the geographic journey to Yonkers obscure their sometimes contentious past. Though white ethnics shared similar histories of hardship in Europe and migration to New York City, they often competed with one another for jobs, housing, and political power, which at times manifested in physical confrontation.[50] Joshua Zeitz has illustrated how these seemingly similar white ethnics held distinctly different world-views: Jews valued dissent while Catholics cherished obedience to authority, which often positioned these groups on different sides of an array of political issues. Though Irish Americans and Italian Americans shared a Catholic faith, they often lived apart not only from Jews but also from each other.[51] And when these blue-collar white ethnics arrived in Yonkers, they were not heartily welcomed. Some longtime residents lamented the "Bronxification" of the city, the increasingly blue-collar character of east Yonkers, and the addition of cooperative apartments and two-family homes in this once single-family milieu. These divides, however, would diminish over time in Yonkers, eclipsed by what George Lipsitz calls a "possessive investment in whiteness," a shared investment in and benefit from race-based housing practices by both the government and the private housing industry.[52] Both longtime middle-class and recent blue-collar white ethnic residents of suburban Yonkers would organize collectively to defend perceived racial threats to this investment in the 1980s. In doing so, they capped a long history of resistance to public housing in the city of Yonkers.

Public Housing and Urban Renewal

New Deal and postwar legislation regarding workers' rights, homeownership, and highway construction served to redistribute people and commerce within the city of Yonkers. Southwest Yonkers, once a thriving industrial sector and home to European immigrants and their descendants, now largely was poor, Black, and Latino. Undeveloped tracts of east Yonkers now accommodated strip malls, single-family homes, and upwardly mobile white ethnics. Moreover, federal and local policy pertaining to public housing placed additional strain on the growing geographic, economic, and racial divides between east and west Yonkers, a rift that pushed the city to the brink of bankruptcy in later decades.

Shortly after launching the Federal Housing Authority, the federal government took responsibility for the construction of low-cost housing via the U.S. Housing Act of 1937. President Roosevelt explained, "We are launching an attack on the slums of this country which must go forward until every American family has a decent home."[53] With a considerable amount of old housing stock in the southwest, Yonkers quickly claimed federal assistance, cleared slums, and constructed public housing in its place. The first neighborhood slated for demolition was "Little Ireland," whose "robust, fun-loving, yet law-abiding" residents resented their association with slum clearance.[54] Mulford Gardens opened in 1940 primarily to working-class and working-poor white ethnic families who had been displaced by this first public housing project. While some resented the slum characterization of their former neighborhood, Mulford Gardens undoubtedly was an improvement over the typical cold-water tenement housing that characterized much of southwest Yonkers. Many early residents were "amazed" by Mulford, its sizable rooms, its hot water, and its steam heat.[55]

Initially, the city's Municipal Housing Authority (MHA) had difficulty responding to the great demand for decent, affordable housing. When the MHA began to receive applications from the general public in 1948 for Cottage Place Gardens, its second public housing project, the early morning line of seventy-five people "more than doubled" in fifteen minutes. In fact, the city had to request additional investigators to assist with the number of applications. In its early years, public housing was intended not for the poorest of the poor but for the "cream of the poor," with potential residents screened though an elaborate point system. Once applicants met the standards for income, employment, and rent habits, as well past histories of residence, juvenile behavior, and social services, they were visited in their home and interviewed. Furthermore, within the context of larger Cold War hostilities between the United States and the Soviet Union, potential tenants had to swear that they were not members of any "subversive" organization. Many Yonkers applicants, largely white ethnic families, did not make the cut. Of the 307 personal interviews conducted by October 1948 for Cottage Place Gardens, only 148 were "apparently" eligible, as "unstable" families characterized by unemployment or juvenile delinquency or headed by a single mother routinely were denied.[56]

When construction began on Cottage Place Gardens, the city intended to reserve one of its buildings specifically for "Negroes." In 1945, the city appointed the Reverend James Clinton Haggard, pastor of Institutional African Methodist Episcopal (AME) Zion Church, to

This Was Mulford . . . .

. . . This is Mulford Now

Figures 1.5 and 1.6. Pamphlet for Mulford Gardens, circa 1930. Courtesy of
Yonkers Riverfront Library, Local History Collection.

the city's MHA, and in this capacity Haggard served as the first "Negro" on a major city board. Undoubtedly his efforts, coupled with those of the newly formed Yonkers chapter of the National Association for the Advancement of Colored People (NAACP), ensured that neither Cottage Place Gardens nor the Schlobahm Houses, which opened later in 1953, racially segregated their residents. In 1956, the Reverend Alger Adams of St. Augustine's Episcopal Church and vice-chair of the local NAACP's housing committee, praised the city for "its actions to date" in maintaining integration in its earliest public housing projects.[57] The construction of public housing in the years that followed deindustrialization and changing racial patterns in southwest Yonkers and the white suburbanization of east Yonkers were a different matter entirely.

The federal government extended its commitment to public housing with the Housing Act of 1949, which authorized the construction of 810,000 units of public housing over the following six years. Later, the Housing Act of 1954 authorized funds for "urban renewal" that cleared and replaced slums with a mix of public and private development. Scholars such as Jill Quandango and Samuel Zipp have illustrated how urban renewal projects typically destroyed more affordable housing than they created and exacerbated deindustrialization through the replacement of factories and warehouses with middle-class apartment towers, hospitals, and cultural institutions.[58] But to many of its contemporaries, urban renewal seemed to offer a possible alternative to the by-products of deindustrialization such as crime, poverty, and expanding welfare rolls, and in Yonkers it was heralded as a "new light, a new hope and a way out" and a "badly needed shot in the arm."[59]

Yonkers embarked on new public housing construction in spurts, or, as characterized by the local press, as a series of "grunts and groans." Under the Housing Act of 1949, the city received federal assistance for 750 units of public housing, but Yonkers would take nine years to finally approve construction sites. And while the city received funds to start urban renewal in 1957, Yonkers forfeited $813,000 because it failed to act for six years.[60] Much of the delay was due to the controversy surrounding the location of future public housing in the city. Yonkers initially supported integrated public housing where there had been a historically small African American population in southwest Yonkers, when its manufacturing industry was fully intact. The city met fierce resistance, however, when proposing sites for newly developed suburban tracts of east Yonkers. Public housing in east Yonkers would have been more cost-effective for the city; land was readily available, so clearance and relocation problems would have been minimal. Undoubtedly, residents were concerned about the potential social costs, as public housing in southwest Yonkers was not immune to the unemployment, crime, and poverty left in the wake of Getty Square's deindustrialization. If anything, these problems were more concentrated in housing projects that historically had been home to the working class and increasingly the poor, as the screening for public housing, like ADC, was liberalized in the late 1960s. In 1968, the MHA began to consider an internal security patrol for its projects because of increasing crime.[61] More important, public housing would racially integrate this part of the city, and race was a concern explicitly raised by Yonkers residents, both Black and white.

Between 1949 and 1956, the Yonkers City Council rejected nineteen out of twenty proposed sites for public housing; the one accepted was located near existing public housing in southwest Yonkers. Although the number of racial minorities still was relatively small, homeowners voiced their racial concerns at local meetings:

> We personally prefer a public referendum with time to acquaint each and every citizen with the full facts on public housing. Where will these tenants come from? How will we provide schools? How much will it cost us over the years? What safeguards do we have against our having to absorb the overflow from Puerto Rico or Harlem? Where will the people go that will have to vacate their private homes?[62]

Residents resisted because they believed public housing would increase numbers of Blacks and Latinos, who at the time were being displaced by urban renewal projects in New York City. Faced with the difficulty of obtaining affordable housing in the Bronx and Upper Manhattan, these groups were finding that nearby Yonkers provided an alternative. There were the few who expressed support for the integration of east Yonkers. Mrs. Milton Eskie, county chairperson of the Anti-Defamation Committee of B'nai B'rith, for example, pleaded, "People fear integration but I feel it is time we took our Negro neighbors into housing outside their ghettoes." But supporters of integrated housing in east Yonkers were outnumbered. In 1957, MHA secretary director Emmett Burke voiced his frustration when he stated, "We cannot compete with the newly formed neighborhood organizations and similar pressure groups unless we rally the applicants for public housing to appear at City Hall."[63]

In 1958, the city of Yonkers finally did approve the only public housing for east Yonkers, Curran Court, a 186-unit complex for seniors on Martin Ray Place and another for families constructed in Runyon Heights, a historically African American enclave. While Black middle-class homeowners mobilized with white homeowners to stop the 335 units initially planned for the area, they were not as successful as other homeowners in east Yonkers had been; 48 units of public housing were constructed in 1960. Though they blocked the original proposal, residents believed public housing was placed there precisely because Runyon Heights was a Black, albeit middle-class, neighborhood, and they criticized the city for placing public housing solely in neighborhoods with Black residents. Edmund Austin Jr., spokesperson for the NAACP, made this clear when he stated, "We are particularly disturbed to find this project being put in a predominantly Negro area."[64]

African Americans in Yonkers not only criticized the city for its refusal to place public housing in white sections of east Yonkers but also underscored how urban renewal disproportionately affected members of its community. Urban renewal projects that began to take shape in southwest Yonkers by the 1960s displaced both Black and white residents. But Black residents faced greater difficulty finding new lodging in bordering white areas, prompting many in Yonkers and in cities nationwide to mock such programs as "Negro removal." At meetings for projects planned for Riverdale Avenue, city officials were asked about "doors closed to Negro families" and, more pointedly, "Where can a Negro family of five find a decent place to live?" The issue was significant enough for the Yonkers Human Rights Commission to ask the city council to go on record against housing discrimination and formally ask citizens "to make known to neighbors whose homes are for rent or for sale that they would welcome residents without regard to race."[65] Racial discrimination indeed was an issue in both private and public housing markets as many white residents refused to rent or sell to Blacks, and the city refused to integrate white neighborhoods of east Yonkers. As the Black and Latino populations of southwest Yonkers expanded during the 1960s, debates over public housing only intensified.

In response to pressure from white homeowner associations in east Yonkers throughout the 1950s, members of the city council refused to publish or discuss a list of potential public housing sites for the city over the next decade. City leaders feared that such a list would cause "undo alarm" and that the public was "not yet ready to accept racial and economic integration on a citywide basis."[66] In 1968, leaders of both the NAACP and the Congress of Racial Equality (CORE) signed letters to the Department of Urban Housing (HUD). They criticized the city for failing to include minority groups and the community at large in the selection of sites.[67] The construction of public housing in segregated neighborhoods was prohibited under the Civil Rights Act of 1968. In Yonkers, this meant that new public housing for those displaced by urban renewal could not be relegated solely to neighborhoods with Black residents, as the city had done in the past. New sites had to be placed across the city, including white east Yonkers. But because HUD allowed New Deal local housing agencies such as the MHA to operate at the local level, they were vulnerable to community pressure and maintained the racial status quo of public housing. And while HUD had the power to withhold funding from cities that did not comply, it was difficult to determine which cities were not in observance.[68] In Yonkers, white homeowners "up in arms" continued to pack local meetings where "bedlam broke loose" over any suggestion of public housing for east Yonkers. Despite warnings from local politicians that their resistance would "add to the racial containment of the city," hundreds of "angry" and "mostly white residents" continued to jam meetings marked by "heated debates" with "racial overtones" that nearly climaxed in physical confrontation.[69] Concerns about a growing impoverished population also intensified. During the 1950s, residents voiced concerns that new public housing in Yonkers would draw poor Black and Puerto Rican residents from New York City. Now residents were concerned about the arrival of those similarly displaced by urban renewal projects in White Plains. In 1975, the city council requested the Westchester County Department of Social Services to declare a moratorium on relocating welfare recipients to Yonkers.[70]

Yonkers hardly was unique in its resistance to the racial and class integration of its white, middle-class neighborhoods. The city's suburban neighbors in Westchester County, because they lacked large-scale manufacturing, also lacked old, working-class housing and neither needed nor availed themselves of federal funding for public housing and urban renewal. On the other hand, older, former industrial sections of Westchester County like Yonkers, but also Mount Vernon, New Rochelle, and White Plains, badly required assistance. In wealthier suburban tracts of Westchester County, zoning laws, building codes, and land-use regulations precluded the construction of inexpensive housing, and working-class groups typically were unable to live in these areas because of commuting expenses and higher housing costs.

In 1968, New York State created the Urban Development Corporation (UDC), which held the authority to develop and finance housing of "all sorts" unbound by local land-use and permit requirements. White residents quickly organized against the mere 100 public housing units planned for their middle- and upper-class towns. This county-wide mobilization was notable for the desire to "keep out those people . . . the scum from the cities." In response to their pressure, Governor Nelson Rockefeller issued a moratorium on the plan, and the state legislature later withheld funding for UDC, repealed its power to override zoning and local land-use codes, and, more important, gave local towns the power to veto projects, which they immediately did.[71] Wealthier suburban tracts of Westchester County were no different than Yonkers in their resistance to public housing; they were, nonetheless, able to pressure government, in this case New York State, to maintain the existing racial status quo. Yonkers, however, would be held liable for its actions, a fate that its neighbors would not meet until the new millennium.[72]

The Court Case

In 1980, the Yonkers branch of the NAACP sued the city of Yonkers, its board of education, and the Yonkers Community Development Agency (the local liaison for the Department of Housing and Urban Development) over the segregation of the city's public schools. Unlike school desegregation lawsuits in other cities, the NAACP made the unprecedented argument that public schools were segregated in Yonkers because housing was segregated. After nearly a hundred days of trial, eighty-four witnesses, thirty-nine depositions, and thousands of exhibits, one thing was clear: Yonkers was indeed segregated. Twenty-three of the city's thirty-four public schools were either 80 percent minority or white; the southwest quadrant contained 97.7 percent of the city's public housing and 80.7 percent of the city's minority population.[73]

The city maintained that public housing segregation was unintentional and argued that projects were placed in areas where the housing stock was the most dilapidated and in need of urban renewal. In addition, the city argued that HUD encouraged segregation because the agency pressed for project locations in areas with low land acquisition costs. Testimony from Yonkers's own politicians challenged the city's refusal to acknowledge the role of race in its decisions to locate public housing solely in the southwest. Former city official Alfred De Bello acknowledged at trial that his "constituents equated public housing with minorities and . . . race was definitely a factor in much of the opposition that arose during the site selection process." Former council member Edward O'Neill insisted that nothing in the public record confirmed that race did play a role, although aforementioned public housing debates of the 1950s and 1960s suggest otherwise. He did, however, acknowledge that racial opposition was "certainly nothing anybody would put into words."[74]

Because it did not want to be found liable for supporting housing policies that could be deemed racist, HUD entered into an agreement with the NAACP in 1984. But the case still needed to be made that Yonkers independently was liable for segregating its residents. Michael Sussman, attorney for the NAACP, got his chance during the actual trial. In 1980, the city responded to requests for suitable public housing sites with fourteen locations, two of which HUD considered suitable. The city, however, permitted one of the sites to be privately developed into a shopping mall on McLean Avenue, and the other location was privately developed into condominiums. Several committee members appointed by the city council to screen developers admitted to Sussman that the group's purpose was to circumvent the development of public housing.[75] That this happened during the trial, in addition to the testimony of former city officials, surely influenced the epic 657-page decision of Judge Leonard B. Sand against the city of Yonkers in 1985.

The judge's order regarding public housing was twofold. Phase one immediately required the city to construct 200 units of public housing east of the Saw Mill River Parkway, a number earlier agreed to by both the city and HUD. In phase two, the city was to establish a fair housing program and develop a plan to encourage private developers to build 800 additional units of low- and moderate-income housing. Furthermore, a federal monitor was appointed to oversee the desegregation of public schools by way of busing and magnet schools. When Yonkers failed to propose sites for the court-mandated housing by the fall 1986 deadline, Sand appointed Oscar Newman as housing master and ordered him to make a list of potential sites within ninety days. Best known for *Defensible Space*, a critique of high-rise public housing, Newman maintained that public housing in the United States had failed because residents were isolated from each other and from the community at large. His plan for Yonkers, which included low-rise, low-density townhouses scattered throughout the city, was one of the first of its kind in the United States.[76]

Shortly thereafter, the Second U.S. Court of Appeals upheld Judge Sand's ruling. In January 1988, the city council, after nearly five hours of being denounced as "wimps, liars and snakes," voted to comply with both phases of the housing order and begin designating sites for its implementation. At Saunders High School, 800 angry residents jammed the gymnasium to watch a televised broadcast of the vote, as the council's chambers could not accommodate such a crowd. "You promised us an appeal! You promised you'd never settle!" shouted residents.[77] They were particularly angry with council members who had campaigned that previous November to fight Judge Sand's order and now reneged on that promise. While resistance to public housing was nothing new in Yonkers, this recent manifestation was noteworthy both for the scale of homeowner mobilization and for its discourse.

Unlike in the past, when neighborhood organizations mobilized in opposition to public housing proposed for their immediate area, Save Yonkers, which boasted 100,000 members, emerged as an umbrella organization of forty-three civil groups to fight the desegregation order. And unlike earlier battles in which race explicitly was expressed in public debate, when the controversy exploded again in 1988, white homeowners insisted that race had nothing to do with their opposition. "We're not racists," they publicly maintained at city council meetings and through the press.[78] To underscore this point, many recounted relationships with people of color. President of Save Yonkers Jack O'Toole, in an editorial for the *Herald Statesman*, insisted, "I know many people here who have associations with many fine black people in the armed forces, at work, in church, in volunteer and sports activities." Interestingly, O'Toole referred to interracial exchanges in semipublic realms of work or church. Home and school, however, were not mentioned but were at the same time the literal sites of this desegregation battle. The latter part of his editorial is more telling: "Sadly most residents of public housing happen to be black. . . . We will not watch our hard-earned property values undermined or our quality of life destroyed without a fight!"[79]

Residents of Yonkers were not unique in their opposition to public housing or in the articulation of their defense. In northern U.S. cities, especially where interracial interactions in workplaces, stores, public transportation, and accommodation were not uncommon, whites mobilized when the segregation of more intimate realms of home and school was challenged.[80] Integrated schools and housing did not merely endanger neighborhood racial homogeneity. Because these sites were more private, they could foster close, personal, and possibly sexual relations. Though never voiced publicly, integrated schools and housing also had the potential to test the racial boundaries of white families. In Yonkers, nonetheless, white homeowners typically defended segregated neighborhoods in terms of property rights, part of a larger racial conservatism emerging in the United States at large. This discourse grew in both the north and the south as early as the 1950s, in response to the civil rights movement, which had begun to successfully discredit racial stereotypes and discrimination.[81] At the same time, the United States was increasingly neoliberal, shifting public resources to private individuals and corporations in the name of economic growth. This larger shift in the political economy was possible precisely because proponents maintained that privatization would reward all consumers, irrespective of their race or ethnicity, as long as they espoused market-oriented values and choices. In the early twentieth century, white homeowners typically defended segregated neighborhoods in explicit terms that highlighted the supposed inferiority of Blacks and their racial predisposition to laziness, sexual licentiousness, and crime. But in the decades following

World War II, the language of property replaced the language of race in the defense of segregated neighborhoods; stories about racial character were reworked into stories about property. In Yonkers, homeowners did not self-identify as white and seldom identified public housing residents by race (although there were a few racially coded references to "Harlem" and "bodegas"), but they did describe racial aptitude in relation to property.

As self-described "homeowners" and "taxpayers," white homeowners stressed how they "scrimped," "worked," and "saved"; they got to live in east Yonkers, where the houses are "well-kept," because of "pride in home, property and strong family values." In marked contrast, "public housing residents" were "unsanitary" and "dangerous" and equated with "crime, rape and drugs."[82] These supposed differences between white homeowners and public housing residents—the latter publicly imagined though never publicly described as Black or Latino—could be attributed to superior values and choices, and not race-based treatment in housing and employment markets in both the public and the private sector. After all, to revisit the language used by O'Toole, public housing residents "just happen to be black," and by extension, homeowners in Yonkers just happened to be white. Although larger structural forces created federally subsidized white, middle-class suburbs apart from decaying Black urban ghettos, residents of the former attributed these differences to free-market forces and insisted upon "color-blind" government housing policy; as a result, white homeowners frequently articulated their opposition to desegregated housing in terms of overbearing government. Throughout the controversy, residents referred to the American Revolution and likened themselves to colonists oppressed by tyrannical British rule. Members of Save Yonkers staged a mock Tea Party outside city hall, with approximately 125 protestors waving American flags and wearing tea bags dangling from their ears.[83] Whether articulated as opposition to government tyranny or defense of property, this new rhetoric nonetheless still defended racially segregated neighborhoods, regardless of how vehemently white homeowners insisted that their opposition had "nothing to do with race."

Indeed, there were those who saw through this racially coded rhetoric. In a letter to the *Herald Statesman*, one observer maintained that if homeowners "really were honest, they'd carry signs like segregation forever." Yonkers was called "Little Mississippi on the Hudson," and Martin Kilson, a political scientist at Harvard University, lamented that "they have created a southern climate of massive resistance."[84] Much to the chagrin of white homeowners who defended segregated neighborhoods, the Knights of the Ku Klux Klan distributed pamphlets near one of the proposed public housing sites and posted signs "all over" east Yonkers that read "Keep Yonkers White."[85] Though white homeowners were not defending segregation in such racially explicit terms, they nonetheless were fighting to keep east Yonkers white, and they would go to great lengths to do so. "Whites will violate the law to keep blacks out of their neighborhood, whites will pay huge fines to keep blacks out of their neighborhoods and whites might even go to jail to keep blacks out of their neighborhoods," one Black resident of southwest Yonkers later remarked to a local journalist.[86]

The mobilization of white homeowners against racial integration in Yonkers during the 1980s, which was larger and more cohesive than movements past, was shaped by the greater presence of blue-collar white ethnics who fled New York City's deindustrialization, changing racial demographics, and urban renewal. The many who moved from the Bronx were not only first-time homeowners but often first-generation homeowners. They would not take lightly any perceived threat to the first and greatest financial investment of their lives. Their tenuous entry into this middle-class milieu shaped an unwavering spirit of resistance, newfound cooperation, and collaboration with other Bronx white ethnics. This experience also informed their class resentment toward wealthier neighbors in Westchester County, especially Judge Sand. Hundreds of protestors gathered outside of his thirty-two-acre property with signs that read "Integrate Pound Ridge!"[87] Sand lived in a town like many others in Westchester County that up to this point had successfully self-isolated from working-class residents, public housing, and legally mandated integration.

Though they often shared the same neighborhoods and a desire to protect property values, some longtime middle-class residents of Yonkers still perceived blue-collar white ethnics as outsiders. City councilman Edward Fagan Jr., who voted against complying with the desegregation order, reminisced fondly about "old Yonkers," before the desegregation controversy, but also before "the refugees from the Bronx, the Camaros, two-family homes and not as many children going to col-lege."[88] Though their blue-collar presence was not entirely welcomed by all in Yonkers, recent white ethnic arrivals from New York City made claim to this controversy by underscoring their past experience with public housing. Their stories gave a certain authority to white home-owner opposition by recounting how they witnessed firsthand "beauti-ful projects" that had turned to "garbage." In doing so, they attempted to discredit public housing more broadly, and the desegregation order specifically. At the same time, white ethnics were unwilling to compro-mise. Many, after moving within the Bronx before moving to Yonkers, were unwilling to move again. While they attributed the aftermath of urban renewal and deindustrialization in the Bronx to the poor choices and values of public housing residents, they both feared and forewarned that the construction of public housing in east Yonkers would "be just like the Bronx."[89] As a result, they brought a degree of urgency in their calls for the city council to defy the desegregation order, which is what it eventually did.

The experience of white ethnic "Bronx refugees" added a new gloss to the desegregation controversy of 1988. Their numbers and presence in Save Yonkers successfully pressured members of the city council to vote in early August 1988 against the 800 additional units of affordable housing mandated by phase two of Judge Sand's housing order. In a poll conducted for the *Herald Statesman*, 64.3 percent of Yonkersresidents opposed the court ruling, 63.5 percent opposed public housing, and 50.9 percent backed members of the city council who voted against the order.[90] Dissenting council members now were in contempt of court and faced $500-a-day fines, while the city faced fines starting at $100 per day, which would double daily and wipe out the city's $337 million budget in three weeks. Because of the potentially crippling effect of the fines, the State Emergency Control Board declared Yonkers to be in a financial crisis. With daily fines of $1 million and a first round of layoffs looming, alongside mounting pressure from the Committee of Organizations to Preserve Law in Yonkers (COMPLY), a multiracial, bipartisan coalition of homeowners, the city council eventually voted in September 1988 to comply with Judge Sand's order. Not only did the episode cost the city $12 million in legal fees, nearly $500,000 in fines, and almost $3 mil-lion in lost federal aid, but Yonkers also lost opportunities for economic development. Because the city was slow to comply with the construction of the first units, Judge Leonard Sand issued a moratorium on new development of city properties, which prohibited Yonkers from assisting private developers with zoning changes, variances, tax abatement, and development bonds. This temporary ban, coupled with bad publicity over desegregation, delayed much-needed investment. According to John Zakian, former executive director of the Yonkers Industrial Development Agency, potential investors used the bad publicity over desegregation to negotiate terms to their advantage. Though Yonkers attracted some light manufacturing in the late 1980s, economic development in the city did not gain momentum until the 1990s.[91]

Dismayed by the city council's response to the desegregation controversy, in 1989 the citizens of Yonkers voted to change their city manager model of government to one that relied on a strong, elected mayor. Terrence Zaleski, the first to hold office under this new plan in 1991, received only 36 percent of the vote because of a three-way race. His administration was punctuated by a difficult power struggle with the city council, directed by majority leader John Spencer, who later would succeed Zaleski in 1995 (and was a Republican hopeful for Hillary Clinton's U.S. Senate seat in 2006). Described by the *New York Times* as a "law and order Republican in the mold of Rudolph W. Giuliani," Spencer began his career as a fighting, hard-drinking construction worker before getting into real estate development and local politics. His first priority was to free the city of its desegregation lawsuit.[92] In 1996, Mayor Spencer met with Judge Sand and agreed to a plan that would allow the city to use its own agencies and existing units to comply with its public housing obligation. Because Sand ruled that the state's Urban Development Program was partially responsible for the segregated housing pattern in Yonkers, New York State would designate 740 units and pay half of their $32 million dollar cost. Since then, the city had successfully lobbied to reduce the number of units to 600. Of the 100 units per year promised over six years, the city provided only 233 units by the time John Spencer left office.[93] Part of the delay stemmed from the city's strict color-blind, class-based interpretation of the housing order, and as a result, 30 percent of the new public housing units went to white families. Both the Department of Justice and the NAACP appealed to Judge Sand, who agreed that the city's actions deliberately defied the intent of the original order to racially integrate east Yonkers. The city lost its appeals to both the U.S. Court of Appeals and the Supreme Court in 2001. Because of these delays, the city fell behind on the construction of the units.[94]

The original units, spread over seven sites, were met with mixed results. Though scattered-site housing had no detectible price effect on nearby privately owned housing, as predicted by opponents of court-ordered desegregation, little integration has occurred. *New York Times* reporter Lisa Belkin, who closely followed the Yonkers controversy, found that the scattered-site residents are "visitors in their new neighborhoods, and they have almost no interaction with the white homeowners whose world they were sent to change." Furthermore, residents have tended to retain the social networks forged in southwest Yonkers and usually attend church and patronize businesses in their old neighborhoods.[95] Judge Sand, however, maintains the intention of the court order never was integration. "Yonkers," he explained, "is technically desegregated. A group of people . . . is now allowed in where before it was deliberately kept out. But Yonkers is not integrated. . . . Time might accomplish that. A judge cannot."[96] In 2002, the city reached an agreement with the NAACP over the desegregation of its public schools. The state agreed to finance $300 million over five years to improve the performance of Black and Hispanic children who now make up a majority of students in the Yonkers school system. As a result of the agreement, federal monitors could be removed, and the city therefore was potentially free to end busing and magnet schools. In 2007, the city reached a final settlement with the NAACP and completed the last of the 600 units it was required to create.[97]

* * *

The postwar challenges of deindustrialization and desegregation left an indelible mark on the city of Yonkers. Rather than comply with court-ordered segregation, many white residents left the city or sent their children to parochial schools. North and east Yonkers were (and still are) predominantly white, and southwest Yonkers, the city's former industrial core, still had significant concentrations of poverty. Writing for the *New York Times* in 2006, Fernanda Santos offered a particularly vivid account of "boarded-up homes and empty storefronts, rotten wood and peeling paint."[98] As the city worked to reach agreements with the NAACP over the desegregation of its public schools and housing during the first years of the new millennium, the median household income in southwest Yonkers was $24,780 a year, substantially lower than for the city of Yonkers as a whole ($44,665), and approximately one-fifth of Yonkers residents in public housing, which was disproportionately located in this area, lived below the poverty level. Working-class immigrants, however, still were drawn to Yonkers because of its affordability and proximity to New York City. Southwest Yonkers witnessed an influx of migrants from Mexico, Central America, and the Caribbean, while large numbers of Irish immigrants made southeast Yonkers their home beginning in the early 1990s. Unlike earlier immigrants who found in the United States a favorable immigration policy and in the city of Yonkers well-paying manufacturing work, Yonkers's newest arrivals largely were undocumented workers in New York City's service economy.[99]

Yonkers is trying to be a "great city" once again. The agreement reached between the city and the NAACP over the desegregation of its public schools and housing, coupled with Mayor John Spencer's ability to persuade the state to remove the financial control board that had been in place intermittently since the 1970s, signaled to some that Yonkers was ready for a rebirth. In a gesture meant to symbolize a clean break with its troubled past, the city recast itself as a "City of Vision" during the late 1990s. New economic investment eventually followed. By the end of John Spencer's second term in 2003, north Yonkers had witnessed the arrival of Stew Leonard's, the self-proclaimed largest dairy store in the world, and the movement of big-box stores such as Costco and Home Depot. Projects in southwest Yonkers included the $53 million conversion of a former Otis Elevator building into a library and headquarters for the board of education, a refurbished Metro-North train station, the construction of a waterfront esplanade and luxury waterfront rental units, as well as the sprouting of new bars, restaurants, and banks in and around Getty Square. In 2004, the city unveiled a $3.1 billion agreement to bring a minor-league baseball stadium, new retail and office space, and more high-end residences to southwest Yonkers. Similar to the campaign launched a century earlier, the "City of Vision" is positioning itself as a less-expensive alternative to neighboring New York City.

The city's long history of contentious class and increasingly racial politics contours the implementation of these plans. These policies, which will displace working-class and working-poor Black and Latino residents of southwest Yonkers, are informed by the bitter legacy of desegregation. The city's history also shaped the reception of undocumented Irish newcomers as they arrived in southeast Yonkers when plans to bring new investment began to take shape during the early 1990s. In such a racially charged environment, where white residents either moved from Yonkers or moved their children from the city's public schools when faced with court-mandated desegregation, one might presume that the movement of white immigrants would be welcomed by those who made doomsday predictions about the impact of forced integration on property values. To the contrary, undocumented Irish immigrant men and women were subjected to surveillance by the Yonkers city council and police department. Though the city's history of contentious class politics can shed light on this development, the history of the Irish in the United States is equally instructive.

2

Good Paddies and Bad Paddies

*The Evolution of Irishness as a Race-Based
Tradition in the United States*

In 1863, the first recorded St. Patrick's Day celebration transpired in
the city of Yonkers. After attending mass at St. Mary's, "handsomely
dressed" participants marched through the streets and avenues of Getty
Square in the city's southwest quadrant. Every residence "proudly" displayed American flags. A St. Patrick's Day ball was added in 1876, and
by the end of the century, Yonkers could boast of several Irish organizations. Although parades became less common during this time, Yonkers celebrated St. Patrick with nine-course banquets and lectures as
well as Irish-themed plays and performances. By World War II, city hall
marked St. Patrick's Day with the adornment of green suits and ties, the
distribution of potted shamrocks, a junior high school assembly on the
life of St. Patrick, and a "Shamrock Shenanigans" dance at a local high
school. A decade later, the city of Yonkers revived the St. Patrick's Day
parade tradition.[1]

Why were Yonkers parade participants "handsomely dressed" in
1863? What did nine-course meals have to do with St. Patrick? These
local manifestations of Irishness that emphasized respectability were
part of a larger transformation in how the Irish were viewed and
came to view themselves. To comprehend this trajectory, this chapter

looks first to Irish encounters with British and later U.S. empire in the nineteenth century. In this context, the ideology of race, which was entrenched in domestic respectability, was a mighty weapon used to subjugate the Irish, but race also played an essential role in how they would forge their own social identity. From this experience, a good Paddy model stressing Irish racial aptitude emerged, characterized by order, hard work, and family, which corresponded to a specific configuration of race, class, and gender, in addition to loyalty and faith. Ever present in Yonkers's 1863 St. Patrick's Day celebrations, this model for Irishness served as a benchmark for the descendants of early parade participants, as well as subsequent generations of Irish immigrants in the twentieth century. Conditions, however, both in Ireland and in the United States informed how well they would sustain this paradigm.

This chapter then turns to the young Irish men and women who left Ireland for the United States following World War II, albeit in smaller numbers than their nineteenth-century predecessors. Arriving initially in New York City, they made the "white flight" to Yonkers by way of the Bronx and Upper Manhattan in later decades. These immigrants came of age in postcolonial Ireland and enjoyed programs in the United States aimed at expanding the middle class. Together these circumstances ensured that this cohort could be good Paddies, a version of Irishness reinforced, moreover, by the larger ethnic revival under way in the United States. This chapter also considers those who arrived in Yonkers beginning in the early 1990s and were not as fortunate as their predecessors. Changes in U.S. immigration law as well as the wider political economy encouraged a largely undocumented, working-class migration, which would challenge the good Paddy Irish model. Together these distinct Irish migrations to Yonkers shed light on the larger evolution of Irishness as a race-based tradition in the United States. At the same time, these episodes reveal Irishness as a thoroughly contingent identity, shaped by a steadfast assemblage of race, class, and gender. These variables, which do not align neatly, warrant consequences in the city of Yonkers.

Encounters with Empire

As early as the colonial era, both Irish Protestants and Catholics migrated to America, but the latter became a growing presence in

New York City and bordering Westchester County beginning in the early decades of the nineteenth century. In port towns such as Yonkers, Irish women worked in private homes as domestics, while Irish men labored on farms or loaded ships. After Ireland witnessed significant population growth across the eighteenth and early nineteenth centuries, the subsequent pressure on land access prompted many to look elsewhere for opportunity. Anywhere between 800,000 and 1 million people left Ireland for North America after the end of the Napoleonic Wars. But after a series of famines in Ireland during the 1840s, the Irish presence in Yonkers, as elsewhere, increased. In 1850, Yonkers had an Irish population of 756; that number grew to 11,889 by 1900. In a city of 47,931, nearly one in four were either Irish-born or the children of Irish immigrants. Though their numbers did not rival those in Manhattan, the proportion of Irish people in relation to the overall population in Yonkers did.[2] These immigrants made a significant geographic journey from colonial Ireland to growing industrial cities such as Yonkers, but their encounters with race along the way ensured an equally important social crossing.

The concept of race is generally accepted in academic circles as a social construct, a way of thinking about physical difference that has no biological basis. Race, however, is more than an ideology; the ways that human bodies are represented are deeply rooted in larger structures of power, which determine how resources are distributed. Not only does race have structural and cultural dimensions, but also, as a social construct, the meaning of race can change over time.[3] The Irish, once depicted as a racially inept "other" under British rule, and later racially adept in nineteenth-century U.S. society, present an illuminating example of race as a sociohistorical process.

Early British accounts depicted the "wild Irish" as cannibals, murderers, and sodomites, serving to justify both the invasion and the colonization of Ireland in the twelfth century. By the time of the Protestant Reformation, religion had become the language with which to establish difference and bar Catholics from serving in the army, owning land, or having a profession or a Catholic education. Within the larger context of European capitalist and colonial expansion in the nineteenth century, as Britain forged an empire under the reign of Queen Victoria, the innate difference between the Anglo or British and Celtic or Irish "races" increasingly justified colonial rule in Ireland.[4] Developments at the time in pseudosciences such as physiognomy gave these distinctions additional weight. Race, however, did not merely replace ethnicity as a social category with which to establish difference, nor was race solely a substitute for class; rather, ethnicity, in this case "Irish" and "British," was informed as much by race as it was by class and gender.[5]

The British, like their European counterparts, "imagined" themselves as not only a distinct race but a *white* race, which required a culturally or socially identified "other." Postcolonial feminist scholars such as Ann Laura Stoler and Anne McClintock have illustrated how what people did in private helped to establish the boundaries of race.[6] Maintaining these racial boundaries, moreover, required cordoning off sexuality, because unbridled sexual relations potentially could produce mixed offspring and thus blur rigid racial divides. The sexual behavior of women was scrutinized as they alone were deemed gatekeepers of the white race. The children they were expected to bear would determine the quality of the racial stock. Properly raised children required a clean household (and the employ of servants) but also an orderly household, organized around a specific configuration of race, class, and gender. A respectable household was a racially homogeneous, middle-class household with a family-rearing wife and a wage-earning, hardworking husband. This respectable household was characterized equally by the Protestant faith. Households arranged in this particular manner were loyal and were composed of reliable members of an adept white, British race. Not only the Irish but many "others" in Britain and its colonies—homosexuals, the working class, Jews, and prostitutes—fell miserably short of these racial expectations and were subject to racial hazing; that is, they were marked as racially substandard.

Because skin color, a marker so commonly used to establish racial difference was not available as a signifier of difference in Ireland, exaggerated simian features were used to represent the Irish race, a member of which was discernible by a "retreating forehead . . . large mouth and thick lips . . . great distance between nose and mouth . . . nose short, upturned, frequently concave, with yawning nostrils."[7] In addition, these "Irish" features were accompanied by a set of supposed behavioral markers. If members of the white, British race required clean, orderly homes, then the racially inferior Irish were represented typically as living in dirty and disheveled hovels; if middle-class, British domiciles required hardworking, temperate husbands and caring, orderly wives, the "disorderly" Bridget and the "lazy" Paddy, who preferred getting drunk over work, inhabited working-class Irish homes. Domestic standards did not coordinate private life alone; they also provided the basis for these racial opposites, which justified the larger extraction of wealth from Ireland and the larger unequal distribution of resources achieved by British colonialism and capitalist expansion.

On the other hand, the disorderly Bridget and the drunken Paddy sometimes could be considered charming. After all, the British would have difficulty incorporating the Irish within their empire if they were too repugnant. That Irish caricatures could be both negative and positive worked to justify British rule in Ireland; the Irish were awful enough to need British intervention but were not beyond repair.[8] To this end, in 1831 the British Parliament agreed to establish a primary school system to counter the "Irish Problem" years before it established a similar program in England. In these schools, Irish children were instructed entirely in English and were punished for lapses in Gaelic. Furthermore, instructors inspected their pupils every morning for their "cleanliness and neatness." Highly regimented class periods introduced by a bell emphasized the "great rule of regulation and order." Young girls learned to sew while young boys were trained in manual labor. These government-sponsored primary schools worked Irish children into loyal, English-speaking subjects and created a future generation of male wage earners and female makers of clean and orderly homes.[9] Clearly Irish children had the potential to learn certain racial expectations. Unschooled Irish adults, on the other hand, were a different matter entirely.

The emotional, blundering, confused but entertaining "stage" Irish, the more positive side of the Irish racial caricature, had been present in British comedies as far back as Shakespeare, but as the Irish challenged repressive British policies in Ireland, especially toward the end of the nineteenth century, they increasingly were portrayed as dangerous. Paddy no longer was amusing but rather was drunk and potentially violent, while Bridget and her inept housekeeping no longer was funny; the numerous offspring she produced were equally threatening. Just as British women were considered gatekeepers of the white race, Irish

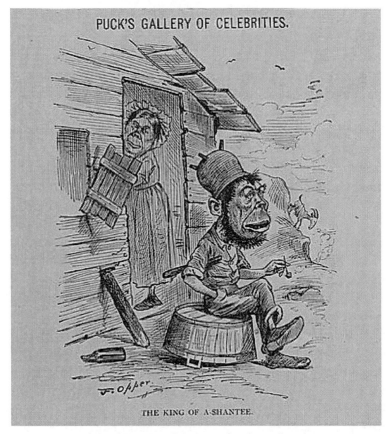

Figure 2.1. Frederick B. Opper, "The King of A-Shantee," *Puck*, 10, no. 258 (February 15, 1882): 378.

women, as members of a substandard race, had the potential to flood these racial gates.[10] These representations of the Irish as dirty, lazy, and drunk, as well as violent and overly fecund, illustrate not only the ways in which what people did in private determined racial aptitude but also how Ireland was a testing ground for racial standards that would circulate in Britain's "other" colonies.[11]

Life in colonial Ireland worsened during the Great Famine, in which more than 1 million people died from starvation or famine-related illness in the ten years that followed a series of potato blights beginning in 1845. Over that decade, approximately 500,000 or more were evicted from their homes and more than 2 million Irish, about one-fourth of the pre-Famine population, went overseas; roughly 1.5 million of them made the United States their home. Between 1851 and 1921, more than 4.5 million people left Ireland; nearly 4 million arrived in the United States.[12] The Irish continued to migrate in the following decades because of the significant changes instituted in Irish society. Prior to the Great Famine, Irish men and women tended to marry young and sustained a livelihood cultivating potatoes on subdivided family land, which allowed Irish peasants to support large families, all of which proved disastrous with potato blight. After the Great Famine, the Irish married later than in earlier periods, and families were less likely to subdivide their land, which instead was inherited increasingly by a single, male heir whose future wife would require a dowry. The money brought from an incoming wife could then finance the dowry of an eldest daughter. As a result of these changes, second sons and daughters had to look elsewhere for both economic opportunities and marriage prospects. These factors sustained migration after the immediate years of the Great Famine and left an indelible imprint: no other group of immigrants to the United States contained as many women.[13] In the United States, Irish women in large numbers found work in domestic service, as this type of employment provided both employment and lodging. Irish men found work as manual laborers, securing accommodation in tenements and boardinghouses. These Irish men and women may have escaped the economic, political, and social limitations of life in post-Famine colonial Ireland, but they would soon find that they left behind neither white racial expectations nor racial hazing.

Like its British counterpart, American identity conveyed a set of racial expectations shaped equally by race, class, and gender. The future of the United States as a *white* nation was predicated likewise on loyal and orderly households that were racially homogeneous and middle-class and that contained Protestant family-oriented wives and hard-working, wage-earning husbands; they were guided equally by the good morals of the Protestant faith.[14] As in Great Britain, this particularly domestic construction of racial fitness reached beyond the private sphere into U.S. society. These racial expectations informed various reform movements in cities such as New York to save female prostitutes and intemperate males. They governed the relocation of orphaned immigrant children from cities to "proper" homes in the American

West, as well as the removal of nonorphaned Native American children from their parents to government-sponsored boarding schools. These standards encouraged racial boundaries in the Jim Crow South and the Southwest, the scrutiny of poor whites, as well as the forced sterilization of the "unfit," including the "feeble-minded," convicts, and poor, single mothers. They governed "cleanliness" campaigns against Mexican "others" along the U.S.-Mexico border and against Chinese "others" in cities such as San Francisco. Furthermore, these standards justified an array of colonial projects in Mexico, Puerto Rico, and the Philippines.[15]

Like these many "others," Irish immigrants fell short of white racial expectations in the United States. First and foremost, the increasingly Catholic migration from Ireland in the early decades of the nineteenth century challenged the Protestant character of good faith in the United States. In 1834, nativists attacked a Massachusetts convent, and Catholic churches increasingly became targets in Philadelphia during the 1840s. The growing popularity of the "escaped nun genre" helped fuel this anti-Catholic sentiment in the United States. Rebecca Reeds, a self-described convent escapee, sold 10,000 copies of her story, *Six Months in a Convent*, to enthusiastic readers in Boston during the first week after its publication in 1835. One year later, *The Awful Disclosures of Maria Monk* buttressed Reeds's titillating accounts of sexual orgies. With 300,000 copies sold before the Civil War, Monk's claims included a mother superior forcing nuns to have sex with priests, as well as the murder of offspring produced by such liaisons.[16] Anti-Irish sentiment found organizational support in the secret Protestant fraternal Order of the Star Spangled Banner, or the Know-Nothings, to its contemporaries. Although this nativist group elected officials at both local and state levels, they did not fulfill their national agenda to lengthen the time required for naturalization and bar the foreign-born from holding office. Because domestic standards guided racial fitness, closer interactions with Irish Catholics also were cause for concern. Irish women who worked in the American homes of the Protestant middle and upper classes threatened to destabilize domestic order. Female employers feared that their families might be poisoned, or that their children might be taken to a secret Catholic baptism.[17] In reality, the Irish who migrated prior to and during the Great Famine were poor Catholics at best. Many never had received the sacrament of Communion; others had to be taught the sign of the cross. Sunday mass attendance was as low as 40 percent in the 1860s. According to U.S. Catholic historian Jay Dolan, nineteenth-century Irish immigrants appeared to be "Catholics in name and nothing more."[18] Nonetheless, Irish Catholicism, in addition to Irish nationalism, encouraged uncertainty about their loyalty to the United States.

Many American nativists feared that the hierarchy of the Catholic Church, especially the authority of the pope, would threaten the relatively new democratic form of government in the United States. Would Catholics be more loyal to their pope than to the president? If so, Catholicism seemed incompatible with democracy, and as a result, Catholics were not to be trusted. While religion provoked doubts about the loyalty of these Irish newcomers to the United States, their experiences with other institutions also were cause for concern. In colonial Ireland, Catholics and Protestants alike sought independence from Great Britain. Despite a failed rebellion in 1798, Irish people on both sides of the Atlantic continued to champion for greater Irish freedom. Under the leadership of Daniel O'Connell in the early decades of the nineteenth century, many sought to repeal the 1801 Act of Union and achieve greater Irish autonomy within the British Empire. The Young Ireland Movement, increasingly impatient with O'Connell's moderate goals, launched its own failed rebellion in 1848. More radical national movements emerged in its wake, such as the Fenian Brotherhood in New York City, which sought complete Irish independence from British rule. Rival Fenian factions twice invaded Canada, in 1866 and 1870. While their goal to provoke war between the United States and Great Britain never was achieved, such devotion to Ireland, and the framing of their migration as forced exile rather than choice, certainly raised questions about Irish loyalty to their adopted country, as did their membership in the Democratic Party.[19] Largely denied suffrage under British colonial rule, many working-class Irish men exercised the right to vote in the United States, and in many American cities, the Irish commanded powerful political machines. Irish participation in the urban ranks of the Democratic Party, especially New York City's Tammany Hall, is legendary, as are allegations of fraud and corruption. While political machines indeed exchanged votes for jobs and services by way of schools, hospitals, and orphanages, they did so decades before federal and state governments actively provided for the welfare of their citizens.[20] Nonetheless, Irish-led political machines prompted suspicion regarding whether these newcomers could be trusted with democracy in the United States.

In addition to faith and loyalty, the Irish fell short of white racial expectations for order and hard work. Beginning in the early decades of the nineteenth century, Orangemen, who drew from the ranks of the Protestant Scots-Irish, paraded in New York City on July 12 to celebrate the 1690 victory of Protestant King William over Catholic King James at the Battle of the Boyne (a controversial celebration that still takes place in Northern Ireland). A confrontation that ensued between paraders and Irish Catholic protestors in 1870 left 9 dead and 150 wounded. The following year, after troops were summoned to protect paraders, soldiers opened fire to quell Irish Catholic protestors, killing 60 and wounding 100. In addition to these incidents, Irish canal and railroad workers used collective violence on "numerous" occasions to demand better wages and protest fraudulent contractors. Such outbreaks stemmed from a larger tradition in Ireland, whereby Irish peasants violently challenged evictions by English landlords. This tradition also shaped violence, sabotage, beatings, and assassinations across Pennsylvania's coalfields during the 1860s and 1870s.[21] Certainly, these episodes did not quell American fears about the Irish. Moreover, Irish-led protests in the United States, which occurred within the larger context of industrial expansion, created both the conditions and concerns about Irish hard work and that of the American working class more generally.

The United States became rapidly industrialized and urbanized by the close of the nineteenth century. With the shift from craft to factory production, the status and livelihood of tradesmen declined, while a wealthy industrial elite expanded, aided by the government's "laissez-faire" approach to business regulation and taxation, as well as its use of local, state, and federal force to quell labor disputes. Increasing gaps in wealth typically were attributed to the free hand of the market. Rather than shifts in the larger political economy, poverty often was attributed to personal shortcomings, commonly the lack of thrift or a good work ethic. In popular discourse, the poor were depicted as lazy spendthrifts who drank rather than saved their wages. Workplace drinking was not uncommon in the early decades of the nineteenth century.

Employers, for example, often paid workers with whiskey. But with the onset of a more regulated, efficient workplace, intemperance became a cause for concern. In this context of industrial expansion and declining craft status, working men expressed their class pride by way of a rough masculinity, in behaviors such as drinking and fighting. Patricia Kelleher maintains that Irish men were so "tightly associated" with this culture because of their disproportionate location in low-paying wage work.[22] While larger structural factors made it difficult for Irish immigrant and native-born working-class men to earn a decent living, hard work was an additional benchmark for white racial fitness that the Irish had missed. Moreover, the larger political economy would shape Irish immigrant households in the United States.

Nuclear families sustained by wage-earning husbands and child-rearing wives often were untenable within the larger nineteenth century, whereby Irish immigrants were looked upon with suspicion and often relegated to low-paying work. The hard conditions of industrial labor, especially workplace accidents, left many Irish widows in their wake. This, coupled with the desertion of many male breadwinners, created a "striking" number of female-headed Irish households. On the other hand, Irish households that were able to conform to the nuclear ideal were deemed too large, as fears of growing Irish political power resulted in characterizations of Irish women as particularly fertile breeders. In reality, the aftermath of the Great Famine encouraged the Irish to marry later, if at all. According to historian Hasia Diner, this served as an effective form of contraception.[23] Nonetheless, Irish families were deficient: they either lacked a male wage earner or were too large, and Irish membership in the Catholic Church certainly did not counter this characterization. Celibate Catholic nuns and clergy did not conform to racial expectations for a nuclear family either, and the popularity of the "escaped nun genre" certainly illustrates this suspicion. Catholic nuns, however, posed a particular threat to America's gender order. As leaders of convents, they could exercise a degree of autonomy away from male oversight. Jenny Franchot has shown in her analysis of the 1834 Massachusetts convent rioters that court discourse often depicted the mother superior as culturally deviant, that is, too masculine in appearance and character.[24] Surely, many Irish men and women failed to meet the very classed and gendered expectations for racially sound households, but even more important, and perhaps even more alarming, they did not always embrace white racial homogeneity, which was a particularly egregious transgression in the United States.

Unlike in Great Britain, the presence of a more heterogeneous population—Native Americans, African slaves, and varied Europeans—required the United States to be somewhat more flexible in defining who was eligible for American citizenship. According to a 1790 congressional statute, naturalization was extended to "free white persons." In contrast to colonial Ireland, working-class Irish men could become citizens in the United States, which allowed them to vote and enjoy other advantages such as property rights. Migrants of color, however, were not as fortunate as the Irish. In response to increased migration from China and Japan, Asian immigrants were deemed ineligible for naturalization in 1870. The Page Act of 1875 fundamentally barred Chinese women from entering the United States, undoubtedly a device to prevent the establishment of long-term Chinese communities. Additionally, the Chinese Exclusion Act of 1882 did just that, excluded Chinese laborers from entering the United States until World War II.[25]

The value of white racialness, however, had an earlier precedent in American legal history. The Constitution specified an unprecedented array of freedoms and at the same time upheld the institution of slavery, a contradiction that has been called the great "paradox" of American history. This paradox, moreover, established a "bipolar" racial order, which projected worthy citizens as "inherently white." In marked contrast, African chattel slavery encapsulated the antithesis of worthy citizenship. This bipolar racial order, anthropologist Aihwa Ong explains, became a national ideology, serving to affirm white citizenship and at the same time disparage those associated with African servitude in the United States.[26] Even after the Fourteenth Amendment extended citizenship to American-born men of African descent in 1868, free Blacks were subject to brutal violence and were disenfranchised socially, politically, and economically in the Jim Crow South. Those who managed to escape soon found that the North also could be unforgiving, as they encountered job discrimination, segregated neighborhoods and schools, and mob violence when they sought to challenge these very real racial boundaries.[27] All newcomers, according to Ong, must navigate this specific construction of racial difference that disparages people associated with African slavery in the United States. When the Irish first arrived in the United States, they did not adhere strictly to his particular racial order.

In cities such as New York, Irish immigrants typically worked as domestic servants and manual laborers, jobs that were relegated to free Blacks. Irish immigrants and free Blacks shared similar jobs and the same neighborhoods, such as the Five Points and Seneca Village (which was demolished for the construction of Central Park), but they also enjoyed similar cultures of leisure. Tyler Anbinder has argued that tap dancing was invented in the Five Points, evolving from Afro-Irish interactions in neighborhood saloons and dance halls. Similar arguments have been made about blackface minstrelsy in the nineteenth century. Though typically understood as a form of white racist mockery and lampoon, according to Eric Lott this performance was at the same time a cultural hybrid, "a simultaneous drawing up and crossing of racial boundaries . . . to repress through ridicule their interest in black cultural practices."[28] The participation of working-class Irish men in this cultural form, as both performers and spectators, should be viewed in this light. Cross-racial desire extended well beyond commercial culture into the domestic sphere as many Irish immigrants shared beds and organized households with their Black neighbors. The larger political culture reflected American anxieties over this racial blurring in work, leisure, popular culture, and households. African Americans and Irish immigrants typically were depicted as similarly repulsive to the American public. Some accounts of the day referred to the Irish as "niggers turned inside out," while people of African descent were described as "smoked Irishmen."[29] The zealousness with which the Irish were racially hazed for disregarding white racial homogeneity significantly would shape how the Irish came to see themselves in the United States.

Becoming Good Paddies

As newcomers in a relatively young, heterogeneous nation structured according to race-based resources, the Irish had to make a very firm and public commitment to white racial homogeneity in the United States. David Roediger has maintained in his pioneering work on working-class Irish immigrants and race that the Irish arrived in the United States

Figure 2.2. Thomas Nast, "The Ignorant Vote," *Harper's
Weekly*, December 9, 1876.

during the nineteenth century with a blank racial slate. More recent
work, however, illustrates that the Irish certainly were exposed to various racial orders prior to their arrival. British colonial rule, for example, exposed Ireland to the African slave trade, and many Irish subjects
served as administrators and soldiers in India. Surely these endeavors
underscored the importance of white racialness. Furthermore, historian
Timothy Meagher has shown how nineteenth-century Irish peasants
were versed in racism and used epithets such as "nagur."[30] But neither
racial knowledge nor racist sentiment was enough. More yielding than
Great Britain in determining *who* was eligible for white citizenship, the

United States was less flexible in *how* one established white racial aptitude. If anything, a more diverse population made white racial homogeneity all the more carefully safeguarded in the United States. In this setting, where a bipolar racial order was so entrenched socially, economically, and politically, Irish immigrants disparaged blackness, African Americans specifically, collectively, publicly, even violently, to assuage concerns about their lack of regard for America's racial order.

Indeed, the Irish achieved this in a variety of ways. On an institutional level, the Irish as a whole did not support the abolition of slavery. Abolitionists certainly were hostile to Irish newcomers. Protestant members of abolitionist groups, for example, often compared chattel slavery to the slavery of Catholicism. Lack of Irish support for this movement nonetheless signaled a very public and collective distance from enslaved Africans. At the same time, Irish men participated in violent attacks against free Blacks, and Irish women refused to work with Black domestics. Together these actions conveyed an everyday allegiance to white racial homogeneity in the United States.[31] More notoriously, the 1863 Draft Riots stressed Irish contempt for African Americans. Free Blacks not only were lynched on the streets of New York City, but those who blurred racial divides by way of interracial relationships also were targeted.[32] In this nineteenth-century context, Irishness became self-defined as a specifically white identity in the United States. The racial purging of neighborhoods that occurred as a result of these incidents has had greater implications for Irish American culture in the United States. Literary scholar Lauren Onkey maintains that the racial purging of African Americans is an important theme, even an "obsession," in many Irish American literary works. And race shapes how Irishness is celebrated on St. Patrick's Day, the most Irish of days (in the United States at least). The Irish are so removed from comparisons and liaisons with nineteenth-century free Blacks that African Americans such as Eddie Murphy, Shaquille O'Neal, and Toni Morrison, who have Irish surnames, are not considered Irish. In marked contrast, Afro-Irish singer and actress Samantha Mumba was the grand marshal of Dublin's St. Patrick's Day parade in 2003. While a U.S. senator, Barack Obama had to lobby for a place in Chicago's St. Patrick's Day parade. On a warmly received visit to the Republic of Ireland, the president reflected on the difficulty of securing a place in the Chicago parade by stating, "I'll bet those parade organizers are watching TV today and feeling kind of bad." Certainly, these biracial constructions of Irishness are unlikely to be displayed on St. Patrick's Day in New York City or any other U.S. city, for that matter, in the near future.[33]

Racist actions might assuage distress over Irish adherence to America's racial order, but they were not enough to fully establish racial aptitude in the United States. The Irish had to meet other racial standards such as faith, loyalty, hard work, and family and were better positioned to do so by the end of the nineteenth century, as increasing numbers entered the ranks of America's middle class. Although Irish immigrants continued to arrive in the United States after the Great Famine, for the first time the American-born second generation outnumbered the Irish-born, and as a result, Irish American identity was in a period of flux. According to Timothy Meagher, it "was hard to deny that, among some Irish Americans at the turn of the century, attitudes about a respectable standard of living, proper conduct, and their public image were clearly changing."[34] In this context, the Irish responded more forcefully and successfully to their racial hazing, and in doing so, they forged a model for Irishness in the United States.

Historian Joseph Lee has addressed the myriad ways in which the Irish responded to racial stereotyping in the United States: they tried to emulate Americans, they fought racial characterizations on their own terms, and they also refined the actual stereotypes.[35] Though I prefer using racial hazing over racial stereotyping to discuss Irish encounters with British and later U.S. racial schemes, Lee's model is a useful framework with which to understand how the Irish sought to establish their racial aptitude in the United States. In the case of racial homogeneity, the Irish adhered to this standard, as their racial attitudes upon arrival might be deemed ambivalent at best. Adherence to a strict bipolar racial order was a rather new expectation, and in the context of America's nineteenth-century slave republic, the Irish could disparage African Americans with relative ease. On the other hand, loyalty, faith, and by extension family had long been the benchmarks used to marginalize the Irish under both British and American regimes. In the U.S. context, with liberal citizenship and property laws for white males, the Irish were better positioned to counter their racial hazing and claim adherence to these standards on their own terms. If anything, they demonstrated in their own unique way how the Irish not only met but surpassed their American counterparts in these benchmarks. As far as order is concerned, in many ways the Irish acknowledged, even possibly endorsed, this supposed racial shortcoming, as such is necessary to fully establish racial competency in the United States.

The Irish fiercely challenged the fury directed against their allegedly backward faith. They were unapologetic for their Catholicism and boasted that their faith was superior to Protestantism. Church leaders, such as William Henry Cardinal O'Connell of Boston, challenged the Puritan theology of wealth and underscored the spiritual bankruptcy of material accumulation. Catholic charity workers similarly defended their values and efforts over those of their Protestant rivals, who, they maintained, used volunteer work to demonstrate their wealth. When visiting the poor after work instead of during their leisure time, Catholics insisted on having purer motives when helping others. In addition, popular Catholic works such as Mary Sadler's *The Blakes and the Callaghan's* (1858) warned of the spiritual risks of American materialism. In this context, some Irish Americans emphasized their religious rather than their ethnic identity, as the former could be associated with the refinement of French aristocracy, and the latter with Ireland's impoverished peasants.[36] The physical growth of the Catholic Church only strengthened this emphasis on the superiority of the Catholic faith.

Because of a growing Irish immigrant population, the Catholic Church built more churches, hospitals, elementary and secondary schools, and colleges, institutions where a more favorable view of the Catholic Church undoubtedly was proffered. This growing Catholic Church fostered a more solidly Irish Catholic identity, safely away from potentially corruptive Protestant influences. By the end of the nineteenth century, Irish Catholics more regularly attended mass, received communion, and attended parish missions. In addition, the Catholic Church encouraged families to incorporate holy water and candles as well as the rosary into their everyday rituals.[37] The growing infrastructure of the Catholic Church promoted not only more regular religious participation but also the growth of an Irish American middle class, a relationship historian Kerby Miller argues cannot be "underestimated." Such expansion, especially in education, promoted employment as well as upward mobility.[38]

By 1900, Irish Americans achieved occupational parity with native-born Americans; by the second decade of the twentieth century, they had surpassed the national average in college attendance and graduation.[39] Undoubtedly immigrant toil and sacrifice created opportunities for the American-born generation that followed and flourished. Though hard work certainly played a role, race-based structural advantages certainly assisted this achievement. Irish immigrants had access to political and economic resources denied to both migrants and native-born people of color. As a result, the Irish were extended opportunities to demonstrate their propensity for hard work in ways that others were not. In doing so, they could appear over time to have a particular procilivity for hard work. As a result, the Irish were better positioned to demonstrate their racial acumen in the United States. While some Irish Americans admired the American Protestant work ethic, others continued to warn that too much hard work and ambition would unmoor Catholics from their spiritual grounding. Mary Francis Egan's turn-of-the-century adult fiction, for example, consistently warned of material temptation as Patrick Dormand, one of her characters, was tempted by enormous wealth to give up his religion. Those who heeded such a warning, and achieved material success without the trappings of excessive material accumulation, could present Irish American success as purer and more noble than that of their Protestant counterparts.

Over time, Irish Americans acquired the tools with which to establish family-centered households. The aforementioned public distancing from people of color ensured that they adhered to the correct racial order, but they also adhered to the correct class and gender order: in other words, a household supported by a wage-earning husband and child-rearing wife. Race-based structural advantages extended to Irish men carved a middle-class economic position that racial fitness was so dependent upon, while Irish women, during their tenure as domestic servants, learned what constituted "respectable" American households. In racially homogeneous American homes, Irish women sometimes were considered more desirable than African American domestics precisely because of Irish proximity to white racial aptitude. That they could leave domestic service upon marriage was a manifestation of Irish American success. More important, Irish women could take what they learned about American respectability into their own racially homogeneous, middle-class, properly adorned households, but also beyond them, organizing parish fairs and engaging in charity work that rivaled their Protestant counterparts.[40] Nothing illustrates emerging Irish racial aptitude more than the emergence of the term "lace curtain" Irish in the 1890s. David Roediger maintains that the presence of white curtains in industrialized neighborhoods conveyed respectability but, more significantly, operated as "flags of whiteness," a way to signal a standard of living that made "whiteness visible" quite literally, in homes. Lace and linen imported directly from Ireland undoubtedly were cherished items in many Irish American homes. The terms "lace curtain" and "shanty" typically have been used to make class distinctions among the Irish. Though usually understood as a class distinction, references to proper households, adorned no less in Irish linen or lace, indicate a racial distinction, a self-conscious mark of *Irish* racial aptitude.[41]

Though women demonstrated Irish racial fitness by way of properly adorned, "lace-curtain" households, they were at the same time subject to a scrutiny that evaded their male counterparts. Irish women as domestic servants had access to American homes and thus a particular knowledge of racial standards that men did not. Tensions over this access were reflected in the mocking of Irish women who too closely resembled their Protestant counterparts, especially if they hired their own domestic servants. Nowhere is this better demonstrated than in Irish American popular culture. In vaudeville sketches and plays, the overly ambitious Irish character typically was represented as female.[42] Though Irish women were scrutinized within the community for being too ambitious, and thus too similar to Protestants, Irish Americans nonetheless typically extolled the moral superiority of their women. Despite being represented as overly fertile, single Irish female chastity was praised. Birth control and divorce were castigated as examples of Protestant self-interest and selfishness, while large families, which characterized Irish American life well into the 1950s, were heralded as morally superior.[43]

The Irish similarly defended their loyalty to the United States on their own terms. While nativists feared that the hierarchy of the Catholic Church would corrupt democracy in the United States, Irish Americans fired back, casting anti-Catholic bigotry as un-American. Though Irish nationalism raised questions about loyalty to the United States, many within the community believed Irish independence would elevate the status of the Irish in America. Furthermore, the Irish discussed nationalism within a decidedly U.S. context, drawing parallels between Irish and American efforts to break free from British rule.[44] While Irish participation in the New York City Draft Riots of 1863 cemented loyalty to America's bipolar racial order, it nonetheless raised questions about Irish willingness to fight on behalf of the Union, as did allegations of Irish desertion and passing information to Confederates. Christian Samito, however, has argued that Irish participation in the Civil War cemented ties to the United States. He maintains that toleration for Catholic religious practices within the military actually nurtured an Irish *American* identity. In this context, American chapters of the Fenian Movement began to emphasize their loyalty to the United States at their meetings and in their song lyrics. Publications such as David Power Conyngham's *History of the Irish Brigade* (1867) helped underscore Irish loyalty to the United States, as did war monuments dedicated to Irish military service.[45]

As the second generation of Irish Americans grew, so too did organizations such as the American Irish Historical Society (AIHS), which countered questions about loyalty with accounts of Irish battlefield bravery. Established in 1897 with the goal of circulating more favorable accounts of the Irish in American history, theAIHS hosted gatherings that typically underscored Irish military contributions to the United States. Annual dinners identified Irish signers of the Declaration of Independence and soldiers who fought both in the American War of Independence and the U.S. Civil War.[46] In addition to military service, the AIHS stressed Irish longevity in the United States. In a lecture titled "Irish Firsts in American History," Michael O'Brien, the organization's historiographer, described the construction of the first lighthouse on the Atlantic coast, as well as the first woman to receive a pension from the U.S. government for services rendered during the American Revolution.[47] Together, these accounts, which stressed military service and longevity, offered the Irish as particularly loyal to the United States.

With faith, hard work, family, and loyalty, the Irish responded to their racial hazing by demonstrating how they were adept, even superior to Protestants. Order, on the other hand, was a somewhat different matter. Many Irish illustrated their commitment to order by scrutinizing the behaviors of their own people, especially drinking behaviors. Many Catholic parishes formed temperance organizations in the United States by the 1880s, and the Irish American Total Abstinence Movement soon was bigger than the temperance crusade in the United States. By the late 1890s, nearly 100,000 members had taken a pledge to abstain from alcohol.[48] Increasing numbers of sober Irish would challenge their racialization as disorderly drunks, yet the scrutiny of this behavior in other Irish nonetheless confirmed its existence. By policing behaviors that American Protestants found unacceptable, Irish American temperance activists seemed to confirm this characterization of the Irish. Nonetheless, Irish temperance organizations in the United States were decidedly different than their Protestant counterparts, as they had the indelible imprint of the Catholic Church. Often they were organized by priests in church quarters, and they often incorporated religious practices such as Holy Communion. Although Irish temperance organizations initially were male, women increasingly joined their ranks by the end of the nineteenth century.[49]

As people from a largely agricultural society, the Irish did not drink more than their British or American counterparts. They were more likely, however, to succumb to higher rates of alcohol addiction and disease, as well as higher rates of mental illness.[50] This perhaps can be explained by the harsh realities of immigration. As immigrants abroad, the Irish tended to drink more than in Ireland. Richard Strivers has located Irish drinking within the larger process of immigrant incorporation within the United States. He argues that the Irish transformed their racial characterization as drunkards into that of the happy drunk, internalizing this more positive characterization to be more fully accepted. Only by accepting its caricature, he explains, could an immigrant group be deemed "predictable and safe."[51] While there were those Irish Americans who never would accept even this modified caricature, others who did were enough to convey that the bad Irish Paddy had been tamed. By accepting a more positive racialization, the Irish conveyed their acceptance of an American order that sorts and caricatures an array of "others." By displaying, and therefore acknowledging, a particular caricature from this order, they no longer were relegated to the bottom. They still were Paddies, but *good* Paddies, nonetheless, who conformed to white racial expectations in the United States.

Irish American organizations collectively promoted a more cohesive good Paddy Irish image. The Ancient Order of Hibernians (AOH) formed as a fraternal Catholic organization in 1836 to counter aforementioned nativist attacks directed against the Irish in America.[52] It too similarly pressed for greater attention to Irish contributions in the United States. Mary F. McWorter, national chairperson of the AOH's Ladies Auxiliary, proposed special Irish history summer schools for elementary school teachers and encouraged members to read Irish literature to their children. The *National Hibernian*, the organization's national newsletter, included articles on the history of the Irish in the United States, accompanied by questions for home study.[53] These efforts to articulate a more favorable account of the Irish in the United States, though directed at its members, also reached a larger audience. Less than ten years after its inception, the AIHS had issued several bound volumes to its members and also to public libraries, historical organizations, and universities. By its seventy-fifth anniversary, the AIHS had amassed 30,000 volumes on the Irish.[54]

While these organizations differed somewhat in their membership and mission, they nonetheless used similar terms to describe the Irish in the United States. Thomas Lonergan, president of the AIHS, explained, "The Irish are a most important element in our composite citizenship. Why? Because they stand for law and order, for virtue and patriotism, and for home and family and for God and country."[55] Eileen Ryan, president of the AOH Ladies Auxiliary, reflected comparably in 1915:

> After a few years of struggle, bitter and severe and with the courage of their race . . . many of these same princely pioneers within a short space of time saw the men of their race holding many of the highest positions in the land, ecclesiastical and lay, and enjoying the comforts procured for them by self-sacrificing fathers and mothers. . . . bravely they went forth to die for the land of their adoption.[56]

Irish county organizations in the United States, which first formed in the 1840s around local Irish affiliations, utilized similar language. In a 1904 address to members of the County Sligo Association, Dr. J. C. Hanan stated, "When I came to this country . . . Irishmen at that time had but little education, some none and they were formed for hard work, yes, slaving work, but today you see Irishmen in a different state, they are businessmen, clerks, bookkeepers."[57] These depictions of the Irish as loyal, orderly, hardworking, and family-oriented are neither random nor incidental. They conformed to white racial expectations in the United States and corresponded specifically to the ways in which the Irish Paddy had been depicted as lazy, disorderly and racially suspect. These descriptions should be viewed as a deliberate response to Irish racial hazing. In stressing Irish respectability, these representations were at the same time accentuating Irish racial fitness.

Irish ethnic organizations themselves were configured around the correct class and gender order. Although they varied, the AIHS, the AOH, and various Irish county organizations organized yearly banquets, balls, and dinners. Clearly evoking middle-class respectability, these organizations also espoused distinct gender conventions. The AOH and various Irish county organizations had separate ladies' auxiliaries. Individuals honored by these organizations and those who addressed these groups, the more prestigious and public roles, were reserved for men, while women typically engaged in supporting roles, educating their children in Irish history, or organizing dances and socials. Any Irish American woman unsure of her proper role needed to look no further than publications such as the *Irish American Advocate*. There she could find accounts of socials led by Irish American women, including "daintily served" refreshments served by a hostess adorned in "Irish point lace." Similarly, Irish women were warned not to "tether" husbands by the fireside: "If he's the breadwinner by day do not twist life out of him by making him a servant at night."[58]

Attention to Irish respectability and its subtext for racial aptitude also could be found elsewhere, especially in Irish American publications. In Kathleen Conway's *Lawlor Maples* (1901), immigrant John Lawlor secures a white-collar position through "hard work," while his wife organizes an "orderly" home adorned with "patterned carpets, mahogany and horsehair chairs." Prolific Kate Clearly similarly attended to Irish respectability in her stories, including accounts of American-born children "scandalized" by old clothes. Additionally, the Catholic Church advanced Irish respectability, in guidebooks including *The Mirror of True Womanhood* and the *Book of Instruction for Women of the World*, as well as its growing number of publications in the United

States, including journals, magazines, and newspapers. While these publications targeted women, the church also offered all-male masses, societies, and athletic leagues.[59] That the Catholic Church publicly endorsed American proscriptions for domestic order only underscored Irish loyalty and racial fitness.

By the end of the nineteenth century, access to race-based resources gave Irish immigrants the tools with which to establish orderly, family-oriented households, supported by hardworking husbands and child-rearing wives. A deliberate and public Irish distancing from African Americans suggests that these households adhered to the correct racial order. Various Irish ethnic organizations, themselves organized around the correct class and gender order, emphasized these traits as well as Irish loyalty in various self-representations. Together these factors, coupled with attention to Irish respectability, by both Irish American writers and the Catholic Church, allowed the Irish to champion their racial aptitude in the United States. By emphasizing their racial fitness, the Irish had made themselves into good Paddies in the United States. They did so, however, by working with the standards that initially deemed them racially substandard. In shaping their Irishness to meet the larger racial expectations for being American, they affixed these same standards to being Irish, and thus Irishness became part of a larger race-based tradition in the United States. Initially joined to white racial fitness, the race-, class-, and gender-laden traits of order, hard work, and family, in addition to loyalty and faith, now would be the benchmark for Irish American identity.

Thus, this evolution of the good Paddy Irish model can contextualize the descriptions of early St. Patrick's Day celebrations in Yonkers. Attention to "handsomely dressed" participants, elaborate balls, and equally intricate menus was not arbitrary but corresponded to this long trajectory both in Ireland and in the United States where private or domestic matters—how their households were organized—were used to challenge the racial fitness of the Irish. Widely circulated representations of the racially suspect Irish as dirty and lazy, with the drunk and violent Paddy and the disorderly Biddy, were countered at the St. Patrick's Day celebration in Yonkers by attention to orderly participants and the religious faith of those who attended mass before the festivities. The very public display of American flags underscored the loyalty of this once-suspect group. While the St. Patrick's Day parade is an indication of how this group understood itself as Irish, these characteristics—order, religious faith, and loyalty—were at the same time indicative of how the group stressed its racial aptitude. Developments at the turn of the century, however, had the potential to thwart these efforts.

Tantalizingly Close to the Mainstream

As a self-image emerged in Irish America more in line with white racial expectations, increasing numbers of immigrants from southern and eastern Europe began to arrive in the United States. The presence of more recent arrivals served to elevate the Irish in the United States. Historian Nell Irving Painter warns, however, that this evolution "came with such reluctance and with so many qualifications and insults . . . that the commentary was far more likely to castigate new immigrants than welcome the old." The growing presence of these newcomers unleashed a new wave of nativism at a time when the Irish were, in the words of Lynn Dumenil, "tantalizingly close to the mainstream."[60] In the wake of a severe economic downturn beginning in 1893, the American Protective Association (APA) grew to 2 million members during that decade, drawing largely from the ranks of American-born businessmen and midwestern workers. In addition to its calls for immigration restriction, the APA demanded free nonsectarian public schools and the abolition of tax breaks for Catholic property. Members also boycotted Catholic merchants and took oaths not to vote for Catholic politicians. Clearly these efforts intended to curb the power of the Catholic Church, which now was a firm and potentially expanding institution with the arrival of new immigrants from southern and eastern Europe. The number of Catholics in the United States grew from 310,000 in 1830 to 18 million by 1920.[61] This nativist movement was given the additional weight of the Immigration Restriction League in 1896, whose members included businessmen, politicians, and upper-class academics who also lobbied Congress for immigration restriction.

These organizations found support in publications such as the *Menace*, which by 1915 could boast of a circulation three times greater than the largest daily newspapers in New York and Chicago combined. Similar anti-Catholic newspapers gave "substantial" attention to the escaped nun stories of the previous century, reports of children abused at the hands of church leaders, as well as graft and corruption.[62] Hostility toward immigrants only intensified as the United States inched closer to entering World War I. Irish Americans, though initially restrained in their treatment of Great Britain in their local press, could not contain their anger after the failed Irish Easter Rising in 1916. Such hatred for America's ally certainly revisited old questions about Irish American loyalty once again. In a speech honoring Commodore James Barry, President Woodrow Wilson praised the Catholic founder of the U.S. Navy but also condemned Irish Americans who required "hyphenated names because only half of them came over."[63]

Antiforeign sentiment reached fever pitch after World War I, when the Ku Klux Klan's campaign for "one-hundred percent American-ism" helped rally support for the national prohibition of alcohol, the elimination of private schools in Oregon (which later was overturned), the defeat of Catholic Al Smith in his 1928 bid for the presidency, and congressional restriction of European immigration. In this context of growing anti-Catholicism, a specifically Irish identity merged with a militant Catholic identity, "broad enough," Timothy Meagher maintains, to "encompass Catholics of all backgrounds." This transformation took shape in the Knights of Columbus and the National Welfare Catholic Council, which fought anti-Catholic rhetoric and legislation during that era. Congress nonetheless enacted immigration quotas that favored northern and western European nations, including the Republic of Ireland, over countries from southern and eastern Europe.[64]

More favorable treatment under U.S. immigration law was paralleled by more positive images of Irish Americans in popular culture. The ape-like, dirty "Paddy" and the disorderly "Bridget," once stock characters in the pages of *Harper's Weekly*, largely vanished in the United States by the early twentieth century; so too did comparisons with African Americans.[65] If anything resembling these earlier caricatures emerged, Irish Americans now were better positioned to fight them. Irish American organizations pressured MGM studios to modify unflattering depictions of the Irish in 1927 films such as *Irish Hearts* and *The Callaghans and the Murphys*. After the latter prompted public disturbances in New York City and Yonkers, MGM withdrew the film. As a result of these protests, which signaled Irish American strength, Hollywood was forced to censor stories that might offend Irish Americans and introduced a production code with the assistance of community leaders. Not surprisingly, film representations of the Irish improved. Christopher Shannon has argued that "the drinking, the fighting, laughing and crying that once marked the Irish as savage, now stood as a sign of Irish humanity."[66] Irish fighting was transformed in film from a destructive force to a vehicle for redemption, and the Catholic priest soon emerged as a leading figure. These changes, Shannon maintains, helped pave the way for Irish American assimilation in the postwar period.

By the middle of the twentieth century, more Irish Americans had made themselves into good Paddies in the United States. A series of government initiatives enacted by the New Deal expanded access to union membership, college education, and homeownership, allowed scores of working-class white ethnics to organize middle-class and thus more orderly households. These largely race-based structural advances allowed scores of Irish Americans to carve a middle-class position that racial fitness was so dependent upon. With their economic standing and thus racial fitness elevated, representations of Irish Americans only continued to improve. Milton Barton, a "leading expert" in the emerging field of U.S. immigration history, offered a positive discussion of the Irish, while textbooks such as *Our America* underscored contributions of Irish American soldiers during World War II. And during America's Cold War with the Soviet Union, Catholics became increasingly prominent in films, magazines, and television. Catholics in the United States, once deemed a threat, now helped "ease" Americans, according to Anthony Burke Smith, into a new postwar social order that condemned godless communism and esteemed consensus and domesticity. While Catholics more broadly were represented in a positive light, subjects represented in popular culture usually were Irish American. At the same time, Irish Catholic organizations such as the AOH launched "intense" campaigns against American communists, which only served to reinforce associations between Irishness, loyalty, faith, and order.[67] Within this context, the city of Yonkers revived its St. Patrick's Day parade tradition in 1955. As the Irish in America inched closer to full racial fitness, the benchmarks for Irish American identity were buttressed by new Irish arrivals in the United States. Conditions, however, both in Ireland and in the United States, determined how well later generations of immigrants to Yonkers could sustain the good Paddy Irish model during the twentieth century.

More Good Paddies

Though the economic horizon looked especially grim in southwest Yonkers with the loss of manufacturing in the decades following World War II, many found in north and east Yonkers a suburban retreat from parts of Upper Manhattan and the Bronx. Arriving during the city's post–World War II phase of suburbanization were upwardly mobile white ethnics—Irish, Jews, and Italians—fleeing the same forces of urban renewal, changing racial demographics, and deindustrialization in New York City that had transformed Getty Square in southwest Yonkers. Some of the Irish in this postwar migration to Yonkers were immigrants who left Ireland for New York City during the 1950s.[68] These "Irish white flighters" could easily meet the racial expectations for being Irish.

The Irish who migrated to New York City during the 1950s came of age after Ireland's civil war and the subsequent establishment of the Irish Free State in 1923, which shaped their reception in the United States. In an attempt to form a financially and politically independent nation, Irish politicians sought to create a self-sufficient rural economy based on agriculture as they equated industrialization, urbanization, and consumption with Great Britain. Free of British rule and arguably racial caricatures, the new nation promoted its fitness for self-rule with Gaelic language, dance, and sport as well as the Catholic Church and the nuclear family. The Irish government promoted the latter with family allowances and enforced proscribed roles for women as wives and mothers to future Irish citizens as divorce and contraception were prohibited, and a ban on married women in public service employment was in effect until 1973.[69]

Recent scholarship illustrates how Irish policies actually worked to undermine family life. Unmarried mothers typically were sent to mother and baby homes, while more "hopeless" cases, that is, those with more than one illegitimate child, sexually active women, or victims of sexual abuse, as well as those deemed wayward or simple, were detained in Magdalen asylums for extended periods of time, even life.

And "no child," Moira Maguire argues, "was more disregarded in policy and everyday practice than the illegitimate child," who typically was institutionalized, boarded out to a foster family until the age of fifteen, or sent overseas for adoption. Among U.S. servicemen stationed in Great Britain, Ireland gained a reputation as a "happy hunting ground" for healthy, white babies. In this climate, unwed expectant mothers often traveled to England to give birth.[70]

This strict emphasis on the nuclear family, in addition to agriculture and high protective tariffs, inhibited the development of a prosperous economy in Ireland. In the early decades of the twentieth century, land in Ireland still was inherited primarily by a single male heir. With scant industrial development, noninheriting siblings could not establish livelihoods and thus had to look to foreign, rather than Irish, towns and cities for employment. Ireland's large nuclear families only heightened pressures to emigrate. More than 500,000 men and women left cash-strapped Ireland between 1946 and 1961.[71]

Prior to the creation of the Irish Free State, emigration from Ireland could be blamed on British polices. After independence, Great Britain no longer could be held responsible. Although emigration provided a safety valve, ridding Ireland of its surplus labor, an exodus of Irish people exposed the shortcomings of the newly formed state. Even more troubling was the considerable shift in Irish emigration as Great Britain, rather than the United States, became the destination of choice. Immigration restrictions of the 1920s, the Great Depression, and World War II weakened immigrant flows from Ireland to the United States. Irish self-rule, and a severe British labor shortage, cast Britain in a more positive light. Though some racial caricatures lingered, the Irish were more favorably received after World War II, especially when nonwhite migrants entered Great Britain in greater numbers. Furthermore, the short geographic distance between Great Britain and Ireland made for a more affordable journey and allowed migrants to make regular return visits. Nonetheless, high emigration rates prompted the Irish government to enact an array of social and economic programs beginning in the 1960s. Until then, its young people looked elsewhere for opportunity.[72]

Of the approximately 500,000 who left Ireland at this time, approximately 70,000 immigrated to the United States.[73] With enhanced enforcement of the 1891 "likely to become a public charge" ushered in by the Great Depression, these migrants usually were sponsored in the United States by a family relative, with whom they often lived upon arrival. Many of the men in this migration found work in civil service or the building trades, while many of the women found work in the expanding service economy as waitresses and clerks in companies such as New York Telephone. Though their numbers paled in comparison to earlier waves of nineteenth-century Irish migrants, their presence, albeit smaller, was felt in New York City, where they gave new immigrant life to U.S.-based ethnic organizations such as Irish county associations and the Ancient Order of Hibernians. They also enjoyed institutions such as the *Irish Echo* newspaper and the Gaelic Athletic Association (GAA), the latter of which sustained regular Irish football and hurling competitions.[74] On most Sunday afternoons, Gaelic Park in the Bronx was packed with enthusiastic Irish sport spectators.

As young people in Ireland, this generation typically socialized in alcohol-free dance halls. Intemperance was not widespread because beer and spirits were expensive in cash-poor Ireland and because many were "pioneers," making a pledge for the sacrament of Confirmation to abstain from alcohol until they reached the age of twenty-one. Though rooted in religious devotion, temperance in postcolonial Ireland surely was shaped by racial caricatures about Irish drinking that accompanied British rule, as widespread sobriety worked to establish Irish suitability for independence.[75] Many in this generation brought their enthusiasm for dance halls to New York City. The City Center, which opened on Fifty-Fifth Street, between Fifth and Sixth Avenues in 1956, was considered one of the foremost Irish dance halls in the United States. On a typical Saturday night, as many as 2,000 people would hear traditional ceili music and old-time waltzes. Unlike in Ireland, these dance halls did serve alcohol. Some in this generation kept their pioneer pledge for life, while others, if they did drink, tended to do so in moderation.[76] Having come of age in a postcolonial Ireland that stressed temperance, the nuclear family, and devout Catholicism deemed them good Paddies prior to their arrival, but their experience in postwar America would serve to reinforce this Irish model.

Unlike many native-born people of color, as white immigrants, this Irish cohort could enjoy a series of government initiatives that expanded access to union membership, college education, and homeownership, which undoubtedly put them on the fast track to middle-class economic prosperity.[77] Many Irish men in the 1950s migration obtained well-paying unionized work that allowed their spouses to leave the workforce upon marriage, raise children, and create an orderly middle-class household. Furthermore, many Irish men were drafted into the military, only serving to establish their loyalty to the United States. The Catholic Church equally was expansive in postwar New York, and members of this cohort usually enrolled their children in the growing parochial school system. While these Irish immigrants undoubtedly arrived in the United States with their own racial knowledge and language, Frank McCourt's memoirs suggest that a racial slur such as "spic" may have been a new addition to their vocabulary.[78] And that they left increasingly Black and Latino neighborhoods in New York City underscored their adherence to white racial homogeneity. Undoubtedly this generation of Irish immigrants established both their faith and their loyalty and maintained their households in the correct race, class, and gender order. As a result, those in this migration who moved from neighborhoods in the Bronx and Upper Manhattan to suburban, largely segregated tracts of north and east Yonkers during the 1970s went unnoticed. They were not subject to racial hazing because they could easily meet the racial expectations required of being Irish in the United States. And a recent local oral history project suggests that members of this cohort saw themselves in ways that conformed to the good Paddy Irish model. Most interviews stressed family, military service, the "moral uplift" of the Catholic faith, and their work ethic.[79] Clearly they were seen and saw themselves in terms that conformed to the good Paddy Irish model. A larger cultural movement under way in the United States, moreover, would give an additional gloss to this standard.

The Good Paddy Revival

Perhaps no other event signaled Irish racial aptitude in the United States more than the election of John F. Kennedy as president in 1960. While there were some lingering questions about Catholics in popular and academic discourse, his election nonetheless conveyed the compatibility of "Irish Catholic" with "American." Kennedy's civil rights agenda, which was enacted after his assassination, intended to assist oppressed people of color, but it actually worked to promote Irish Americans and white ethnics more generally. The success of the civil rights movement during the 1960s legitimatized a logic of group oppression and group rights in the United States. White ethnics used this reasoning to minimize their own position in the white power structure that increasingly was coming under attack. Nathan Glazer and Daniel Patrick Moynihan's book *Beyond the Melting Pot* (1963) augmented this trend. Their study disputed the University of Chicago's model of assimilation, long an accepted paradigm for understanding social groups in the United States. "Perhaps the meaning of ethnic labels will yet be erased in America," they explained, but "it has not yet worked out this way in New York."[80] Their emphasis on cultural difference, however, minimized the unequal treatment of groups in the larger U.S. political economy and their different outcomes. As a result of this oversight, group success, rooted no less in domestic standards, was attributed to cultural aptitude, while group failure was explained in terms of cultural pathology. Though they lamented why the Irish had not been more successful in the United States, Glazer and Moynihan clearly underscored Irish aptitude, in marked contrast to their treatment of Puerto Rican and Black failure, which they attributed to "weak families" and a "lack of motivation and self-help." Though Puerto Rican and Irish immigrants shared a colonial history and religious faith, Glazer and Moynihan depicted the island of Puerto Rico as "defective" and characterized the Catholic Church there as "weak." Even if they did not meet Glazer and Moynihan's standards for success, the Irish undoubtedly came across as more family-oriented and more hardworking, orderly, and faithful than their Puerto Rican and Black counterparts.

Moynihan himself reinforced the ethnic divide between cultural aptitude and cultural pathology two years later in his report *The Negro Family and the Case for National Action* (1965). Moynihan located Black urban poverty in poor family structures and blamed households headed by single females for a "tangle of pathology," including welfare dependency, unemployment, illegitimacy, and divorce. Though his job creation proposal did not result in any significant policy change, this report received considerable media attention, and Moynihan's earlier collaboration with Glazer is still heralded more than forty years later as a classic.[81] Together they shaped how white ethnic groups would be understood in U.S. society and how they would understand themselves.

Glazer and Moynihan's work informed a larger shift in U.S. collective identity. Matthew Frye Jacobson argues that racial whiteness, "long the key to American belonging and power relations," shifted from "Plymouth Rock whiteness" to "Ellis Island whiteness." As a result, the "downtrodden but determined greenhorn" became incorporated within the larger, racially defined, national collective.[82] This shift was reflected by the 1965 changes in immigration law, which abolished the previous national origins quotas favoring northern and western Europe over southern and eastern Europe. This transformation undoubtedly encouraged an "ethnic revival," marked in recent years by multiculturalism in school curricula and a demand from consumers for all things ethnic.[83] More broadly, this development influenced (and continues to influence) debates about affirmative action, welfare, and immigration, as well as narratives about the history of the Irish in the United States.

The admonition"No Irish Need Apply," for example, is commonly understood as an accompaniment to nineteenth-century job announcements, yet Richard Jensen argues that there is no historical evidence for its use.[84] Evidence of discrimination, however, can be found in classified ads with wording such as "Woman wanted to do general housework . . . English, Scotch, Welsh, German or any other or color except Irish." This is likely the basis for "No Irish Need Apply" ("NINA") that many Irish Americans believe was posted on signs in factories and construction sites. How this shorthand gained currency is unclear, but it probably was popularized by a song of the same name in 1863.[85] While this slogan may have originated in the nineteenth century, it undoubtedly gained currency within the larger U.S. shift from "Plymouth Rock whiteness" to "Ellis Island whiteness" and the consequent valorization of the "downtrodden but determined greenhorn." This construction of the Irish as particularly downtrodden is what Diane Negra calls a "racial fantasy."[86] The "NINA" myth resonates with so many Irish Americans precisely because they are so far removed from nineteenth-century encounters with discrimination and oppression. This version of "Irish," Negra maintains, offers a "guilt-free ethnicity." Irish racial fantasies divert Irish Americans from their own position in the larger white power structure that increasingly was brought under attack, and therein resides its appeal.[87] This racial fantasy is indulged in an array of contemporary Irish American texts that typically equate Irish colonization and African American slavery, obscuring the race-based structural advantages enjoyed by the Irish as well as Irish racism in the United States. Such omissions, Catherine Eagan argues, cast Irishness in the United States in terms of both "racial innocence" and "multicultural belonging."[88]

Irish American comparisons between the Irish immigrant and African American experience are meant to highlight *Irish* suffering; similarities do not necessarily elicit sympathy for African Americans. Nowhere is this more apparent than in Irish American distaste for Bernadette Devlin, a civil rights activist from Northern Ireland. The struggle for Catholic civil rights in Northern Ireland drew inspiration from the civil rights movement in the United States. Devlin, for example, visited Angela Davis in prison on a trip to the United States and criticized Irish Americans over Boston's school integration controversy during the 1970s. When she was scheduled to address a 1969 event organized by Irish Americans in Detroit, African Americans who also arrived to hear her speak were turned away. To show her solidarity with oppressed people of color, Devlin refused to begin until they were admitted. When Devlin made comparisons between Catholic oppression in Northern Ireland and Black oppression in the United States, some Irish American audience members left in protest.[89]

Whether motivated by racial fantasy or racial innocence, there is a material cast to renewed interest in Irish ethnicity. The number of Irish-themed retail stores in the United States doubled during the 1990s and there is at least one such store in most states.[90] This trend has inspired many costly "root visits" to Ireland in search of family histories, with interest not in lineage to Irish kings but to Irish peasants.[91] Attention to the latter is indicative of Irish American interest in Irish downtroddeness and undoubtedly indulges a racial fantasy. While a trip to Ireland may offer a deeper ethnic connection than a mass-produced Irish product, these trips reveal more about national racial politics than a desire for deeper knowledge of family history. Catherine Nash maintains that pursuits of family histories also can be read as a "reactionary appeal" to a white European identity and growing anxieties about the changing cultural composition of the United States.[92] Perhaps the most remarkable indication of this interest in Irish downtroddeness can be found in the U.S. South, where many people of Scotch-Irish descent are beginning to self-identify solely as Irish.[93] This trend, which emphasizes Irish privation and obscures Irish privilege, has real consequences in the United States whereby violent, racist agendas are advanced under the guise of Irish cultural symbols.[94] Irish downtroddeness also has implications for the Yonkers Irish. The addition of hardship served to augment the good Paddy Irish model. As a result, the Irish in the United States were recast as *particularly* hardworking, loyal, and orderly because they endured adversity. In reifying the Irish as racially adept, undocumented, working-class Irish immigrants who began to arrive in Yonkers by the 1990s would be marked as particularly aberrant.

Bad Paddies on Arrival

The Republic of Ireland tried to reverse its long history of economic stagnation and emigration that continued after the creation of the Irish Free State by modernizing its economy. Membership in the European Economic Community in 1973, subsidies for foreign companies, and the expansion of credit and social welfare programs, especially in the realm of education, brought capital and jobs to Ireland during the 1960s and 1970s. The by-products of these efforts, 23 percent inflation and nearly 20 percent unemployment, troubled Ireland in the 1980s. Approximately 360,000 men and women, many of whom were college-educated, left Ireland between 1981 and 1991. While most, like their 1950s predecessors, went to Great Britain, approximately 50,000 "new Irish" immigrants entered the United States.[95]

This generation came of age in an Ireland that would be unrecognizable to their 1950s predecessors. Not only was Ireland part of an international community, but its citizens were better educated and exposed by way of television to other parts of the world. And a series of scandals during the 1980s began to unravel the authority of the Catholic Church. With the ban on contraception removed and the expansion of financial resources to unwed mothers, there appeared to be a greater tolerance not only for sex but also for children conceived outside of marriage. They left an Ireland that was concerned less with establishing Irish respectability, and they arrived in a changing United States. For an earlier generation of Irish immigrants, the opportunities in the United States seemed endless. These Irish newcomers, in contrast, arrived when the United States was transitioning from a manufacturing to a service economy and government subsidies for social services were being scaled back in favor of privatization. Not only did this generation of Irish immigrants (and their U.S. counterparts) find less economic opportunity than their predecessors, but they did not have the same access to legal residency. The overhaul of immigration law in 1965 mandated close family relations or preferred skills instead of "national origins" quotas. As a result, many young Irish entered the United States as tourists and overstayed their holiday visas, finding work within the informal economy as construction laborers, bartenders, waitresses, and nannies, giving new life to neighborhoods in the Bronx, Queens, and Manhattan where the Irish-born population had been in decline for decades.[96] The *Irish Voice* was launched in 1987 as a new paper for this generation whose experiences differed greatly from those of their immediate predecessors.

These circumstances would shape the way this generation forged an Irish community in the United States. Without close family ties or access to structural support, bars in New York functioned as "community centers" for this generation.[97] They provided a space to network for jobs, cash checks, and host fund-raisers for the injured and the sick, crucial functions for those without access to union halls, banks, and health care. Acquisition of housing could be difficult for these newcomers because apartment leases often required social security numbers; as a result, apartments could be overcrowded, housing several roommates.[98] With their future in the United States uncertain, many planned to return to Ireland eventually, making the purchase of household furnishings and comforts both costly and pointless. Moreover, because marriage and children would only compound the difficulty of undocumented life, many in this generation preferred casual sexual encounters. And instead of regular attendance at mass, their interaction with the Catholic Church was more likely through Project Irish Outreach, an organization formed in New York City in response to heightened immigration restriction in the United States at large. Under these conditions, both in Ireland and in the United States, this generation of immigrants could not organize their households around the correct class and gender order or establish their loyalty to the United States or their faith in the Catholic Church, putting them undoubtedly at odds with other Irish in the United States.

The most bitter and public conflict between Irish immigrant newcomers and their predecessors concerned New York City's St. Patrick's Day parade and whether Irish lesbians and gays could march in this festivity under a separate banner. The Irish Lesbian and Gay Organization (ILGO) formed in 1990 to provide a safe space for lesbians and gays of Irish descent. Many young men and women had left Ireland during the 1980s precisely because of their fear of "coming out," only to find that they had to be closeted in New York's Irish communities. Anne Maguire, a Dublin native and founding member of ILGO, explained, "There would be no job, no place to live, no relief for loneliness if the community was aware of our homosexuality."[99] ILGO, however, allowed its members to be both Irish *and* gay. After marching in New York City's Lesbian and Gay Pride Parade, ILGO applied to march in the city's St. Patrick's Day parade, which was (and still is) organized by the Ancient Order of Hibernians. After initially being denied entry because of "municipal restrictions," ILGO was placed on a waiting list. Later, in 1991, the group marched with Mayor David Dinkins and Manhattan's Seventh Division of the AOH, only to be met with shouts and jeers such as "Faggots. Queers. You're not Irish. You must be English!" Such comparisons to Great Britain revealed how some viewed homosexuality as not merely abhorrent but treasonous to Irish American identity. Indeed ILGO's alliance with Dinkins challenged the racial homogeneity of the parade, while its strong lesbian direction tested the traditionally male leadership of the parade, as well as its heteronormativity. Compared with the Ku Klux Klan, ILGO was cast in continuous court battles as the antithesis of Irishness because homosexuality was contrary to Catholic Church doctrine. Subsequentially, ILGO was not permitted to march in future St. Patrick Day parades in Manhattan (although gays and lesbians are welcome in the Queens St. Patrick's Day parade, as well as in parades across Ireland).[100]

In addition to this bitter battle over the correct Irish order and faith, academic studies of these Irish newcomers revealed an array of everyday tensions. Linda Dowling Almeida's history of the 1950s and 1980s Irish in New York City revealed clashes over unpaid phone bills, questionable work ethics, and "bleary-eyed" nannies showing up for work on a Monday morning "too tired" to care for infants and toddlers.[101] Mary P. Corcoran's study of the 1980s Irish included more evidence of conflict: "The older Irish think that the new Irish lack morals because they see couples living together, they see people drinking, being rowdy and disturbing the neighborhood. They don't understand why the new Irish don't come in and actively participate in their civic clubs and county associations."[102]

While these differences were understood as generational, the specific language used is more telling. References to laziness, drinking, potentially threatening public behavior, and unmarried partnerships correspond to the ways in which this generation fell short of the racial expectations for being Irish. These traits, however, had a particular resonance in the United States during the 1980s.

The broader neoliberal shift in the United States economy from manufacturing to service and the rollback of social programs in favor of privatization, which resulted in the upward redistribution of wealth, accelerated under a series of "culture wars" during the 1980s and 1990s. Appeals to agendas of race and gender resulted in the realignment of politics to the right, and the rhetoric that enabled this transition was that Americans had less not because of the loss of industry or government subsidies for wealthy individuals and corporations but because of the excesses of the 1960s—women's and civil rights movements in particular. People of color, ever the scapegoat of economic decline, were not referenced specifically by race or ethnicity. Instead, racially coded terms such as "welfare queens" and "illegal aliens" gained currency and mobilized support for dismantling programs like welfare and affirmative action. Linkages between these racial outsiders with an array of social problems such as crime, drugs, and urban violence worked to advance the privatization of social services and the policing of inner-city youth and the U.S.-Mexico border, and also underscored "proper" American households as white and middle-class. The concomitant resurgence in religious fundamentalism and the crusade against homosexuality and women's rights added a religious and heteronormative gloss to this raced and classed notion of respectable households.[103]

Descriptions of undocumented Irish newcomers that emphasized indifference to work, less traditional sexual mores, hard drinking, and potentially violent behavior illustrate how members of this group were

marked as bad Paddies because they failed to meet the racial expectations for being Irish. This disparity between the 1950s and 1980s Irish
was more striking, and perhaps more alarming to some given the larger
"culture wars" of the 1980s, whereby racial ineptitude was firmly associated in popular discourse with people of color. Like their nineteenth-
century predecessors, these Irish newcomers shared a class and cultural
proximity to people of color, and they too threatened to blur existing
racial divides in the United States. Though the racial fitness of Irish
newcomers was questioned by older Irish immigrants, they still enjoyed
a degree of race privilege, as they usually received more desirable and
better-paying jobs than their Mexican, Central American, and Caribbean counterparts.[104] The new Irish, nonetheless, presented an interesting paradox. They first settled in neighborhoods of the Bronx, Queens,
and Manhattan where the numbers of Irish-born had been in decline
for decades, serving to literally reproduce this population, but their version of being Irish threatened to unhinge existing associations between
the Irish and racial aptitude. There would be consequences to these disparities in nearby Yonkers.

* * *

As Irish newcomers moved into Woodlawn Heights in the north central Bronx, settlement spilled over into the bordering McLean Avenue
section of southeast Yonkers. Their arrival was marked by the mid-
1990s with the establishment of distinctly Irish businesses, such as
bars, restaurants, coffee shops, travel agencies, and an Irish butcher,
and an array of products, including candy, soda, newspapers, and even
imported bread, could be found in most local delis. Gaelic names such
as the Granuaile, the An Bodhran, or An Sioppa Beag adorned some of
these establishments. The Aisling Irish Center opened in 1996 to meet
the needs of this growing community. In less than a decade, southeast
Yonkers had been transformed into an ethnic enclave, prompting some
to refer to this section as "Little Ireland."[105]

As plans to bring new investment to Yonkers began to take shape
during the early 1990s, hard drinking by bad Paddies, primarily undocumented Irish men and women, was first subject to surveillance by the
city council and police department. As redevelopment plans began to

materialize less than a decade later, a "Guinness pub," a franchise in an increasingly popular Irish-themed bar and restaurant chain and more in line with the good Paddy Irish model, was considered as part of what would become a $3.1 billion arrangement to bring a minor-league baseball stadium and retail and office space, as well as luxury housing and upscale consumers, to the city's former industrial waterfront in southwest Yonkers. These plans, part of a larger neoliberal agenda based on aggressive privatization and policing, would reveal the real consequences of bad Paddy digressions in the city of Yonkers.

3

Bar Wars

Irish Bar Politics in Neoliberal Ireland and Neoliberal Yonkers

During the early 1990s, the southeast section of McLean Avenue witnessed the arrival of several stand-alone drinking establishments that were patronized largely by working-class, undocumented Irish immigrant newcomers. This shift marked the arrival of bad Paddies in the city of Yonkers. In response to homeowners' complaints, the city council issued a moratorium on new bars in 1996, and a heightened police presence was dispatched to quell potential bar-related trouble. Conflicts between the Yonkers Police Department and bar patrons ensued, which in one case resulted in a federal indictment against two officers for violating the civil rights of the Irish immigrants in their custody. These episodes were extensions of the city's historic indifference to members of its working class, but the event that followed was less predictable. In the early years of the new millennium, rumors began to circulate that an Irish Guinness pub was planned for the Getty Square neighborhood of southwest Yonkers. In step with a $3.1 billion agreement, the Guinness pub would be part of larger strategy to bring a more affluent, largely white demographic (including good Paddies) to this working-class and working-poor Black and Latino neighborhood. Though the Guinness pub never materialized, how can we make sense of this incongruity?

How could Irish bars be policed in southeast Yonkers and at the same time function as a possible tool for developing southwest Yonkers? These are the questions that frame this chapter.

These contradictory Irish bar politics are constitutive of this neoliberal moment in time. By "neoliberal," I again refer to policies that channel public resources away from social services like schools, public housing, and welfare in the name of promoting economic growth and government efficiency. In cities like Yonkers, they take shape by way of tax subsidies for private corporations and citizens to promote development in economically depressed and often crime-plagued areas. At the same time, aggressive privatization usually is accompanied by forceful or "zero tolerance" policing to assure potential developers and consumers that their investment is safe.[1] While neoliberalism certainly casts a global web of capital, goods, jobs, and people, I am interested specifically in its intersections between the Republic of Ireland and the city of Yonkers, New York. This chapter first traces the policies in Ireland that allow for the export of Irish products like Guinness pubs and working-class, largely undocumented immigrants who live along McLean Avenue in southeast Yonkers. I then examine how Guinness pubs could be desired by the city of Yonkers while Irish immigrant bars and their patrons also were policed. Though the chapter is concerned with the policies that fuel this inconsistency, I also chart the history of public drinking in both Ireland and the United States to explain why bars, and not festivals or churches, are the site of this contradiction.

By examining the separate treatment of Irish bars and, by extension, Irish people, I show how these policies are accentuating class disparities within the Yonkers Irish community. My critical treatment is in line with the growing body of literature on how neoliberal urban redevelopment models, though masked in promises of economic growth, actually accentuate existing inequality.[2] By examining how working-class Irish immigrants and bars are policed, however, I do not want to suggest that they encounter neoliberal forces in the same way as Yonkers's working-class communities of color. Quite the contrary, though undocumented Irish immigrants occupy a comparable class position, and receive similar treatment by the city, racial hierarchies certainly place them in a privileged position. But in a city like Yonkers, marked by a long history of class and increasingly racial tensions, support for redevelopment is what anthropologist Neil Smith would call "revanchist," embodying "a revengeful and reactionary viciousness" toward people of color accused of "stealing" the city from white residents.[3] Redevelopment in southwest Yonkers should be considered in this light, as a form of revenge against Blacks and Latinos for "taking" Getty Square from its former white ethnic residents, but also as retribution for the costly desegregation suit that nearly bankrupted the city. This "reactionary viciousness" reared its ugly head at a televised Yonkers town hall debate in 2006. When a young African American man questioned where the city's minorities would shop if Getty Square were to become home to high-end retail, he was dismissed angrily and charged with "race baiting" and "using the race card." In fact, one white male audience member was so angered by this question that he had to be restrained physically by other audience members.[4]

Redevelopment in Yonkers has everything to do with race. In my analysis of neoliberal Irish bar politics, race is not, as white and middle-class Yonkers residents suggest, a ploy used by the African American community. Instead, race is an agent of neoliberalism, serving a larger "racial project" that keeps white structures of power intact.[5] Neoliberal policies in Yonkers, which will create a more policed, privatized, and unequal city, find widespread support precisely because they assess and value different cohorts of urban dwellers. In this case, a Guinness pub is possible in southwest Yonkers because it could appeal to white, affluent consumers and displace working-class Black and Latino residents. Disguised as an "ethnic" experience, this purportedly color-blind policy can appear less racist.[6] And Irish immigrant bars and patrons were policed aggressively during the 1990s because they had the potential to make predominantly white and middle-class sections of southeast Yonkers less class-exclusive, and therefore less racially exclusive. My examination of these different outcomes offers neoliberalism as more than mere policy, but as a condition of everyday life. In showing the human costs of this type of development, my work corresponds to examinations of urban communities under this logic.[7]

Neoliberal Ireland

In 1994, Ken Gardiner, an investment banker at a London branch of Morgan Stanley, made a comparison between the Republic of Ireland and the "tiger" economies of Southeast Asia. Since then, "Celtic Tiger" has been used to describe the unprecedented economic growth that began in Ireland during that decade. The Republic of Ireland, once considered one of the poorest members of the European Union (EU), quickly became one of its wealthiest. During the 1990s, the Irish economy grew at an annual rate of 7.5 percent, with the rate hovering slightly over 10 percent by the end of the decade.[8] But the Irish economy came to a screeching halt by the end of 2007. Fueled largely by the extension of credit, concomitant booms in construction and real estate were followed by massive busts. Between 2002 and 2008, for example, Ireland was building twenty-one housing units for every 1,000 people, in comparison to an average of seven units for every 1,000 people in western Europe. During the boom, a house that once cost €76,655 jumped to more than €300,000 in 2007. When the crash hit at the end of that year, Ireland had 266,332 unoccupied housing units. Unemployment reached 12 percent in 2009, and some forecast rates as high as 17 percent. With so many employed in construction, workers in this field were particularly hard hit. With banks on the brink of insolvency because of bad loans, the Irish government rescued "almost all" of the country's lending institutions, a bailout thought to be one of the world's largest. Faced with a banking crisis, a shrinking tax base, and greater demand for social services, the Republic of Ireland accepted a costly bailout from the EU and International Monetary Fund (IMF) in 2010. With the unemployment rate hovering at 14 percent and 30 percent of the nation's homeowners holding negative equity, the Irish people largely will shoulder the burden of sustained tax increases and public spending reductions in order to repay the national debt, which was expected to grow to 114 percent of GDP by the end of 2012.[9]

Although citizens, politicians, and academics alike angrily questioned Irish economic policy after the severe downturn that began in 2007, critical questions raised by scholars during the boom went largely unheeded. In Irish popular discourse, economic growth under the Celtic Tiger largely was attributed to neoliberal government policies during the 1980s that emphasized education in information technology (IT) skills as well as "social partnership" agreements, which curbed public resources, wage costs, and union power in favor of using tax cuts to encourage corporate investment and consumer spending. Some scholars at the time, however, pointed to the nation's earlier use of neoliberal models during the 1970s. After Ireland joined the European Economic Community in 1972, low corporate tax rates attracted many western European corporations. After these companies divested and relocated from Ireland during the 1980s, when the terms of their tax abatement expired, growth declined and unemployment soared. With an unemployment rate of nearly 20 percent, one of the highest in all of Europe, many young people left Ireland for the United States and cities like New York. The movement of capital and jobs from Ireland created an opening for U.S. corporations seeking new markets for computers and health care technology, an interest that peaked after the creation of a single European market in 1992. Ireland's low corporate tax rate of 10 percent was raised to 12.5 percent in 1996 but still was quite low in comparison to rates of 30 or 40 percent elsewhere. This meant greater profits for U.S. corporations, but also easier access to a larger European market.[10] But by tracing the Celtic Tiger back to the 1970s and the subsequent downturn of the 1980s, scholars, largely dismissed as radicals or naysayers, were able to suggest that the growth of the 1990s was unexceptional and potentially fleeting.

While considerable economic growth did occur in manufacturing sectors dominated by U.S. corporations, job growth in Ireland occurred largely in construction and service, areas in which part-time work, poor job security, and weakened labor rights (as a result of social partnership agreements) prevailed. As was occurring elsewhere, unskilled, largely nonunionized jobs outpaced highly skilled, well-paying, white-collar jobs. The movement of Irish women and teenagers into the workforce (448,000 in 1996, up from 212,000 in 1971) helped meet the demand for unskilled labor but forced Ireland to make the unprecedented move of looking elsewhere for its labor needs. In 1993, Ireland issued 1,103 work permits; by 2001, that number stood at 35,431. Not only drawing workers from Latvia, Lithuania, and Poland, Ireland's purported wealth lured asylum seekers and refugees from eastern Europe and Africa. In addition, the Irish government launched a campaign aimed at luring emigrants back home, and in 2000 Ireland held the first of many international job fairs to attract skilled workers.[11] Growing economic inequality in Irish society, moreover, paralleled this disparity in the job market.

During the Celtic Tiger, critics underscored one of its most striking features, a decrease in both private and public consumption in Ireland.

Irish public consumption, which totaled 16 percent of Ireland's GDP in the early 1990s, dropped to 12 percent by 2000. Public education and health care felt the effects of this trend. Ireland had the second-lowest per capita spending on primary education, while 23 percent of its citizens were illiterate, the highest rate in the European Union (EU) at the time. And in the realm of health care, Ireland had the fewest hospital beds per capita in the EU. Private consumption, which made up two-thirds of Ireland's GDP in 1990, fell to less than one-half in 2000.[12] Scholars located this change within the income disparity fostered by unequal job growth. Overall spending, while down in Ireland, relied mostly with borrowed money. In 1992, personal sector credit represented 42 percent of personal disposable income; by 2001 it had risen to 71 percent.[13] Luxury spending, on the other hand, increased. Second to the United States in its percentage of low-wage workers, the Republic of Ireland also was second to the United States in being the most unequal society in the Western world.[14]

While the expansion of Ireland's economy brought new people into the country, the outward migration of people reflected the nation's growing class inequality. Newly affluent Irish citizens took "shopping holidays" to New York City in search of luxury items and real estate. In response to this trend, the city of New York launched a campaign urging Irish residents to "shop while the dollar drops." To facilitate this, the U.S. federal government, at the urging of New York's mayor Michael Bloomberg, approved a new air traffic route to run three weekly flights from JFK International Airport to the west of Ireland. Irish men and women from rural and working-class backgrounds, however, also were on these same flights, coming in search of better-paying work, albeit in smaller numbers than their predecessors.[15]

These economic transformations in Ireland had an important impact on government policy. Increases in violent crime, like murder, paralleled growing Irish inequality. In response to this, and as a way to assure potential investors that Ireland was safe for investment, the Irish government officially embraced "zero tolerance" policing in 1997. This style of policing, which favors the strict enforcement of smaller offenses such as panhandling and disorderly public conduct, had been popularized in New York City by Mayor Rudolph Giuliani and police chief William Bratton. Based largely on the "broken windows" theory of James Q. Wilson and George L. Kelling, zero tolerance policing attributes larger crimes to society's tolerance for smaller ones. Zero tolerance came to Ireland by way of

Dublin native John Timoney, Bratton's deputy, who worked as a security consultant after retiring from the New York City Police Department. He helped Ireland's Fianna Fail's party create a zero tolerance platform before returning to power in 1997. This resulted in an increase in proceedings against prostitutes and beggars, and 2,000 new prison spaces were created in Ireland between 1997 and 2000. One Irish scholar quipped, "The fact that many tigers in the developed world end up in cages is an ironic reminder of the penal realities of contemporary Irish society."[16] Not only did Ireland become more class-stratified, but the most marginal in Irish society were bearing the brunt of these neoliberal policies.

In response to rapidly changing demographics during the Celtic Tiger, Ireland changed its citizenship laws. Though I will discuss debates regarding this issue in chapter 6, a few points are worth noting here. Because of its history of emigration, the Republic of Ireland had been quite generous in granting citizenship. Anyone of Irish descent with a grandparent born in Ireland can become an Irish citizen, and prior to the Celtic Tiger, Ireland was the only member of the EU to grant citizenship to anyone born in the country, irrespective of parental origin. In 2004, however, Irish voters overwhelmingly supported doing away with the constitutional provision that allowed for the latter practice.[17] The aforementioned global flows of capital, people, and goods into Ireland prompted a legal narrowing of who is Irish but also cultural nationalism. With the onset of the Celtic Tiger, the Gaelic language, as well as traditional Irish music and dance, became popular in Ireland, and this was paralleled by a market confidence in selling Irish products. The Irish Tourist Board aggressively promoted Ireland and an array of Irish products, including films, music, food, and crystal, earned profits abroad, especially in U.S. markets.[18] I am particularly interested in the popularity of one Irish export, the "Irish pub concept" or "Guinness pub," as it also is known, once rumored for southwest Yonkers. Before we can trace the evolution of the traditional Irish pub into a global commodity, a brief history of public drinking in Ireland is in order.

Reinventing the Irish Pub Tradition

Pubs, long considered to be an essentially Irish institution, actually are a cultural product of British colonialism. People of English descent primarily patronized early taverns, alehouses, and public houses in colonial Ireland. Native Irish drinking patterns, in contrast, were less fixed by space and time and tended to take place outdoors along springs and rivers, atop hills, or in woody areas. Moreover, they usually were cyclical, coinciding with special occasions such as a bountiful crop or a religious celebration. The consumption of alcohol indoors, however, was a widely revered sign of Irish hospitality. In rural parts of Ireland not fully incorporated under British control, women usually produced beer or ale for travelers who could spend the night on the floor by a warm fire. As these drink shops, or "shebeens," became popular in the sixteenth and seventeenth centuries, they met the scrutiny of the crown, as they gained a reputation for harboring Irish rebels. Government efforts to regulate and tax these types of establishments, coupled with restrictions on outdoor drinking, made the consumption of alcohol in government-regulated public houses more common in Ireland by the end of the nineteenth century.[19]

British colonial polices not only shaped where people drank but also shaped how people drank in Ireland. Binge drinking did exist in Ireland prior to this time and usually accompanied a successful harvest, as in many agricultural societies.[20] But as British policies tightened, and despair worsened, binges became extended. The despair of a colonized people worsened during the Great Famine, after which Ireland witnessed a significant loss of population and a per capita increase in alcohol consumption. The consumption of alcohol, however, not only provided an escape from the misery of post-Famine Ireland. For a colonized people under British rule, the distilling of grain for *potin* (pronounced "poteen") provided cash for those with few economic options, and during the most difficult of times, the consumption of alcohol provided inexpensive sustenance.[21]

After the devastating impact of the Great Famine, Ireland witnessed a delay in marriage and a stricter separation of the sexes whereby homosocial mingling became the new norm.[22] This social divide was quite literal in the traditional Irish pub, where Irish men typically enjoyed inexpensive entertainment, an information exchange, and a meeting site for trade unions and political organizations. Women and children, if they entered at all, did so through a snug, a separate space cornered off from the rest of the pub. These divides only began to unravel during the 1960s and 1970s when Ireland tried to modernize its economy. Improvements in education, membership in the European Economic Community, and the influx of foreign investment created jobs and brought capital to Ireland. During this time of prosperity, many pub owners in Ireland expanded their establishments, replacing snugs with larger lounges in which popular bands could perform and greater numbers of patrons could be served. Live entertainment brought men, women, and children into public houses where heterosocial mingling had become more acceptable.[23]

Though these neoliberal forces opened the traditional Irish pub to new patrons, at the same time they also threatened to undermine pubs. Not only foreign investment but also foreign styles of socializing entered Ireland during this era. Younger Irish men and women may have had greater access to the pub, but they were drawn instead to the European-style discotheques that were becoming popular across Ireland. New advancements in communication, telephones and television especially, lessened the role of the pub as an important information exchange. And with the "social partnership" agreements undoing labor rights, union and political organizing in pubs became less common. While some might attribute waning pub patronage to a 2004 smoking ban, the decline was in place many decades prior. The Celtic Tiger only hastened the traditional Irish pub's demise.

In the midst of frenzied real estate speculation under the Celtic Tiger, Irish pubs were sold for record prices and pub owners were under enormous pressure to meet their costs. Faced with higher prices in the pub, Irish consumers purchased less expensive alcoholic beverages in off-licenses for home consumption. As a result, Ireland's off-license trade doubled.[24] Not only were more Irish people drinking at home, they also were drinking more. In 1990, Ireland had the lowest per capita consumption of alcohol in all of Europe, but by 2004, Ireland had the highest rates of binge drinking. While contemporaries attributed the latter to affluence under the Celtic Tiger, Irish scholars underscored the aggressive marketing of alcoholic beverages and the Irish government's extension of drinking laws to lure tourists into cities like Dublin. Irrespective of its cause, the Irish government responded to this trend with a crackdown on drunk driving, which put additional pressure on dwindling pub patronage.[25]

Not only did the traditional Irish pub face a tenuous future within a larger neoliberal context, but so too did Guinness, Ireland's traditional beverage. For years, this dark stout had been sold in bottles, but in 1961, draft Guinness began to flow from pressurized kegs and taps. This new Guinness product, however, surely looked unappealing next to the lagers and wines that began to flow into Ireland from other parts of Europe. The Arthur Guinness Company faced the challenge of popularizing a new product that was largely confined to pub consumption, at a time when both the pub and the beverage faced a new, more competitive market. Its answer was to export the entire pub. In 1992, Guinness joined forces with the Irish Pub Company, a Dublin-based firm specializing in Irish pubs for export. Mel McNally, the company's founder, traveled Ireland in search of pubs that once dotted the Irish landscape but were succumbing to the aforementioned neoliberal forces. McNally narrowed down what he found into three basic categories that would serve as the model for his Irish pub designs: the Country Cottage Pub, the Victorian Pub, and the Traditional Pub Shop, and later added two additional designs, the Gaelic Pub and the Brewery Pub.[26]

Once an investor chooses from one of these five styles, the pub is constructed in Ireland, disassembled, and shipped within eighteen months. Replicating Irish pub design, however, is not enough. Irish food, music, beverages, and staff also are necessary to create what the Irish Pub Company says it actually sells, an Irish pub experience. With this goal, Irish Pub Company consultants assist investors with menu development and also put them in touch with Irish food suppliers. Menus might include traditional fare like a full Irish breakfast (eggs, rashers of bacon, sausages, tomatoes, and mushrooms), Irish stew (baby lamb shank, potatoes, and vegetables in a traditional broth), or more interesting "Irish" creations like Celtic Chicken (chicken with prosciutto, fontina cheese, and sage beurre blanc).[27] The Irish Pub Company insists that its pubs sell beverages that provide pure Irish flavor such as Guinness, naturally, but also Harp, Jameson, Bushmills, and Bailey's Irish Cream. In addition, the company puts investors in contact with Irish employment agencies to secure an Irish staff, as well as a network of Irish musicians to provide a lively background sound track. Since opening its first venture, the Irish Pub Company has launched approximately 1,500 "Guinness pubs" and outlets in Europe, Asia, and the United States. While some of these establishments opened in Ireland, usually in popular tourist destinations, there is a great market for them abroad.[28] The same neoliberal forces that are making pubs obsolete in Ireland are creating a demand for them overseas, especially in the United States. To understand why pubs are becoming so popular in American cities, we must examine Yonkers and view it specifically as a neoliberal city.

Neoliberal Yonkers

Thus far we have examined the neoliberal state, how privatization and policing were employed at the national level to commodify Ireland, export Irish products abroad, and market Ireland as a place for corporate and consumer investment. We will now look at the neoliberal city and the commodification of Yonkers. The Republic of Ireland made a significant leap from an economy based on agriculture to a service-oriented economy, largely skipping wide-scale industrialization. Yonkers, on the other hand, witnessed the shift from manufacturing in the southwest to retail in north and east quadrants of the city. In its wake, Getty Square, the city's former industrial core, became a poor, largely Black and Latino ghetto, surrounded by white suburbs. The city of Yonkers is trying to expand its service economy, using tourism especially to sell Yonkers both to corporate investors and to affluent consumers. While the Republic of Ireland and the city of Yonkers share the same economic goals and employ the same neoliberal policies, the commodification of cities like Yonkers, Matthew Ruben has argued, is largely dependent on making appeals to the "American suburban consciousness."[29] Rumors of a Guinness pub are but one component of a larger campaign to lure white, middle-class consumers from suburban tracts of Yonkers and Westchester County at large. Before we examine how the city markets itself, a brief discussion of what Yonkers specifically envisions, as well as the policies that make it possible, is in order.

As discussed in chapter 1, the loss of manufacturing, Smith Carpet and Otis Elevator in particular, devastated southwest Yonkers. New economic growth in retail and home construction in undeveloped tracts of east and north Yonkers did not recoup the loss of the city's industrial base. The city's costly desegregation battle with the NAACP during the 1980s stalled efforts to lure new investment. With new government structure and leadership, however, conditions began to change in Yonkers. Under Mayor John Spencer, the city settled its federal lawsuit over the desegregation of its public schools and housing, and New York State's emergency control board was removed. By the end of Spencer's tenure, big-box stores like Home Depot and Costco opened in Yonkers, while new construction began in and around Getty Square. Yonkers's vision of economic development was reflected in its new appellation, "City of Vision."

Redevelopment continued to accelerate under John Spencer's former deputy, Phil Amicone, who took office as mayor in 2004. That year the city signed a $3.1 billion agreement to bring a minor-league baseball stadium, retail and office space as well as high-rise luxury housing in and around Getty Square's former industrial waterfront. At the helm of this deal are Louis R. Cappelli, Westchester's "hottest" developer, the Struever Brothers, known for their work in Baltimore, and Fidelco Realty of New Jersey. Even Donald Trump expressed interest in collaborating on this project.[30] Because of the city's nineteenth-century roots, automobile access to its waterfront is particularly limited; as a result, the city of Yonkers has an additional $153 million plan to facilitate traffic by redeveloping its main artery, Ashburton Avenue. Plans for this project, which has been called the Ashburton Corridor, include widening Ashburton Avenue itself, rehabilitating existing retail space, and tearing down seventy-year-old Mulford Gardens, the city's first public housing project. A mix of low-income, market-rate rentals and first-time home-ownership opportunities are expected to be offered in its place, with promises of priority to former residents of Mulford Gardens.[31]

Other major plans for the city include Ridge Hill Village, a $600 million "lifestyle center," as it has been called, that will include luxury retail and housing off the New York State Thruway in the city's northeast quadrant. Bruce Ratner, developer of the $3.5 billion plan to construct the Atlantic Yards in Brooklyn, is developing Ridge Hill. Other redevelopment plans for the city included a $225 million project that brought video lottery terminals (VLTs), or slot machines, to the Yonkers Raceway and a $105 million project to renovate the fifty-year-old Cross County Shopping Center, both located in the southeast section of the city. Indeed, scholars of tourist cities would call this a "trophy collection" of redevelopment projects.[32]

Much of this local development is funded by way of Empire Zones or Empowerment Zones, state and federal programs, respectively, that give tax subsidies to promote development in economically depressed areas. In New York, Industrial Development Agencies (IDAs), non-profit entities sanctioned by the state, assist developers with an array of services ranging from coordinating government subsidies, issuing low- or no-interest mortgages, or negotiating payments-in-lieu-of-taxes (PILOTs). Based on market-rate assessment of the property to be developed, developers agree to make a set payment to the city, in lieu of taxes, over an extended period. In the case of the Yonkers Raceway, for example, the track will pay a base payment of $2.5 million per year for five years, plus a variable payment based on what the track earns from its casino. Though PILOTs guarantee payment to local authorities over a set period, businesses reap the greater benefit because these arrangements lower their overall tax expenses. Though the city of Yonkers stands to lose potential tax revenue over time, these plans and policies largely have been favored by a "growth coalition" of union workers, developers, government officials, and private citizens because of the jobs and sales tax revenue that these projects promise.[33]

In conjunction with tax subsidies, the city of Yonkers stepped up its police enforcement. Even though most components of these redevelopment plans are architecturally self-contained "tourist bubbles," the city needs to assure potential investors and consumers that Yonkers is safe for investment. Crime-plagued Getty Square largely has been the target of these efforts. In 2005, the city created a special police task force to combat crime in this area before officially embracing a zero tolerance approach in 2006. At the same time, the city considered a youth curfew to stem violence and gang activity, as well as a baggy-pants ban by way of a "decency" ordinance. Yonkers expanded these zero tolerance efforts to include the policing of Latino immigrant day laborers along Yonkers Avenue, one of the two avenues that connect suburban southeast and urban southwest Yonkers. The latter development illustrates how preemptive racial profiling police tactics are necessary to inspire white suburban confidence in urban areas.[34]

With the near collapse of the U.S. housing market in 2008, the city of Yonkers made up for budget shortfalls through increased property taxes, reduced services such as garbage collection and school programs, and layoffs, especially in the board of education. Yonkers residents have been asked to pay for more and receive less, while businesses have demanded greater concessions from the city. The Yonkers Raceway and Kimber Gun Manufacturers, for example, asked the city for tax breaks in order to expand their facilities. And as Ridge Hill added retailers such as Lord and Taylor and Whole Foods to its "lifestyle complex," a federal jury convicted former city councilwoman Sandy Annabi of bribery and corruption charges for accepting cash and gifts to change her vote on this project. Indeed, Yonkers may still be the "city of hills where nothing is on the level." Despite these setbacks, and reservations from the Westchester County Planning Commission about the financial underpinnings of redevelopment slated for Getty Square, the city of Yonkers continues to forge ahead with plans to aggressively court the American suburban consumer.[35]

The American Suburban Consciousness

Projects and policies alone are not enough to lure white, middle-class and affluent consumers into an environment long pathologized in public discourse as a crime-plagued, violent Black ghetto. Getty Square, after all, is mocked colloquially in Yonkers as "Ghetto Square." Cities like Yonkers are sold to potential consumers by appealing to suburban dissatisfaction. Aided by government homeownership programs, highway construction projects, and increasingly affordable automobiles, the United States became a suburban nation in the decades after World War II. While homeownership may have represented attainment of the American Dream for many, in recent years urban boosters have compellingly underscored the limits of suburban living. The car-dependent lifestyle is countered in Yonkers, for example, by calling attention to the convenience of having shops and restaurants within walking distance and the availability of public transportation. In 2004, the city refurbished its Metro-North railroad station and restored ferry service from Yonkers to lower Manhattan. Like a century ago, Yonkers maintains that is has the same conveniences as neighboring Manhattan, but without the high cost.[36]

But even before the commodification of postindustrial cities, suburbia was criticized by its contemporaries for being bland. Sociologist Lewis Mumford described suburban development as "uniform, unidentifiable houses, lined up inflexibly, at uniform distances, on uniform roads . . . inhabited by people of the same class, the same income, the same age group, witnessing the same television performances, eating the same tasteless pre-fabricated foods from the same freezers."[37] This uniformity also included racial uniformity, as government homeownership programs largely excluded people of color. This race-based structural inequality resulted in the erasure of urban, ethnic loyalties and the forging of a white, middle-class suburban identity.[38] In addition to racial and cultural conformity, the suburbs encouraged a retreat from community. Surely large, subdivided homes offered privacy, but many suburban residents experienced isolation, especially women and children. With the greater availability of consumer items, there was no need to leave the suburban home. Sociologist Ray Oldenburg warns, however, that the lack of informal public life in suburbia has created a lifestyle wracked with material accumulation and boredom.[39]

Postindustrial cities have presented themselves as the answer to these suburban dilemmas. Components of urban life have been brought to the suburbs by way of "New Urbanist" architecture, and urban campaigns have sought to lure suburbanites into the city itself. In contrast to the bland, homogeneous suburbs, cities promise excitement or "riskless risk" in an array of "cultural experiences," from the culture associated with art, museums, festivals, and heritage to the culture associated with ethnic groups.[40] Yonkers boosters, for example, market culture in calling attention to the city's refurbished public library, events such as Riverfest, public art along the waterfront, and many ethnic restaurants. In addition, the city promotes its industrial heritage by way converting former warehouses into residential housing and its plan to daylight the Saw Mill River, which once provided power for Yonkers's manufacturing. Fitting nicely with these larger plans, a Guinness pub could promise not only a cultural experience but also the excitement of seemingly spontaneous urban interactions.

Part of the Guinness pub's appeal is that it promises an ethnic experience and taps into a larger "ethnic revival" under way in the United States since the 1960s. As discussed in chapter 2, this trend has been shaped by civil rights legislation and the greater acceptance of cultural pluralism, as well as the cultural homogenizing effects of wide-scale suburbanization. This shift has been marked in academia by a change from assimilationist to pluralist approaches to study immigration, by the use of multiculturalism in schools, and by consumer demand for all things ethnic. The latter trend undoubtedly parallels larger global trends whereby people increasingly fabricate a sense of self in what they buy.[41]

Since Ireland's unprecedented economic expansion, Irishness has been an increasingly marketed identity under the Celtic Tiger, not only as a destination for tourists or foreign investment but as a source of products for export, especially for the U.S. market. As discussed, there has been an increasing demand for all things Irish, and the growing popularity of Guinness pubs in the United States is part of this larger trend. Since Guinness and the Irish Pub Company first popularized the "Irish pub concept," the Irish Pub Company launched its own U.S. venture, Fado (pronounced "f'doe," which means "long ago") Pub Inc., in Atlanta in 1996. With establishments open in Austin, Chicago, Columbus, Denver, Las Vegas, Philadelphia, Seattle, and Washington, DC, the Irish Pub Company intends to double its U.S. presence.[42] The company's success sparked an array of supporting industries, competing chains, and designers that are racing to spread the Irish pub concept across the United States. One of its competitors, Claddagh Irish Pubs, topped restaurant chain growth in 2004, while Irish pubs more generally are recognized as a growing trend by restaurant market researchers. The Irish pub concept might even be coming to a private home near you. Tired of hosting Super Bowl parties with 130 guests scattered throughout their home, one Florida couple spent $500,000 for the Irish Pub Company to build an Irish-themed pub in their backyard.[43]

Though Guinness pubs first were popularized in Europe, part of their popularity in the United States stems from the some 40 million Americans who claim Irish ancestry.[44] In a global environment of increasingly commodified forms, a promise of greater "authenticity" undoubtedly resonates with many consumers. The Irish Pub Company was not the first to launch an Irish bar and restaurant chain in the United States. Bennigan's first popularized Irish-themed food such as the "O'Connor Monte Cristo" and the "Turkey O'Toole," as well as green decor, walls, and shamrocks beginning in 1976. American-based constructions of Irishness, however, draw the ire of the Irish Pub Company. Founder Mel McNally maintains, "It is not enough to put a few shamrocks on the wall and call yourself an Irish bar."[45] And the Irish Pub Company will go to great lengths to deliver on its promise of a "true Irish experience." At the Nine Fine Irishmen in Las Vegas, the largely American-born staff was trained to "think and feel Irish." After a series of activities that included role playing to think Irish, as well as information sessions on Irish sports and culture, potential staffers were quizzed daily and weekly on what they had learned. After the successful completion of a competency test at the end of their training, staffers received an Irish "passport" to vouch for their authenticity.[46]

While the company's emphasis on authenticity clearly is an appeal to the modern quest for finding "real" experiences, the very tradability of these pubs threatens to render them commonplace. Already parts of Europe appear to be saturated with the Irish pub concept. In addition, critics have challenged the authenticity of Irish representations within these establishments. Some mock the faux fireplaces, while others question the sanitized, apolitical version of Irish history presented in some of these pubs. Nonetheless, studies suggest that meaningful cultural exchanges can exist in these commercialized spaces even when consumers know that mass-produced Irish pubs are not the "real" thing.[47] The pub itself does not have to be Irish, and neither do its customers.

Great efforts are made so that the decor, food, beverages, and staff appear Irish, but the Guinness pub experience is meant to have a universal, urban appeal. One of the main components of urban life is that strangers come into contact with each other, which is a source of both fear and excitement for city dwellers. The Irish Pub Company's promises to forge community are meant to allay these fears, while at the same time amplifying the sense of excitement for patrons. Fado Pubs, for example, maintain that they provide a space in which customers can "relax," enjoying "pleasure in company" and the "hospitality that exudes naturally from members of their staff." One does not have to be Irish to encounter this sense of community or the thrill of "dancing on the tables" as promised by Raglan Road at Downtown Disney. This is an experience that can appeal to the bored, isolated suburbanite, irrespective of his or her ethnicity, and it helps explain the appeal of the Guinness pub within the growing "experience economy" more generally.[48]

But if the pub does not have to be "authentically" Irish and neither do its customers, what is so appealing about a Guinness pub? In a self-consciously ethnic space, where neither the site nor the participants need to be Irish, the appeal lies in its subtle invocations of race. In chapter 2, I traced the evolution of the good Paddy Irish model in the United States. Within the larger nineteenth-century context of British colonialism and U.S. racial slavery, the working-class, Catholic Irish were deemed racially inept. In the United States, however, they were able to overcome their racial hazing by adhering to standards such as hard work, loyalty, faith, family, and order, which had been used to assess their own racial fitness. In this way, the Irish transformed themselves into good Paddies, but they also engaged in hard drinking, an important component of their bad Paddy racial caricature. Though not without controversy or conflict, self-perpetuation of this caricature facilitated an important exchange whereby the Irish accepted America's social order, and Americans, albeit grudgingly, accepted the Irish within that larger hierarchy. Moreover, I also discussed adaptations of Irishness as racial fantasy in U.S. popular culture. In an array of cultural texts, nineteenth-century Irish immigrants typically are represented as victims of oppression, rather than oppressors, which allows contemporary Irish Americans to minimize their own racial privilege.

These trajectories intersect within the Guinness pub, where the two sides of Paddy are very much present. The good Paddy is literally embodied by Guinness pub customers, typically white, middle-class consumers. While visitors do not have to be Irish, Guinness pub investors undoubtedly have the approximately 40 million Americans who claim Irish ancestry in mind as potential customers. Playful references to hard drinking in the Guinness pub, however, are a bad Paddy digression from the good Paddy model embodied by pub customers. Patrons are promised at Raglan Road in Orlando, for example, that they will have "sore heads" after a night of "mayhem." Even "drunk chicken" is served on the premises. That good Paddies come to a Guinness pub and participate in a bad Paddy digression reveals how race operates in this space. Intoxication and boisterous behavior marked the nineteenth-century working-class Irish as racially inept. Yet assimilated Irish and other white ethnics reference these traits in a setting that evokes both a downtrodden Ireland and Irish people of the past. They embrace Irish drinking caricatures precisely because they are so far removed from the experience that shaped them. White consumers' participation in a bad Paddy digression is a brief departure from their own position in the larger race-based power structure. In embracing a racial caricature, these good Paddies can appear less culpable and less racist. This is one of the reasons Guinness pubs are popular with consumers and neoliberal cities alike. While it never materialized, the Guinness pub proposed for southwest Yonkers would be touted as being in step with the area's other ethnic restaurants. The city's deliberate emphasis on ethnicity obscures the larger racial project embedded in aggressive redevelopment. More visible in the wake of the civil rights movement, race-based advantages, Hamilton Carroll maintains, were remade to be hardly visible at all. White privilege, he explains, is distinct for its ability to recuperate hegemony through the articulation of difference or, in this case, Irishness.[49] On the ground in Yonkers, emphasis on ethnicity obscures the way in which redevelopment plans will replace working-class Black and Latino residents with white, affluent consumers. Guinness pubs can indulge cities like Yonkers in racial fantasies of their own, that is, making Getty Square white again, without seeming racist.

While commodified Irish pubs could be part of a larger plan to lure white, middle-class suburbanites into a Black urban space, other Irish drinking establishments in Yonkers were treated quite differently. The same neoliberal forces that could bring a Guinness pub to southwest Yonkers also brought young, largely undocumented immigrants to the city's southeast section beginning in the early 1990s. Their arrival was marked by several stand-alone drinking establishments along McLean Avenue serving mostly Irish immigrant men and women. In 1996, the city of Yonkers issued a moratorium on the construction of new drinking establishments, and by this time there had been two well-publicized altercations between Irish immigrants and the Yonkers Police Department. How could this be? After all, these establishments fit into the city's larger use of culture to promote development. What could be more cultural than patronizing an ethnic establishment not only staffed but

also patronized by Irish immigrants? And what evokes the city's industrial heritage more than a stand-alone drinking establishment, akin to
the nineteenth-century saloons that once dotted Getty Square? While
white, middle-class suburban consumers may occasionally enjoy a bad
Paddy digression on St. Patrick's Day, while on vacation, or on a lei-
surely weekend visit to a Guinness pub, these gestures are moderated by
the cost, in addition to the presence of food and family. The establishments that opened on McLean Avenue, however, are stand-alone bars
and encourage hard drinking, fights, and indifference to work. These
behaviors fall short of the racial expectations for being a good Paddy
and are subject to scrutiny by the city. So as to better contextualize these
establishments, let us first examine a brief history of public drinking in
the United States.

Public Drinking in the United States

Though Irish immigrants gained a negative reputation for drinking in the United States during the nineteenth century, most Americans liked to drink. Since the colonial era, Americans drank alcohol
either in taverns, which served as an important institution for lodging
and feeding travelers, or more commonly at home, where alcohol was
both produced and consumed. Drinking and work often mingled in an
environment where water was unsafe to drink and tea and coffee were
expensive luxury items. According to historian Jack Blocker, "Everyone
drank, even infants were given a 'toddy' to keep them quiet." Americans drank the most in our nation's early decades, with a per capita
consumption of 5.8 gallons in 1790, which reached 7.1 gallons by 1830.
Newcomers to the United States beginning in the mid-nineteenth century merely added to an established drinking landscape. Germans popularized lager, while Irish widows sold alcohol as they did in Ireland, in
"shebeens," or unregulated drink shops.[50] Industrialization and urbanization, however, changed the way people drank in the United States.
Industrialization took men outside the home to work in a factory environment where drinking on the job was frowned upon. This, coupled
with the regulation of the unlicensed liquor trade in grocery shops,
ensured that the consumption of alcohol would be increasingly public and male. The advent of hotels primarily for lodging transformed

taverns into barrooms or "saloons," derived from the French *salon*, meaning large social hall, where working-class men consumed beer and spirits. The prevalence of these establishments has led scholars to characterize the period between 1870 and 1920 as the "saloon era" because "millions upon millions" of people patronized them.[51]

Contemporaries criticized saloons for encouraging separatism as they tended to be exclusive along lines of class, gender, race, ethnicity, and even occupation. "Poor men's clubs," as saloons also were known, in many ways actually encouraged acculturation to the United States. Exclusivity ironically fostered community by bringing together men of similar backgrounds. Drinking customs, such as clubbing, whereby patrons took turns buying drinks for those in their company or contributed to a drinking fund for the entire group, worked to bolster solidarity. In addition to this social role, saloons served other important functions, providing an escape from drab, overcrowded tenement life where patrons could avail themselves of inexpensive food (most saloons offered a free lunch with the purchase of a drink) but also entertainment, as newspapers and playing cards usually were readily available. The saloon not only provided socioeconomic mobility for its immigrant proprietors, but patrons also could cash checks, establish credit, and borrow money. In the absence of union halls and ward offices, male laborers held union meetings and politicians canvassed voters in saloons.[52] In providing a space in which various social, economic, and political resources could be exchanged, saloons were gateways to larger U.S. society.

Though scores of working-class men valued saloons, they played an important, perhaps conspicuous, role in Irish communities. As discussed, the prevalence of alcohol consumption in Ireland was shaped by British colonialism, which partially can explain its presence within Irish communities in the United States. Yet Irish drinking took on a meaning of its own in this new context, both a response to racial hazing and a way to cope with the harsh realities of urban American life. Not surprisingly, in New York City's Irish enclaves, the selling of alcohol had a conspicuous presence. Unlike other working-class saloons, where eating was an equal partner with drinking, Irish establishments were noted for their minimal emphasis on food. And while many immigrant groups enjoyed saloons as a temporary stop en route to greater independence and prosperity, the Irish tended to remain in the retail liquor business across generations.[53]

Despite their important role within many immigrant communities, many Americans found shortcomings in saloons, and efforts to prohibit the consumption of alcohol began to gain momentum by the end of the nineteenth century. Industrialists expected Prohibition to provide for more efficient, more manageable, and less troublesome employees. In cities transformed by working-class immigrants and Black migrants from the American South, native-born middle-class whites hoped Prohibition would restore urban order and reduce crime. And many women trusted Prohibition to protect families from domestic violence and lost wages associated with male intemperance. Undoubtedly informed by degrees of class, race, and ethnic bias, the movement to ban alcohol reveals more about societal anxieties over the tremendous shifts caused by industrialization and urbanization, namely, crime, poverty, labor unrest, shifting demographics, and the changing role of women, rather than the so-called evils of alcohol itself. Prohibition nevertheless gained a boost from World War I, during which Congress mandated liquor-free zones around military camps for better military preparedness. In addition, the unpopularity of Germany and German Americans drew support for closing the nation's brewing industry, which had German roots. Alcohol finally was prohibited nationally with ratification of the Eighteenth Amendment in 1919.[54]

Although it closed saloons, Prohibition did not bring drinking to a halt in the United States. The prevalence of bootlegging, underground drinking in speakeasies, and the growing role of organized crime led to support for Prohibition's repeal, as did the need for tax revenue and job creation during the Great Depression. Though increased lawlessness and economic recession enabled the legal repeal of Prohibition, advancements in science and medicine allowed a cultural shift in society's perceptions about the dangers of alcohol. Once considered a threat to the family, alcoholism increasingly was seen as a result of pathological family relationships. Treatments, like Alcoholics Anonymous, were geared increasingly toward the individual drinker and family, and not society at large. Once America's experiment with sobriety officially ended with the ratification of the Twenty-First Amendment in 1933, moderate drinking, rather than abstinence, would be the new norm.[55]

Though Prohibition officially brought an end to the "saloon era," the seeds of its demise had been planted many years prior. Progressive Era reforms aimed at ending both child labor and political corruption limited visits to in saloons, as did the opening of union halls. The enforcement of building codes made tenements less squalid and thus the saloon less appealing. New forms of leisure, such as movies, radios, and amusement parks, which became popular in the early twentieth century, challenged the saloon's vitality. Perhaps the seeds of demise were located in the saloon itself. Though the saloon helped working-class males become productive members of society, once they became more independent and could obtain well-paying work, own a home, and vote, the saloon became less necessary. And with America's doors basically closed to new immigrants in the 1920s, there were fewer patrons to take their place. Thus the saloons that reemerged after Prohibition were different from their predecessors; they were smaller in number, and the legal ban on the word itself in some locales helped popularize the use of "bars," a new moniker.[56]

But within a larger shift from an urban-centered manufacturing economy to one anchored by service in the suburbs after World War II, drinking changed too. Stand-alone, predominantly male bars in cities lost ground to suburban cocktail parties and family-friendly bar/restaurant chains. Though bars reminiscent of the nineteenth-century saloon certainly remain in urban, working-class neighborhoods, the challenges of deindustrialization and suburbanization have rendered them an endangered species. These changes also were felt in cities like Yonkers. When major manufacturing left southwest Yonkers, most of the once-ubiquitous working-class bars in and around Getty Square closed.[57] Instead, new restaurants opened alongside the growing retail sector on Central Avenue in northeast Yonkers. These establishments, where food, rather than drink, was the focus, would be a site of leisure for middle-class assimilated Irish ethnics, Irish white flighters, and their families. These spaces, however, would not suffice for the city's Irish newcomers. Their proximity to a public drinking culture in Ireland, and their undocumented status, together worked to create an Irish bar revival in southeast Yonkers. To fully understand this resurgence, we must examine the exchanges within these establishments along McLean Avenue.

The Irish Bar Revival in Yonkers

The Irish immigrant men and women who arrived in the United States beginning in the 1980s were raised in a pub tradition. While this partially explains bars' popularity where Irish communities developed, the largely undocumented status of this generation made bars vital. Bars were aptly called "community centers" by sociologist Mary P. Corcoran because they, like their nineteenth-century saloon counterparts, housed many important exchanges. Like earlier saloons, these bars fostered a sense of community by a degree of exclusivity as they were patronized solely by Irish immigrants.[58] Ties with Ireland were forged in immigrant bars by way of music selected for the jukebox and the live broadcast of Irish sporting matches and replays of newscasts. And like nineteenth-century saloons, these bars provided an alternative to sparse living conditions. Because apartment leases often required social security numbers, acquisition of housing could be difficult for newcomers, and as a result, apartments could be overcrowded, housing several roommates.[59] With their future in the United States uncertain, many planned to return to Ireland eventually, making the purchase of household furnishings and comforts both costly and pointless. Therefore, the presence of televisions and air-conditioning made bars more appealing to those seeking affordable entertainment or temporary relief from sweltering apartment heat during summer months. And like their saloon predecessors, regular bar patrons could borrow money and cash checks in these spaces. Because they could not access more formal banking services, these economic exchanges and the social networks that circulated information about housing and jobs were vital. In addition, these bars also were sites of political activity. The Irish Immigration Reform Movement (IIRM) formed in 1987 to publicize the plight of the undocumented Irish and advertised meetings in the local Irish press. Leaflets and flyers were distributed in bars throughout Queens and the Bronx in New York City. Clearly, undocumented life shaped these bars to resemble nineteenth-century saloons, but Ireland's unique pub tradition equally was present in these spaces.

Though bars resembled saloons in function, they more closely resembled pub lounges in Ireland. They often were adorned with elaborate woodwork and Irish crystal; they contained smaller side tables and chairs to complement a long bar, while large windows and hanging flower baskets typically embellished the facade. But, more important, they contained female patrons. Though gender hierarchies certainly existed, female Irish patrons could avail themselves of the networks previously enjoyed solely by previous generations of immigrant men. Their patronage was so important that many bar owners sponsored separate sports teams, including darts, soccer, and Irish football, for their female patrons. More like pubs in Ireland than nineteenth-century saloons in this regard, these bars were more tolerant of heterosocial mingling and were the site of many birthday, wedding, and even christening celebrations.[60]

This mix of nineteenth-century saloon and Irish pub culture could be found in the stand-alone Irish immigrant bars that began to open in southeast Yonkers during the early 1990s. These bars were an aesthetic improvement to McLean Avenue, where aging business storefronts typically were outdated and worn. But the sites themselves and the people within would in many ways be largely misunderstood by other Yonkers residents, including assimilated Irish ethnics and Irish white flighters. Those with access to secure work, family networks, home-ownership, legal residency, and bank accounts did not experience, and therefore could not understand, the vital economic, political, and social exchanges within these "community centers." Nor could they comprehend the more troubling consequence of this milieu: hard drinking.

Like the first significant wave of Irish immigrants in the middle of the nineteenth century whose future in the United States was uncertain, this generation of migrants shared a proclivity to drink, perhaps as an escape from the reality of undocumented life. Though the future may have been uncertain to nineteenth-century Irish migrants, this generation arrived knowing what happened to their predecessors, armed with narratives about the success of the Irish in the United States. Why the Irish were able to make this trajectory is not without controversy, but this history has created a legacy of success that undocumented newcomers often cannot fulfill. Hard drinking by the nineteenth-century Irish has been read as an act of defiance against a society that would not accept them. Hard drinking by Irish newcomers should be interpreted in a similar vein, against a society that welcomed previous waves of Irish *except* them. The cause of hard drinking may be difficult to decipher, but its by-products, indifference to work and job absenteeism, lack of personal thrift, and casual sexual encounters, could be alarming to their contemporaries who associated these traits with racial ineptitude. As a result, Irish newcomers were subject to scrutiny by the city at large.

Policing Whiteness

After a night of drinking at a christening party into the early hours of December 2, 1991, Paul and Bridget Stoker argued in the parking lot of Cornyn's Coach'n Four Steak and Seafood House. They could not decide whether they should drive to their home in Monticello, New York, or stay with friends in Yonkers. Their loud dispute prompted a complaint to the Yonkers Police Department, and officers arrived shortly afterward. Several guests leaving the party at this time questioned the need for nine police officers to answer the complaint. What happened from this point has been contested, yet some results are undisputable. The police arrested seven Irish immigrants on charges including assault, resisting arrest, disorderly conduct, obstruction of government administration, and third-degree escape. St. Joseph's Medical Center in Yonkers treated four police officers for injuries. Of the seven Irish immigrants arrested, Margaret Nolan received fifteen stitches on her forehead, Pat McNulty received thirty stitches to close cuts on his head, and Patrick Lilly was treated for bruises on his back.

The police officers claimed that the defendants physically resisted arrest. The accused charged that the officers were not justified in making any arrests and that they uttered ethnic slurs while they used excessive and brutal force. On December 7, the accused brought a $3 million lawsuit against the Yonkers Police Department, officers at the scene, and their supervisors. Charges against four of the seven Irish immigrants accused later were dropped, while three others were acquitted in 1992. One year later, a federal jury indicted Officers Bruce Nickels and Michael Buono for violating the civil rights of two men and one woman they arrested on December 2, 1991. Nickels was accused of striking Margaret Nolan on the head with his nightstick after she asked why her husband, Colm Nolan, was being arrested. Nickels and Buono were accused of stopping at a Yonkers railroad station while transporting

Patrick Lilly and Patrick McNulty to the city jail on the night in question. The officers allegedly took the men out of the car and beat them repeatedly.[61]

These allegations of excessive force and misconduct were nothing new in the city of Yonkers. Two weeks earlier, two of the arresting officers at the Coach'n Four had fabricated an assault by a Black man against a police officer to conceal a fistfight involving two other police officers in their precinct. This violation ultimately led to their dismissal from the force in 1992. Robert K. Olson, the former police chief of Corpus Christi, Texas, was hired by Yonkers in 1990 to deal with growing incidents like these involving police misconduct. His efforts, which included a complaint investigation committee and collaboration with the FBI into ties between organized crime and city officials, were not well received; Olson survived an assassination attempt by way of a car bomb in 1992. Olson's efforts nonetheless sought to improve the department's relationship with the city's communities of color. Accusations made throughout the Irish American press that the immigrants in the Coach'n Four case were abused by the police because they were Irish surprised some, given the history of Irish immigrants joining the ranks of police departments across the country. Their claim was so powerful that one of the first points made by the defense was to establish the Irish heritage of the officers at the scene to dispel these allegations of ethnic bias.[62]

Despite the shared ancestry of the accusers and the accused, this conflict could have been cultural, stemming from differences in how policing is understood in Ireland and the United States. In rural parts of Ireland, where residents are familiar with their local "guard" on a first-name basis, nine officers responding to prevent a dispute from escalating into a crime would seem excessive. And to Catholic immigrants from Northern Ireland like Patrick Nulty, a police presence could be read quite differently. Unlike in the United States, especially in cities like New York where many officers are of Irish descent, police ranks in Northern Ireland historically have excluded Irish Catholics, and the police force, the Royal Ulster Constabulary (RUC) was seen as an agent of British imperialism. Attendees at the christening party may not have acquiesced and possibly challenged the police presence verbally, and perhaps physically, as many Irish Catholics have done in Northern Ireland.[63]

At the same time, this incident illustrates different understandings of Irishness in Yonkers. Even though most of the officers at the scene shared a common ancestry with their accusers, what they found that night at the Coach'n Four would not meet their notion of Irishness as associated with hard work and family. Men and women drinking in the presence of children into the early hours of a Monday morning, the start of a workweek, would undoubtedly be offensive. Such behaviors were unacceptable, and as a result, those Irish immigrants encountered the same police misconduct and excessive force that working-class and working-poor people of color are so well acquainted with in Yonkers. Several years passed before the conflict that began at the Coach'n Four in 1991 finally was resolved. Officers Nickels and Buono were acquitted of federal charges in 1993, and the city settled its civil suit with the seven Irish plaintiffs in 1997 for $700,000. The incident itself occurred when Irish immigrants were just starting to arrive in Yonkers, but it foreshadowed what was to come. As more Irish immigrants arrived and new bars opened, these establishments and the behaviors associated with them would be policed.[64]

As discussed, the arrival of Irish newcomers in Yonkers was marked by the presence of Irish businesses, especially bars. The largest and most popular of these establishments opened in 1994. A "superpub" by Irish standards, Rory Dolan's contained an enormous bar and restaurant with additional catering facilities. Offering traditional Irish food, served by an Irish-born staff, Rory Dolan's showcased traditional music on Sundays and catered to a diverse, usually American-born crowd, in comparison to its smaller competitors along McLean Avenue. Nevertheless, the New York Times dubbed Rory Dolan's the "liveliest pub in New York," and these words were soon proudly displayed on its facade.[65] The size and popularity of Rory Dolan's and subsequentially other bars in the area, served to magnify concerns about bar-related trouble, especially noise, fights, and parking shortages.

In response to growing complaints from residents, a moratorium on the construction of future bars was first proposed by the Yonkers City Council in 1995. At this time, I was both a Yonkers resident and a graduate student. I followed these events closely, attended civic meetings, and informally interviewed residents for research on social movements in the United States. Most residents expressed support for the moratorium.

One homeowner, for example, explained to me, "I'm Irish too. I like to drink and have a good time like everyone else. I have even been to Rory Dolan's, but do we need ten bars?" His comment was revealing. Despite being an assimilated Irish ethnic, as a middle-class homeowner, he could not recognize the importance of bars beyond being a place in which to "have a good time." The vital exchanges that transpired in bars patronized by Irish immigrants could not take place in larger, busier establishments like Rory Dolan's but only through regular patronage in smaller establishments, hence the number of them. To him, Rory Dolan's was representative of all the Irish bars on McLean Avenue, and more bars simply meant more drinking and more problems.

Incidentally, this resident also was a member of the Hyatt Association, whose members were quite vocal in their support of the proposed bar moratorium. The Hyatt Association first formed in the 1980s to protest the desegregation of Yonkers public schools and housing because its members feared that the movement of working-class Black and Latinos into predominantly white sections of the city would cause property values to decline. Despite losing their fight against integration, property values did not decline, nor was there a massive of influx of minorities into white neighborhoods, as they had feared. The increased presence of Irish immigrant bars, however, served to mobilize their class and race anxieties. The undocumented Irish, as white immigrants, moved with relative ease into this racially exclusive section of the city (though some might have difficulty securing an apartment if required to present a social security number). But as working-class immigrants, their bars and bar-related behaviors could make the area less desirable to middle-class whites, causing property values to decline and at the same making the area more affordable to upwardly mobile Blacks and Latinos, who constituted only a small presence by way of fiercely resisted court-mandated school busing and scattered-site public housing. A decline in property values could weaken the firm racial divide between this predominantly white section of Yonkers and bordering Black neighborhoods in Mount Vernon and the Bronx.

Though Yonkers homeowners did not publicly concede the link between Irish bars and their class and race anxieties, Irish newcomers often did. One immigrant commented on his frustration about the proposed moratorium, "I remember an older lady on Bainbridge Avenue [in the Bronx] who would always complain about the number of bars and amount of drinking going on at that time. I would love to see what she has to say now about her new neighbors." He not only thought that the Irish were more desirable than Black and Latinos because they were white but also thought they should be treated accordingly. That distinction did not go unnoticed at local Hyatt Association meetings. When besieged by complaints from residents about the bars, a local politician responded that "things could be a lot worse," referring to the doomsday predications about desegregation a decade earlier. Though Irish bars and patrons were preferable to an influx of people of color, their potential to make the area less racially exclusive would be firmly managed. With these class and race anxieties mobilized, Yonkers homeowners successfully lobbied their politicians, and the bar moratorium was successfully legislated in 1996.

Members of the city council and Yonkers politicians more generally had their own reasons for supporting a bar moratorium in this part of the city. As discussed, Mayor John Spencer helped resolve the costly desegregation suit with the NAACP that was straining the city's coffers and its reputation.[66] The agreement reached by the city and the NAACP over the desegregation of schools and housing, coupled with Spencer's ability to persuade the state to remove the financial control board that had been in place intermittently since the 1970s, signaled to many that Yonkers was ready for an economic rebirth. New investment followed as a result of these changes, but Spencer's "law-and-order" style was reflected in the city council's bar moratorium for southeast Yonkers, exactly a decade before the city officially embraced "zero tolerance" policing. A legal ban on the construction of new bars sought to keep the area more orderly, and thus more desirable for potential investors.

Local newspapers captured the enthusiasm residents expressed for the city council's action. "Amen to what the City Council did," exclaimed one resident. "This is a family neighborhood, and sometimes there are drunk people falling all over the place." Another, however, more concerned about the impact of bars on property rather than family values, explained, "I have nothing against bars, but the people who come down here to drink don't give a hoot about our neighborhood. They use our doors as urinals, the sidewalks as trash cans and the whole place as a boxing ring for fighting."[67] Their descriptions of the area were

not exaggerated, especially on the weekends. But due to their precarious legal standing, Irish newcomers did not share these concerns of
longtime Yonkers residents and homeowners. Without the same access
to steady employment and homeownership, they were less concerned
with missing work or how noise, litter, and fights might affect property
values over time because their tenure in the United States was uncertain. And they would not be concerned about the impact of public
drinking on children because many did not have children of their own;
a family would only compound the uncertainties of undocumented life.
The drinking culture encouraged by their status prevented many Irish
newcomers from sharing the same values as middle-class homeowners,
and this disparity had consequences in Yonkers. Though the moratorium prevented the construction of future bars along McLean Avenue,
troublesome bar-related behavior did not subside but merely was contained. And as the city's efforts to court outside investment accelerated
under Mayor Spencer's tenure, so too did efforts to police Irish bars and
patrons on McLean Avenue.

In January 1996, outside the Kozy Korner Diner on McLean Avenue,
two Irish men were charged with second-degree assault after they purportedly attacked four police officers who were dealing with a street fight.
Although the accused men did not comment in the press, several eyewit-
nesses explained that the men in question verbally protested the police
beating of an unknown man. The police then physically responded with
nightsticks and mace. This incident was given considerable attention
in both the *Irish Echo* and the *Irish Voice*, since the three men arrested
claimed brutality on the part of the police. Both papers reported that the
accused had visible cuts and bruises on their faces and necks, while one
defendant "limped noticeably" in court. Many people interviewed by
reporters after the incident claimed that police were picking on the men
because they were Irish and expressed contempt for the Yonkers Police
Department. The three men in question pled guilty to lesser charges in
August 1997, and each was ordered to pay a fine of $100.[68]

Though this was the only publicized conflict between Irish immigrants and the Yonkers Police Department to follow the 1991 Coach'n
Four incident, informal discussions confirmed that misconduct and
excessive force continued during the 1990s. In particular, undocumented immigrants I spoke with at the time complained that the police

verbally harassed bar patrons after closing time and demanded to see green cards if they protested. In 2002, the codirectors of a local Irish community center confirmed these allegations. Fearful of deportation, they explained, undocumented immigrants usually returned to Ireland after altercations with Yonkers police officers. My efforts to question officers at the Second Precinct about bars on McLean Avenue yielded no answers, reflecting a broader departmental silence regarding complaints against the police.[69]

Irish bars on McLean Avenue, however, have become less popular and do not constitute the same threat or necessitate the same police presence as they did throughout the 1990s. A more lax enforcement of a separate smoking ban for New York City, in comparison to Westchester County, which includes Yonkers, drew some patrons to adjacent Irish bars on Katonah Avenue in the Bronx.[70] Larger forces, moreover, are responsible for the decrease in Irish bar patronage on McLean Avenue. The efforts of the Irish Immigration Reform Movement, discussed at greater length in chapter 6, helped many of the "new" Irish receive "diversity" visas during the 1990s. With a path to legal citizenship in place, many purchased homes and started families in the area, creating what the New York Times called "a strong middle-class backbone that no longer measures its vitality by the pint and the keg."[71] In other words, they had become good Paddies or, as I discuss in chapter 5, "good Paddies in transition." Others members of this cohort were lured by the Celtic Tiger and used skills honed during their tenure in the United States to capitalize on new opportunities offered in Ireland's expanding service economy. As a result of these changes, neighborhoods in the Bronx, Queens, and Manhattan that became more Irish during the 1980s have more recently become less so.[72] The impact of this broader shift on McLean Avenue has been striking. Once-packed bars are noticeably less crowded. Some establishments have closed or changed hands, while others have tried to recoup their economic losses by turning a blind eye to underage drinking and violations of the smoking ban. Rory Dolan's, the largest bar, and perhaps the biggest target for the scrutiny of the State Liquor Authority, was temporarily closed for violations in 2004 and 2006.[73]

The same forces that drew emigrants back to Ireland during the Celtic Tiger, however, displaced others, particularly those from rural and working-class backgrounds, who continued to migrate to places like Yonkers. The "newer" Irish also were largely undocumented but also less skilled than their immediate predecessors. Because of advancements in communication and computer technologies, this cohort maintains close ties to Ireland and is less likely to join the various ethnic organizations that sustained previous Irish immigrant generations. And with the heightened policing at the federal and state level that occurred after September 11, 2001, this group also is more vulnerable. With provisions of the Patriot Act and stricter requirements for driver's licenses in New York State, this generation faced greater difficulty finding work and cashing checks, as the Irish have done for many years prior because of the networks forged in bars. With greater scrutiny and less support, some members of this cohort have encountered depression, alcoholism, and suicide. As calls to enforce U.S. borders and to deport "illegal aliens" heightened, some returned to Ireland.[74] Those who remained hoped to legalize their status through the efforts of the Irish Lobby for Immigration Reform (ILIR), which like its predecessor the IRIM, held meetings and fund-raisers in local Yonkers Irish immigrant bars. Unlike their immediate new Irish immigrant predecessors, who either changed their legal status or enjoyed short-lived prosperity as return migrants to Celtic Tiger Ireland, this cohort remains in a precarious limbo. With downturns in both the U.S. and Irish economies, these newer Irish immigrants encounter diminished possibilities for legal residency and economic advancement. Their experience in the city of Yonkers and their interactions with other Irish cohorts frame the chapters that follow.

* * *

The bar moratorium in Yonkers is an example of how the city's historic class and race anxieties were managed during the 1990s by way of Irish bar policing, at a time when the city was still coping with the loss of industry and its desegregation battle with the NAACP. The presence of several stand-alone drinking establishments and hard drinking by undocumented Irish immigrants had the potential to make southeast Yonkers less class-exclusive and thus less racially exclusive. As a result, both Irish bars and their Irish immigrant patrons were scrutinized by the city.

Though a recent episode in a long trajectory of class and race tensions, Irish bar politics are a departure from previous conflicts in Yonkers. By juxtaposing my discussion of Irish bar policing with an analysis of the Guinness pub rumored for southwest Yonkers, I show how race and class tensions in Yonkers are more contradictory than ever before. In policing some Irish bars, and potentially privileging others with tax subsidies, this neoliberal moment foreshadows a new era of inequality. However, by looking at the Irish, I seek not to obscure but to emphasize how such policies, as they take more definite shape, will affect Blacks and Latinos, who constitute a far greater proportion of the city's working class. My treatment of Irish bars, when the city was in its early stages of development, is meant to question what the future holds for Yonkers.

In December 2005, a twenty-year-old African American Yonkers resident was shot outside Rory Dolan's. Whether the young man was served alcohol was subject to dispute. He reportedly caused a scene when asked to leave the premises, which warranted the scrutiny of two off-duty New York City police officers drinking at the bar. A physical confrontation ensued in which one of the officers was stabbed and the young man was shot and killed. As the officers later were cleared of any wrongdoing, the incident was illustrative of the racial hierarchies at work in Yonkers. Despite charges of misconduct and excessive force, no Irish immigrant died as a result of an altercation with the police in Yonkers, and those at the Coach'n Four in 1991 had recourse in a civil suit. And Irish laborers who gather for work along McLean Avenue are not scrutinized like their Latino counterparts on Yonkers Avenue. With a trophy collection of projects in place and an official embrace of zero tolerance policing, the future looks frightfully dim in the City of Vision. With strategies that replicate neoliberal policies in cities like New York and Baltimore, the city of Yonkers is merely en route to replicating the same inequality.[75]

4

They're Just Like Us

Good Paddies and Everyday Irish Racial Expectations

"They're were just like us," I am told by Frank, a thirty-four-year-old assimilated Irish ethnic, as he describes the people he met during the first of many visits to Ireland. "It was as if my family never left Ireland." He also added, "I felt like I picked up where they left off one hundred and fifty years ago." When I asked Frank whether he patronized the Irish immigrant bars on McLean Avenue, as a way to possibly reconnect with his experience in Ireland, he told me, "No. They don't really like Americans there." Mary, a sixty-five-year-old Irish white flighter, shared with me how "mortified" she was by her Irish newcomer nephews who stayed with her after their arrival in the United States. "It was unreal," she told me." They were out drinking all night. No work, of course, the next morning. They made me embarrassed to be Irish." "They're just like us," I am told again, but this time by Caroline, a twenty-two-year-old Irish newcomer, to describe her Latino coworkers in the restaurant industry. "Mexicans are just like the Irish," she said." They're Catholic. They like soccer and they love to drink!"

This chapter considers how various Irish cohorts in Yonkers interact with the good Paddy model, so as to understand how it operates on an everyday, lived basis. Specifically, I examine how both assimilated Irish ethnics and Irish white flighters celebrate St. Patrick's Day, the most Irish of days in the United States. Ever attentive to race, class, and gender, these cohorts stress Irish racial expectations of loyalty, hard work, order, religious faith, and family and, consequently, Irish racial expectations. I first analyze assimilated Irish ethnics, whose ancestors typically immigrated to Yonkers in the middle to late nineteenth century. Because they have been in the United States for several generations, they are more fully immersed in this tradition; therefore, they are a fitting starting point for this chapter. I then turn to Irish white flighters, the Irish men and women who immigrated to New York in the 1950s and early 1960s and moved to Yonkers in the decades that followed. In my examination of assimilated Irish ethnics and Irish white flighters, I consider their ethnic traditions alongside discussions about Irish immigrant newcomers, who first began to arrive in Yonkers during the early 1990s. Their practices and discourse are shaped by two very distinct historical trajectories, yet assimilated Irish ethnics and Irish white flighters both disparage Irish newcomers as disloyal, disorderly, lazy, and deficient in faith and family. (In chapter 5, I consider how Irish newcomers see themselves.) By juxtaposing practice alongside discourse, the former stressing who the Irish are and the latter, how Irish newcomers fall short, this chapter is positioned to show how Irishness is *supposed* to be in the United States.

In addition, this chapter reveals how neoliberal policies govern interactions among the Yonkers Irish. Assimilated Irish ethnics and Irish white flighters scrutinize Irish newcomers in relation to market-oriented choices and values, especially in regard to private property. This tension reflects the larger neoliberal emphasis on private consumption but also the greater fraying of collective ties. The larger shift of resources away from public housing, schools, and infrastructure has eroded our sense of civic responsibility. In its wake, members of the seemingly same racial and ethnic group increasingly are estranged from one another. At the same time, this chapter continues to underscore the larger racial project inherent within urban neoliberal policies that will disproportionately displace working-class and working-poor communities of color in the city of Yonkers. Assimilated Irish ethnic and

Irish white flighter discourse is punctuated by race, and ranges from the racially coded to racially explicit. As I have argued in previous chapters, when Irish racial fitness is underscored, people of color appear more racially inept and in need of aggressive policing and privatization. Moreover, my ethnographic examination of the Yonkers Irish, both in this chapter and in the one that follows, treats neoliberalism as a condition of everyday life.

Assimilated Irish Ethnics and St. Patrick's Day in Yonkers

Like many locales that have a sizable number of residents with Irish ancestry, the city of Yonkers hosts its own Irish parade, which is organized by the St. Patrick's Day Committee. The first St. Patrick's Day parade in Yonkers was recorded in 1863, but this tradition fell out of practice by the turn of the century. Assimilated Irish ethnics, the descendants of Yonkers's early Irish immigrants, later revived this tradition in 1955. So it does not compete with, and possibly lose spectators to, the larger St. Patrick's Day parade in Manhattan on March 17, the city of Yonkers hosts its own parade on the first Sunday of March. Because many nearby cities and towns employ the same tactic, there is a St. Patrick's Day parade in the tristate area every weekend in March, prompting some to refer to this month as the "St. Patrick's Day season."[1]

The Yonkers St. Patrick's Day festivities officially begin at 11.30 a.m. with the raising of an Irish flag in front of the city hall entrance on South Broadway, although I am told that some parade participants start the day earlier, with Irish coffees in a nearby home.[2] The flag raising is attended largely by parade honorees, the grand marshal, and eight aides to the grand marshal, all of whom are handpicked by the parade chairman. Each was given a ceremonial sash in green, white, and gold, the colors of the Irish flag, several weeks prior to the parade in a separate ceremony. Members of the parade committee also are here, as are family and friends of the honorees, as well as a few members of the Yonkers City Council. Besides me, this event draws few other spectators. After the flag raising we proceed a few blocks to St. Mary's Catholic Church, also on South Broadway, for a noon mass because the earliest St. Patrick's Day parade participants in Yonkers also began here. This event, however, is better attended and draws local politicians and members of Irish American organizations who will march in the parade, as well as those who plan to watch the parade. Green is ever present to evoke the green fields of Ireland, as are shamrocks, an important symbol of Irish Catholicism.[3] Green seems to be everywhere, in an array of interesting outfits, even on fingernails.

Although many Irish immigrants live in Yonkers, few accents can be heard as we gather to board the bus that will bring us to the beginning of the parade route, at the intersection of McLean Avenue and South Broadway in southwest Yonkers. As we drive down South Broadway, vendors begin to gather along the route, as do Latino and African American residents of the area. There is friendly buzz on the bus, as many praise the lack of rain. I introduce myself as a parade novice and ask fellow travelers to describe the day. "It's a great day," I am told by two middle-aged assimilated Irish ethnic women, who grew up here in Getty Square but moved to northeast Yonkers in the 1960s. "I wish more people could see what a great honor it is to the poor and hard-working Irish who came before us," another adds.

As I exit the bus, I see various groups gathering, preparing to march. There are Irish American organizations, bagpipe bands, marching bands from local Catholic and public high schools, labor unions, and Girl Scout and Boy Scout troops. I march with the Irish Lobby for Immigration Reform,[4] and as we make our way up South Broadway, I notice that the middle of the street has been painted with a green line. As we get closer to St. Mary's, Black and Latino onlookers soon are eclipsed by large clusters of white spectators. The parade route ends just past St. Mary's and city hall in Getty Square, and those finished with marching make their way to bars in the area. They might visit the Waterford Tavern, which has been in the area for several decades, or one of the newer establishments that have opened in part to redevelop the Yonkers waterfront. In these very crowded sites, patrons enjoy pints of Guinness, corned beef sandwiches, and traditional Irish music playing on the jukebox. Some parade enthusiasts have a few drinks before venturing to the St. Patrick's Day dinner that will begin at six o'clock in the Polish Community Center, while others, who do not plan to attend this event, stay for several more hours.

Figure 4.1. The Irish flag at Yonkers city hall. Photograph by author.

The dinner itself is attended largely by the same people who attended the flag-raising ceremony or mass at St. Mary's, mostly middle-class, assimilated Irish ethnic professionals, civil servants, and trade unionists, both young and old. They have attended the St. Patrick's Day festivities here for many years, traveling to Getty Square from neighborhoods in northwest and east Yonkers. We make our way through a five-course meal of foods named after Irish counties, including "chicken à la Kerry," "Galway rolls and butter," and the "rolling bar à la Mayo." The tables are decorated with green napkins, green and gold flowers, and green-checkered ribbons. We are entertained by a local Irish band and Irish step-dancers. After the dinner, those who are not exhausted by the day's events, head to local bars in Getty Square and nearby northwest Yonkers to finish the night.

These crowded sites contain patrons who have remained for several hours after the parade. Traditional music that played earlier on the jukebox has been replaced by live Irish music. Patrons are interrupted by a procession of bagpipers who circle the room and perform a few songs, including "Danny Boy"[5] and "God Bless America." Accompanied by an adult, a small troupe of young, female Irish step-dancers stop by later to perform. The bar's patrons make room for the dancers, who are greeted with wild applause. Some patrons stuff dollar bills into the hands of the young dancers after their performance, as a sign of their appreciation. This scene is repeated in some bars along McLean Avenue in southeast Yonkers on March 17 by those who have attended the Fifth Avenue St. Patrick's Day parade in Manhattan.

Practices such as these during the St. Patrick's Day season are typical in Yonkers and undoubtedly other U.S. cities that witnessed an influx of Irish immigrants after the Great Famine. But these traditions, while commonplace, evolved over the course of two centuries. During the early nineteenth century, St. Patrick's Day celebrations in the United States mostly were small private affairs. At that time wealthy Irish Catholics and Protestants largely attended banquets hosted by organizations such as the Friendly Sons of St. Patrick. But by the 1830s, as more working-class and working-poor Irish immigrants began to arrive in the United States, St. Patrick's Day celebrations became larger and more public. In cities like New York, St. Patrick was honored in local neighborhood processions, which usually were linked to a religious ceremony and dinner. With the arrival of famine migrants, local demonstrations became consolidated into a more formal and singular parade. By the mid-nineteenth century, public ceremonies became routine as city people had few large venues in which to socialize. And "no one social group," urban historian Mary P. Ryan writes, "not even the native born, could completely manipulate urban culture." While most antebellum cities hosted an array of public holidays, St. Patrick's Day was on the calendar of "every city," serving to illustrate the growing presence of recent Irish arrivals. The St. Patrick's Day parade, therefore, emerged in this context and projected a particular identity to Irish newcomers and Americans alike. By 1853, the St. Patrick's Day parade in New York City was large enough to stop traffic; by the end of the decade, it drew 10,000 marchers. Because the process of migration often severed familial and communal bonds, parades brought Irish people together, serving to nurture a growing Irish American community. As a result, the United States witnessed 120 annual parades by 1874.[6]

Figure 4.2. Bagpipers performing on St. Patrick's Day in Yonkers adorned with Irish and American flags. Photo by author.

The sheer number of parade marchers and spectators demonstrated the potential power of the Irish in America. Cities like New York could boast of 40,000 marchers and 500,000 onlookers by 1870. Assisted by the beat from several drums, moving in step could convey the impression of even more marchers. By parading beyond the confines of their ethnic enclaves, into residential and commercial spaces not their own, the Irish communicated that they were a force to be reckoned with in the United States. At the same time, these parades countered depictions of the Irish as lazy, disloyal, and disorderly. While an array of organizations marched in the parade, including benevolent societies and the Ancient Order of Hibernians (AOH), the presence of labor unions demonstrated Irish propensity for hard work, while temperance organizations illustrated Irish regard for order, as did the presence of militias, which became an increasingly common presence after the Civil War. Within a nativist climate, conspicuous displays of Irish and American flags communicated Irish loyalty to the United States, as did

conventions at postparade gatherings. Song lyrics increasingly were distributed in English and not Gaelic, while toasts typically honored the
United States. Parades also upheld gender conventions as marchers and
marshals typically were male, while women organized postparade festivities, including picnics and dinners.[7]

While the presence of temperance organizations conveyed orderly
Irish American sobriety, drinking also played a role in St. Patrick's
Day festivities. Parade historians Mike Cronin and Daryl Adair maintain that "drowning the shamrock" was a venerable tradition. Though
shamrocks adorned parade celebrants, they also were placed at the bottom of glasses and covered with alcohol, from which celebrants would
drink. Excessive eating and drinking on this day was not uncommon,
as St. Patrick's Day was a sanctioned respite from the Lenten season
of abstinence. Drinking on St. Patrick's Day, however, was not without controversy. As discussed in previous chapters, the larger process
of racialization shaped how the Irish drank in the United States. Hard
drinking, nonetheless, and drink-related problems like fighting served
to reinforce racial caricatures and threaten the reputation of the Irish.
As a result, many Irish Americans went to great lengths to eliminate
drunken revelry from this very public event. Temperance supporters campaigned against excessive drinking and urged saloonkeepers
to close shop on St. Patrick's Day, while priests also pressed their con-
gregants to refrain. In one case, organizers held the parade in the early
morning, after mass, to deter men from nearby watering holes.[8]

Despite this controversy, St. Patrick's Day parades witnessed a pre-
cipitous decline across the United States during the 1870s and 1880s.
As discussed, the New York City Draft Riots, Molly Maguire trials, and
the Orange Riots hurt the reputation of the Irish. At the same time,
the growing popularity of commercial entertainment in concert halls,
sporting events, and amusement parks drew parade enthusiasts elsewhere. There trends, coupled with infighting among Irish American
organizations and growing parade costs, resulted in both diminishing
parade support and attendance. In the absence of strong leadership,
the AOH assumed control over the parade in cities like New York and
led the parade's revival during the 1890s, in face of growing nativism
unleashed by the economic downturn that began in 1893. The parade
persevered in the early decades of the twentieth century, through

both world wars and the Great Depression, as the United States witnessed a decline in Irish immigration. After World War II, parades celebrated Irish Americans not as a newly emerging immigrant group but as a firmly established ethnic group in the United States. Postwar Irish American ascendance was best illustrated, perhaps, by the attendance of President Harry Truman at New York's St. Patrick's Day parade in 1947, the same year a green line first adorned Fifth Avenue. Surely, the participation of a sitting president confirmed that the Irish were a significant presence in the United States. In the decades that followed, St. Patrick's Day parades were better attended, and cities like New York drew more than 1 million spectators. Bigger turnouts were largely due to the growing commercialization of the parade. With considerable media coverage, advertisers used St. Patrick's Day to sell greeting cards, green hats, and leprechaun-adorned shirts, but also beer and alcohol, making Irishness an identity that increasingly was consumed rather than inherited. After all, everyone can be Irish on St. Patrick's Day. As a result of this historical trajectory, the St. Patrick's Day parade tradition in Yonkers and the United States at large is part ethnic celebration and part secular holiday. And for many Americans of Irish descent, the St. Patrick's Day parade is their singular tradition that is distinctly Irish.[9]

In the sections that follow, I discuss how Irish racial expectations, such as order, loyalty, family, hard work, and faith, are embedded in local St. Patrick's Day practices in Yonkers. Alongside my analysis of each benchmark for Irish racial fitness, I also consider assimilated Irish ethnic discourse regarding Irish immigrant newcomers in Yonkers. As my examination will show, assimilated Irish ethnics do not merely criticize Irish newcomers but pass judgment according to the standards embedded in the good Paddy Irish model. In addition, I consider how these customs also emphasize the racial fantasy of Irish downtroddenness. As I have discussed in previous chapters, this growing trend in Irish American popular culture, which serves to minimize Irish racial privilege, also, as I show here, operates in everyday Irish American life. My attention to Irishness in Yonkers as a racial fantasy, in addition to my close reading of Irish racial expectations in parade practices and everyday discourse, is intended to emphasize the importance of race to everyday Irish identity in the United States.

Order

Attention to order is ever present in the Yonkers St. Patrick's Day parade tradition, in the very structure of the day itself: first mass at St. Mary's, then the raising of the Irish flag at city hall, then a bus ride to the beginning of the parade route, followed by the parade itself along South Broadway to its commencement at Getty Square, and finally a dinner dance at the nearby Polish Community Center. Perhaps the sense of order communicated by the parade is best captured in the "instructions" for parade participants in the official program for the day's celebration. In addition to directives regarding time (PARADE STARTS PROMPTLY AT 1.30. PM) and formation (Marching will consist of FOUR to SIX abreast), there are also standards for marching conduct contained in the official parade program:

> Each contingent will maintain uniform ranks and endeavor to "keep in step" with the music. Nothing of an unbecoming nature which detracts from the dignity of the parade will be permitted. This includes comic hats, advertising, posters and commercial signs. The carrying or consumption of alcoholic beverages while in the line of march is strictly forbidden.

> Proper distance from units shall be maintained. NO gaps will be allowed. All marching units will exercise "EYES LEFT" when passing the Reviewing Stand of the Honorary Chairman and Reverend Clergy at St. Mary's and "EYES LEFT" at the Reviewing Stand at Getty Square where Governmental and Parade Officials will acknowledge salutes.[10]

This regimen, which communicates that the Irish are orderly in the United States, emerged from the tradition of militia parade participation that began after the American Civil War. This public expression of Irish American order is countered by discussions about new and newer Irish immigrants in Yonkers, especially about excessive and disorderly hard drinking. Assimilated Irish ethnics typically do not share occupational and/or family ties with Irish newcomers. Instead, their interactions are informed by sharing the same neighborhood space, typically in southeast Yonkers. As a result, newcomers are discussed in terms of what they represent for the area at large. Most assimilated Irish ethnic informants trace their immigrant history to southwest Yonkers in the middle to late nineteenth century. Their predecessors moved to either northwest or east Yonkers during the city's suburbanization of the 1920s and 1950s. Those who live near McLean Avenue in southeast Yonkers were there before the area became an ethnic enclave. Many are not pleased with this transformation, especially the number of bars and bar-related behaviors. Ken, for example, a forty-two-year-old civil servant asked: "Do we have to have so many bars? I enjoy a good time and I like to drink, but do we need all of them? It gives people a bad impression about the Irish and this neighborhood. . . . Seriously, who would want to buy a house around here?"

Tom, a retired firefighter and second-generation resident of southeast Yonkers, also objected to drinking-related behaviors. As a dog owner, he takes regular walks in the area, at various times, both day and night. He told me, "I've seen it all. Fights, broken bottles, vomit. I even saw a young Irish kid asleep in the ATM. I enjoy a drink myself, but this is ridiculous." His sentiments, moreover, were reinforced by Ann, a secretary from northwest Yonkers. She clarified (my words are included, in italics):

I like going to Rory Dolan's, who doesn't? But there are so many bars.
Why do you think so many bars are a problem?
It just doesn't look good for the neighborhood. They may be fun now, but what about twenty years from now? What will McLean Avenue look like then?
What do you think it will look like?
Well . . . that area is very close to the Bronx. Anyone could move in by that time.

These sentiments about Irish immigrant bars and their patrons seem to counter the good Paddy benchmark for order, yet they nonetheless reify this model. By emphasizing their dislike for disorderly drinking behaviors, assimilated Irish ethnics also highlight who the Irish are supposed to be in the United States. More important, these assimilated Irish ethnics forge a link between Irish newcomers and private property. While Ken emphasizes how a bar-saturated area will be undesirable to future homeowners, Ann reveals that this means *white* homeowners. By referencing the largely Black and Latino Bronx, Ann discloses a local anxiety over the proximity of southeast Yonkers to New York City. If the area is less desirable to white homeowners, the decline in demand might allow upwardly mobile Black and Latinos to move in. Irish immigrant bars and bar-related behaviors, therefore, have the potential to threaten property values. But they also challenge the racial exclusivity of this neighborhood, long a bastion of white privilege so fiercely resisted during the 1980s Yonkers desegregation controversy. As we shall see, Irish newcomers will be disparaged for falling short of other Irish racial expectations, such as loyalty and faith. But more important, discourse surrounding their failure to uphold the benchmarks for Irishness in the United States also reveals their failure to uphold the racial privileges of other Irish in Yonkers.

Loyalty

Similar to their interaction with order, assimilated Irish ethnics publicly stress Irish loyalty to the United States during the Yonkers St. Patrick's Day parade. At the same time, they question Irish newcomer adherence to this standard. Even though an Irish flag is raised at city hall on this occasion, the event represents a larger collaboration with and loyalty to civic institutions and, by extension, the larger U.S. political collective. While the Irish national anthem is sung at the St. Patrick's Day dinner that follows the parade, it is performed in English and not in Gaelic, as is the custom in Ireland.[11] In addition, this rendition is followed immediately by the American national anthem. These gestures of loyalty, which evolved over the course of the nineteenth century, extend beyond the day's festivities to participants who adorn themselves with pins or clothing that contains not only the Irish but also the American flag.

While distinctly American expressions within a seemingly ethnic event appear to convey a dual identity, the consistent inclusion of the former reinforces Irish American loyalty to the United States. Many assimilated Irish ethnics, however, raised concerns that Irish newcomers have not made a strong commitment to their adopted land. They often discussed the Irish immigrant character along McLean Avenue

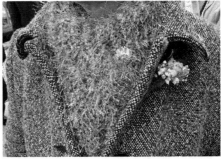

Figures 4.3 and 4.4. Assimilated Irish ethnics convey a dual identity on St. Patrick's Day.
Photos by author.

in southeast Yonkers, as many public displays typically are grounded in Irish rather than American, or even Irish American, experiences. Because they are more fully rooted in Ireland and lack the same duality as ethnic expressions associated with assimilated Irish ethnics, they often are interpreted as disloyal or disrespectful to the United States. For example, Susan, a thirty-two-year-old waitress explained:

> I'm Irish and I'm proud to be Irish, but these people forget that they're in America. Walk down McLean Avenue. There are always signs for some Irish sport. What's wrong with American sports? And all the delis carry Irish products. What don't they want to buy American? And why do they call it the Irish Coffee Shop? This is America. Sometimes I feel like a stranger in my own neighborhood.

Dave, a twenty-seven-year-old tradesman, similarly conveyed a level of discomfort with the Irish immigrant character of the area:

> We were out after work on a Friday night and decided to have a drink in every bar on McLean. Some of those bars are real immigrant bars and they look you at funny if you're not one of them. This is America. I'm an American. I should be able to go into any bar that I want.
> *What happened? Were you refused service?*
> No, but they made it clear that they did not want us there.

These sentiments reveal discomfort with Irish immigrant displays on McLean Avenue, such as the availability of imported Irish products, live satellite broadcasts of Irish sporting events, and solidly immigrant-patronized bars. Indeed, Irish newcomers are assessed as consumers and condemned for their choice of Irish rather than U.S. products. During my interviews, I asked whether maintaining these ties to Ireland might help newcomers adjust to the United States. Not only did they disagree, but Susan and Dave both used race to address Irish immigrant disloyalty.

> DAVE: They just don't want to be American, and they are no better than Mexicans. I was working a job in the Bronx and it was the same thing. Mexican flags everywhere. All the signs in Spanish.
>
> SUSAN: I just think they don't respect the United States. Most of them on McLean are illegal, right? They came here and they knew they weren't supposed to be here. They're just like the Mexicans. No respect for our laws whatsoever.

These outlooks associate Irish immigrant disloyalty with undocumented migrants of color and their supposed racial inferiority. Clearly, these comparisons between Irish and Mexican immigrants are not meant to be complimentary. By likening Irish newcomers to nonwhite immigrants, rather than Irish Americans like themselves, with whom they seemingly share the same racial and ethnic background, they suggest that Irish newcomers are racially unfit. In the discussions that follow regarding hard work, faith, and family, assimilated Irish ethnics more clearly address the ways in which Irish newcomers are racially unreliable. Irish immigrants often are disdained because they are poor buffers against challenges to sites historically associated with white privilege, namely, segregated neighborhoods, schools, and businesses.

Family

Local newspapers, by way of their coverage and photographs, emphasize the Yonkers St. Patrick's Day parade as an event the entire family can enjoy,[12] a feature emphasized by parade participants as well as

Figures 4.5 and 4.6. In contrast to assimilated Irish ethnics, Irish newcomers typically express their identity in relation to Ireland, to their county of origin. Photos by author.

onlookers. "Do you have any kids?" I am asked by a parade organizer. After replying "No," I am told, "Well, when you do, you have to bring them here. It's such a terrific family day." Most of my assimilated Irish ethnic informants stressed the importance of the parade as a family tradition but also its longevity. While Yonkers's St. Patrick's Day parade history is brief in comparison to that of neighboring New York City, assimilated Irish ethnics regularly discuss the permanence of this tradition, describing the parade either as a practice passed down over generations or as a ritual spanning several centuries, connecting nineteenth-century Irish immigrants with twenty-first-century Irish Americans. Alan, a retired accountant, reflected:

> I've been going to the parade since I was a kid. Now I bring my children to the parade, and they bring their children. Four generations in my family have attended this parade.
>
> *Why do you think this tradition has lasted so long in your family? What brings your family back year after year?*
>
> I guess I want my family to know where we came from. It's very easy to take life for granted. You appreciate life more when you stop and think about the Irish immigrants who came to this country starving and penniless. They worked hard so we could have a better life.

Allison, a thirty-eight-year-old former elementary school teacher and full-time homemaker, also attended the parade as a child. She also brings her children to the parade every year. She told me:

Tradition is important to me. My parents brought me to the parade and
now I bring my children. I hope that someday they'll also come
to the parade with their children. It's the glue that keeps the Irish
together.

*Why do you think it's important to have a St. Patrick's Day parade
tradition?*

People need to know how much we struggled, how hard we worked to get
where we are today. People would lose that history and that pride we
have in being Irish.

In their discussion of the parade as a family affair, Alan and Allison
both underscore the longevity of the Yonkers St. Patrick's Day parade
tradition, but they also stress Irish longevity in the United States. For
each of them, the parade is not only a family tradition but a reminder
of Irish immigrants of the past, of their struggle and "hard work." In
discussions of contemporary Irish immigrants, however, longevity and
hard work are noticeably absent.

In the early 1990s, shortly after undocumented Irish newcomers began to live in southeast Yonkers, a "diversity" visa program,
which will be discussed at greater length in chapter 6, enabled many
to change their legal status and become legal residents of the United
States. The new Irish immigrants who eventually started families and
purchased homes are well regarded by assimilated Irish ethnics, but
the newer Irish immigrants who arrived later, without the means
to do the same, are disdained. Nonetheless, both new and newer
Irish immigrants often are discussed in relation to people of color.
Tom, the dog owner displeased with Irish bars on McLean Avenue,
was at the same time satisfied with the presence of Irish immigrant
homeowners:

With the whole desegregation thing, I thought no one would want to move
here, but a lot of the Irish bought homes and fixed them up. I've
got an Irish family on each side of me. Nice people. Nice kids. I was
really heartened to see them move in.

What did you think would happen after the desegregation thing?

I really thought that there would be a flood from across the bridge, but
luckily that didn't happen.

By "across the bridge," Tom refers to the Nereid Avenue bridge across the Bronx River Parkway that connects McLean Avenue in Yonkers to the Wakefield section of the Bronx, a largely residential, West Indian immigrant neighborhood. Though residents of this area share a class proximity with residents in southeast Yonkers, white immigrant homeowners unmistakably are preferred.[13] While most whites in Yonkers maintained during the desegregation crisis that the controversy was rooted in class, and not race, Tom's response suggests otherwise. Margaret, a forty-seven-year-old resident of Yonkers made similar connections:

When did you start to notice that this part of Yonkers was becoming an Irish enclave?

I guess it started with all the Irish bars and the stores, the coffee shop and the gift shop. And then you started to hear more accents on the street. And then those with families bought houses and fixed them up, thank God.

You seem relieved.

Well sure. With the whole desegregation controversy, I thought every Puerto Rican from the Bronx would move here.

Again, new Irish immigrant homeowners are heralded for their investment in local real estate. This seemingly race-neutral, market-oriented choice is discussed in relation to race, as a buffer against the migration of people of color to southeast Yonkers. In this case, Puerto Ricans "from the Bronx" who also are upwardly mobile, are not especially welcome.

Newer undocumented Irish immigrants, on the other hand, who have not been able to change their status, are less likely to make a long-term financial commitment to the neighborhood. As a result, many assimilated Irish ethnics fear that Irish newcomers are transitional neighbors. Mary, a retired nurse, described Irish newcomers who lived on her street:

For years there was an eyesore on my block, just two doors down. But this Irish carpenter moved in with his family and fixed it up. It's really good to see families move in.

How so?

Well, it means people are planning to stay here a while. On the other side
of the street there was this other house, with all sorts of young Irish
coming in and out. There were always new faces. Now section 8
[public housing residents] lives there.

In contrast to assimilated Irish ethnics and new Irish homeowners,
newer Irish immigrants are interpreted as unstable and unpredict-
able residents. While new Irish immigrant home-owning families are
praised for fortifying the racial homogeneity of the neighborhood,
newer Irish immigrants are associated with class integration, and therefore racial integration. Both Irish immigrant cohorts are viewed in relation to people of color, as either a strong or weak barrier to potential
migrants of color, irrespective of their class position or aspirations.

Hard Work

In addition to loyalty and family, assimilated Irish ethnics stress the
importance of hard work in relation to the Yonkers St. Patrick's Day
parade, as well as in their discussions of Irish newcomers. During my
visits to the parade, organizers regularly informed me that the St. Patrick's Day parade is the only parade that does not get "public assistance"
from the city of Yonkers. In this neoliberal setting, a seemingly race-neutral, market-oriented value such as efficiency is expressed specifically in
regard to race. By referencing "public assistance," these assimilated ethnics distanced themselves from communities of color typically associated
with public assistance or welfare.[14] But because of what is assumed to be
"hard work," Yonkers's St. Patrick's Day parade supporters are self-sufficient, and therefore racially adept. Alan and Allison, in their discussion
of the parade as a family tradition, also called attention to hardworking
Irish immigrants of the past. Tom, Mary, and Margaret all stressed the
physical work that new Irish immigrants put into their homes. In marked
contrast, newer Irish immigrants often were deemed lazy, and they
potentially could be outworked by other immigrants of color. Allison,
who previously discussed her family's parade tradition, explained:

"I go to a moms and tots program at our parish a few mornings a
week. . . . Most days there are young Irish guys smoking cigarettes

outside the bars at eleven in the morning. I enjoy a glass of wine but *come on* [her emphasis]. Drinking in the morning? On a weekday? They should be at work."

Whether these men were actually drinking is uncertain, but Allison believes, nonetheless, that this is an unproductive use of time. Newer immigrants also are assailed for not working hard enough. During the interview, Dave, for example, asked me:

Do you know how many delis in the area sell Irish products?
I'm not sure, maybe ten?
Well they're all owned by Arabs. It wasn't always that way. Why can't they hold on to their own businesses?

While there are at least two Irish-owned delis in the area, there were indeed more when Irish immigrants first moved there beginning in the early 1990s. Dave's commentary suggests that Irish newcomers do not espouse suitable market-oriented values, such as a strong work ethic, to maintain a small business. At the same time, his sentiment links Irish newcomers and this seemingly race-neutral value with the racial transition of businesses in the neighborhood. Again, Irish newcomers are deemed poor bulwarks against racial integration and are similarly regarded in reference to faith.

Faith

The importance of faith to the St. Patrick's Day parade may seem obvious, given that the day begins with a mass at St. Mary's; the dinner dance also begins and ends with a prayer. Evolving from nineteenth-century parade practices, these displays of faith, while important to many assimilated Irish ethnics on St. Patrick's Day, are not as important during the rest of the year. Many assimilated Irish ethnics I spoke with maintained that they, like increasing numbers of Catholics in the United States at large, do not regularly attend mass.[15] The Catholic education of their children, however, was important. Frank, for example, a thirty-year-old civil servant explained:

> I wouldn't say I go to church regularly. Maybe once a month? It's hard, my kids have baseball and soccer. Weekends are pretty hectic. But I send my kids to Catholic school. If I don't take them (to mass) on Sunday, I know that they are getting something during the week. Catholic schools teach discipline and morals. Public schools don't do that. And they let anyone in, but I guess they have to. I think my kids are getting a better education in a Catholic school but it's starting to change.
>
> *How so?*
>
> Catholic schools in Yonkers are (pause) how shall I say (pause) becoming more diverse. You have kids going there from the Bronx who don't know how to behave or read. They bring down Catholic school standards.

Frank uses racially coded language to address the racial transition in his children's school. By using the words "diverse" and "Bronx," he conjures people of color without being racially explicit.[16] Other assimilated Irish ethics similarly addressed the Catholic school racial transition in their discussions of faith. Susan, who earlier described Irish newcomer loyalty, also had reservations about sending her three-year-old to a Catholic school:

> I'd like to send Katie to a Catholic school. I went to Catholic school, my husband went to Catholic school. All of our parents went to Catholic school. I know there has been a lot of controversy lately with the church, but they also do a lot of good. We all turned out fine. But St. Bonaventure is getting a little darker, and I think it's only going to get worse.

Like Frank, Susan similarly uses racially coded language to address the racial transition at the local Catholic school. And while discussing this transformation, they both contemplated the role of Irish newcomers:

> SUSAN: I guess that's their choice, but I don't agree. When they don't send their kids to Catholic school, the school has a lower enrollment and they have to make up their numbers. I don't understand why they don't go to the Catholic schools in their own neighborhood.

FRANK: If more of them sent their kids to the local Catholic school, we
wouldn't have the problem kids from the Bronx.

The closing of parish schools in the Bronx may explain why children of
color attend a Catholic school in a nearby, predominantly white Yonkers
neighborhood. Nonetheless, while Susan and Dave stress the importance
of school discipline and moral teaching, they see Irish newcomers as
unreliable consumers of education. In eschewing private education, they
have contributed to the racial transition of local Catholic schools. Clearly,
Susan and Dave do not interpret racial transition as a positive development, and in their discussions of faith, they underscore the importance of
racial homogeneity. This particular quality, which informs everyday discussions about Irish newcomers, also is stressed in the very parade itself.

A Particular Order: Race, Class, and Gender

As discussed in chapter 2, race, class, and gender have long intersected
with racial expectations in the United States. Full racial fitness historically required racial homogeneity, a middle-class position, and traditional gender roles for men and women. The importance of racial
homogeneity animates many discussions about Irish newcomers and
also structures the parade itself, as do class and gender. The dinner
dance most clearly communicates how being Irish in Yonkers requires
a middle-class position, as the meal itself costs $75 a person. Class
privilege is more overtly displayed in the printed program, in which
donors are listed by name and contribution. Those who donate $100
or more are listed as "patrons," while those who give between $50 and
$99 are listed as "sponsors." Smaller contributions, if they exist, are not
acknowledged.

A particular gender order equally is present at the dinner dance,
where more public and prestigious tasks, such as giving speeches, are
performed by men, while women unobtrusively sell raffle tickets to
attendees. The public and prestigious male role extends to the parade
itself, for which grand marshals typically are men. Since the parade tradition was revived in 1955, only four women have served as marshals,
the first as late as 1989. The city of Yonkers is not unique in this regard, as
the neighboring parade in New York City can boast of only three female

marshals. Although women typically occupy a supporting role during the festivities, young girls literally, albeit briefly, take center stage at the dinner as traditional Irish step-dancers. The historical understanding of women as cultural bearers resonates here in the overrepresentation of girls in this performance while boys are conspicuously absent.[17] At the same time, the gender conventions here are undoubtedly heteropatriarchal, precluding other forms of diversity like homosexuality. Should gays and lesbians wish to march under a separate banner in Yonkers, the parade committee likely would bar them, in step with festivities in Boston and New York. Ever attentive to the correct class and gender order, this ethnic event is focused equally on a particular racial order.

When the Yonkers St. Patrick's Day parade tradition began in 1863, southwest Yonkers was an Irish enclave. When the parade was revived in 1955, the city of Yonkers was undergoing rapid demographic and economic shifts, as described in chapter 1. Aided by the G.I. Bill and the Federal Housing Authority, upwardly mobile, working-class, white ethnic residents moved from southwest Yonkers into newly developed suburban tracts of north and east Yonkers. White ethnic residents were not alone in their move. Smith Carpet, one of the city's largest employers, also left southwest Yonkers, but for Mississippi, and was the first of several manufacturers to leave town. African American and Latino workers were moving into southwest Yonkers in greater numbers and were beginning to make inroads into a historically segregated manufacturing industry just as it was beginning to disappear. Well-paying manufacturing work was replaced with unemployment, poverty, and crime, and Getty Square soon was mocked as "Ghetto Square."

This shift in the racial demographics of southwest Yonkers prompts debate among parade participants and spectators alike about moving the parade route to McLean Avenue in southeast Yonkers, an area that has been called "Little Ireland" since the arrival of Irish immigrants beginning in the early 1990s. Whether in favor of or opposed to changing the parade route, this debate is anchored by race. Prior to attending the parade, I asked those more familiar with the parade tradition, "What I can expect to see?" Many expressed regretfully that parade attendance is low. Although the parade route has pockets of few or no spectators, overall attendance is not low, but the attendance of *white* spectators is low, and there is a sizable presence of African American and Latino onlookers. Because Irish identity in Yonkers and arguably the larger U.S. context is understood as a white identity, some expressed a desire to see "more Irish" spectators at the event. One parade enthusiast explained, "I wish there were more Irish faces at the event. I guess the neighborhood scares them away." Indeed, this concern reveals discomfort with the parade route itself, which does not closely adhere to the correct racial order. Many assimilated Irish ethnics and Irish white flighters in Yonkers do not attend the parade precisely because Getty Square is a largely Black and Latino area. Many familiar with the parade explained that is why more Catholic grammar schools from white sections of north and east Yonkers do not march in the parade, but schools in southwest Yonkers do. Thus parade participants are a mix of white residents celebrating their Irish ancestry adorned in green, and students of color who attend local Catholic and public schools. While some might maintain that the latter presence, coupled with a dinner dance at the *Polish* Community Center, deems the Yonkers St. Patrick's Day parade a "multicultural" and arguably racially inclusive event, larger racial hierarchies at work undercut such claims.

Besides local Catholic and public schools in southwest Yonkers, young African American teenagers march in the parade as a step group. Though the "diversity" of the parade is heralded in reference to this presence, the troupe is closely managed and described as the parade's "only problem." One onlooker who attended the parade for decades told me, "This group draws an entourage of people from the neighborhood who follow them with their pit bulls along the way." I also was told, "No need to worry, Jennifer, we have it well under control." As this group marched along the route, paralleled by a crowd of enthusiastic supporters, I discovered how they were "under control." Not only were they placed near the end of the parade, but they were followed closely by a Yonkers police officer riding a bicycle. When the group did not adhere to the aforementioned strict marching conduct, stopping to perform a dance routine instead of following the "EYES LEFT" instructions in front of the reviewing stand, their performance was cut short, and they were told to move along.

Not only are people of color managed at this event, but efforts are made to prevent bad Paddy digressions such as hard drinking, in step with a larger history of dispute over this practice. While the "carrying or consumption of alcohol while in the line of march is strictly forbidden," many do not hesitate to express their distaste for the "trash" that might drink before the parade. Concern about drinking is why many do not want to move the parade to the Irish immigrant section of southeast Yonkers, for fear that a "booze fest" might occur. One parade participant explained that "there are just too many bars on McLean Avenue. If we move it there will be drunk people all over the place." While having a parade along McLean Avenue in southeast Yonkers could boost the presence of white spectators, it also could draw the "wrong kind" of spectator, that is working-class, hard-drinking, single Irish immigrant men and women instead of sober families. These bad Paddy displays could detract from the decidedly good Paddy image of the parade. But there is more to having the parade in southwest Yonkers than preventing an overrun of bad Paddies.

Though some would prefer to have a parade in southeast Yonkers that could draw more white spectators, the white racial identity of the city's assimilated Irish ethnics is reinforced by keeping the parade exactly in the current location of southwest Yonkers. I have argued in chapter 3 that support for neoliberal economic development in southwest Yonkers is revanchist and draws support from many middle-class, white ethnic residents precisely because it will displace African American and Latino residents from this section of the city. Economic expansion in Getty Square is a form of revenge for "taking" this section of the city from former white residents. We should view the Yonkers St. Patrick's Day parade in a similar light, as a way that white, middle-class residents can reclaim southwest Yonkers, albeit just for a day, although the green line that marks the South Broadway parade route might remain visible for many weeks longer. In many ways the parade foreshadows the larger demographic shifts that will occur as a result of aggressive privatization and policing, and many make that connection, explaining that the parade will get more spectators "when the waterfront is finished," a shorthand for an array of projects that will bring more white, middle-class consumers to southwest Yonkers and displace working-class and working-poor residents of color. One parade watcher explained to me, "The parade will definitely be better when they finish cleaning up this place. Once they finally get a better class of people here, more will come to watch the parade."

White, middle-class marchers walking down the St. Patrick's Day parade route, flanked by Latino and African American onlookers, serve a larger racial project that keeps race-based structures of power intact. Many commented to me in a positive light on the presence of local residents. One parade enthusiast commented on the presence of local residents by stating, "I guess you could say they make it a multicultural parade. They buy the Irish flag and wave and cheer as we go by. It's nice. They are very cordial." People of color, largely on the sidelines of this event, wearing green, shamrock-shaped sunglasses, adorned with green beads, cheering as the parade goes by, give a certain authority to the white participants and Irish racial fitness. This narrative minimizes the race and class privilege that allows white, middle-class residents of Yonkers to have a parade where they no longer live. No doubt an uproar likely would ensue if the Yonkers Puerto Rican Parade was moved to white sections of north or east Yonkers.[18] The current parade route also obscures the racist housing policies that segregated the city and required a costly desegregation battle. This spectacle obscures both how race and class segregated the city of Yonkers remains and how urban redevelopment policies will displace these local residents of color. Not only the parade route but also discourse about the Irish in the United States on this day perform the work of a larger racial project.

Irish Downtroddeness

As discussed in previous chapters, in the decades following World War II, European immigrants and their descendants became more fully entrenched in the larger national collective. In its wake, immigrant downtroddenness came to be valorized in the United States. This trend also animates discussions about the Irish during the Yonkers St. Patrick's Day season. Although there are concerns that bad Paddy displays such as hard drinking might undermine the self-consciously good Paddy public image of the Yonkers St. Patrick's Day parade, many gestures, nonetheless, are made to the marginalized status of nineteenth-century Irish immigrants. While the bad Paddy hard-drinking caricature is aggressively kept at bay, narratives of Paddy, victim of British colonial oppression and discrimination in the United States, abound. The parade often was explained to me as a celebration of Irish triumph over persecution and poverty, even "genocide." Commonplace are narratives whereby the Irish were "choked and starved" by the British during the Great Famine of the 1840s, the result of which was a "massive exodus" to the United States, where they faced additional struggle. Sympathetic accounts of nineteenth-century Irish immigrants similarly were told by my assimilated Irish ethnic informants, who typically do not see contemporary undocumented Irish immigrants in the same light. Ken, for example, explained the history of the Irish in the United States:

> "No Irish Need Apply" signs were everywhere. But they, like every other group, had to step up. By spilling their own blood and getting their knuckles bloody from work, their lives got better. They were devoted to their children, their religion, and their country, and now they are the most educated and successful group in the United States.

While this account emphasizes Irish racial fitness by underscoring family, religion, and loyalty, it offers the Irish as a particularly downtrodden yet hardworking group.

These accounts of the Irish in Yonkers are emblematic of how the history of the Irish is told in the United States more generally. As discussed in chapter 2, questions have been raised about the historical accuracy of "No Irish Need Apply." Yet many assimilated Irish ethnics in Yonkers told me that "NINA" could be found at Smith Carpet as late as the 1930s, long after the Irish constituted one-quarter of the Yonkers population. Another maintained that this sign could be found as late as the 1950s albeit in a different form, "No Irish or Blacks Need Apply," serving to equate Irish and African American oppression. This everyday perpetuation of the "NINA" myth attributes existing race and class inequality in Yonkers to "hard work" and obscures the larger structural forces that historically marginalized, and will continue to marginalize, the city's working-class communities of color.

In addition to these narratives, Irish downtroddenness also is underscored in practices associated with the St. Patrick's Day season in Yonkers. Parade organizers and enthusiasts alike make sure that the hard-drinking caricature does not interfere with the decidedly good Paddy public image of the parade. Alcohol, for example, is banned during the

Figure 4.7. "No Irish Need Apply" as it is prominently displayed in a Yonkers
home. Photo by author.

parade, and organizers deliberately keep the route away from the Irish
immigrant section of southeast Yonkers. When the parade ends, however, bad Paddy comes out at night, in the semipublic spaces of the city's
Irish bars and restaurants. Many assimilated Irish ethnics who dislike
Irish immigrant hard drinking during the rest of the year engage in this
practice themselves during the St. Patrick's Day season.

Bars that serve primarily an American-born clientele are particularly crowded during the St. Patrick's Day season, with young and old,
predominantly white, middle-class, male and female patrons. Many
establishments have their walls and ceilings adorned with cardboard
shamrocks supplied by beer distributors. "Shamrocks for a cure," on the
other hand, are usually placed above the bar itself. In exchange for a
one-dollar donation to charity, a patron receives a paper shamrock on
which to write his or her name or a message; during the St. Patrick's
Day season these range from "The Irish are #1," to "Mike Loves Mary,"
to "Car Bombs (Irish not Iraq)." These spaces are crowded, warm, and
loud. The few Irish songs on the jukebox are played repeatedly, and thus
the same songs, usually from the Wolfe Tones, can be heard throughout the night, over and over and over again.[19] While most patrons are
wearing green, usually a green top or shirt, many others put a concerted
effort into their appearance, adorning themselves with pins that read
"Kiss Me I'm Irish," green wigs, tall green-and-white striped hats, or

T-shirts that read, "Who's Your Paddy?" Most people are drinking alcohol, and many are visibly intoxicated.

As I tried to make my way though the crowd, a young male patron bumped into me and apologized with an added, "Top of the morning to you," even though the time was 8:00 p.m. A dance troupe of young girls performed a few Irish steps. The jukebox was turned off (thankfully, a respite from "Tim Finnegan's Wake"). The dance music was supplied by the troupe's chaperone, a parent, I presumed, by way of a portable tape cassette player. The end of the performance was met by wild applause, after which some patrons tried to re-create the dance moves they just witnessed. Visibly intoxicated patrons unfamiliar with Irish dance steps, shuffling their feet on a floor both slick with dropped corned beef sandwiches and sticky from spilled pints of beer, were both comical and annoying as these pseudo-Irish dancers bumped into passersby and knocked down unattended beverages.

Throughout the night I approached various bar patrons as a researcher on the Yonkers Irish, asking questions such as "How should we understand this celebration of Irish identity?" I am told by a self-described "proud Irish American" that "everyone wants to be Irish on St. Patrick's Day. Everyone loves the Irish. We work hard and we play hard. Who doesn't like that?" When I ask how to interpret the overconsumption of alcohol, another enthusiast, whose "great-great-grandparents hailed from County Cork," tells me, "The Irish like to drink. That's just what we do. On St. Patrick's Day when we all celebrate being Irish, I guess we get a little bit carried away."

In previous chapters, I discussed how scholars have interpreted hard drinking by the Irish in the United States. This expression of ethnic identity has its roots in their racial hazing during the nineteenth century, as well as in their experience as immigrants abroad. Quite possibly overstated, excessive drinking has been understood as an act of defiance against Americans who criticized their consumption of alcohol but also their accents and religion. At the same time, the internalization of this caricature signaled to their host society that the Irish accepted America's social hierarchy. In return, Irish Americans were considered less threatening. Nonetheless, this history created a legacy whereby many Irish Americans imbibe to excess on St. Patrick's Day. At the same time, I also considered the role of racial fantasy in contemporary Irish American popular culture. Irish downtroddedness is an increasingly popular theme in an array of texts precisely because these representations serve to minimize Irish American racial privilege. While chapter 3 examined how the hard-drinking caricature and Irish racial fantasy intersect in mass-produced Guinness pubs, the same is true during the St. Patrick's Day season in Yonkers. Drinking to excess in local bars at this time is not an act of defiance as it was for nineteenth-century Irish immigrants. Similar to discourse about "No Irish Need Apply," which underscores Irish victimization, assimilated Irish ethnics perform the Irish hard-drinking racial caricature precisely because they are so far removed from the experience that shaped it. Participating in a bad Paddy digression such as hard drinking is a brief departure from their own position in the existing power structure and minimizes their own racial privilege.

I am not alone in my observation of bad Paddy digressions on St. Patrick's Day. Mass-produced Guinness pubs have commodified the Irish drinking racial caricature to great effect, aiming to extend its use beyond St. Patrick's Day, but so too have clothing manufacturers. "Who's Your Paddy?" can be found printed across the green T-shirts of many bar patrons during the St. Patrick's Day season. While some shirts merely contain this slogan, others also include an angry, red-haired leprechaun. Not only are bar patrons evoking bad Paddy behaviors, but they are literally adorning themselves with a bad Paddy in case their gesture is not fully clear. But there is an additional gloss to the "Who's Your Paddy?" adornment; while it gestures the hard-drinking caricature, it also gestures racial blackness. Irish American racial fantasies not only emphasize downtroddenness but often equate Irish and African oppression in the United States. Irish racial fantasies manifest here in these St. Patrick's Day celebrations in the appropriation of "Who's Your Daddy?" a slang phrase typically associated with African American culture. This use of "Who's Your Paddy?" only underscores Irish American racial privilege. While Black English is the most important source of new slang in white American English, linguist Jane Hill notes that African American appropriations of slang typically are disparaged.[20] Only in this Irish American context can Black slang be playful.

As the same time, assimilated Irish ethnic interest in past Irish oppression as a respite from their own race privilege also is countered by quests for a romanticized Ireland of the past. As discussed in chapter 2, many

Irish Americans embark on roots visits to Ireland, and several of my informants discussed these journeys. Descriptions of these trips typically emphasized the Ireland their ancestors left in the nineteenth century. For example, Amy, a twenty-five-year-old teacher, recounted her first impressions of Ireland: "There were thatched cottages and so many castles. There were too many to keep track of. I will never forget this old house on our way to Killarney. There were animals grazing right there on the front lawn." Her emphasis on the by-products of Ireland's agricultural and colonial past diminishes the way Ireland has modernized. Other assimilated Irish ethnics similarly minimized the lapse of time. Tom similarly described his first meeting with distant relatives: "They made me feel as if I was at home. They were so happy to see me. It was amazing to see so many people who look just like yourself . . . I mean they're just like us."

In these narratives, time has not created a gap between what Amy and her ancestors experienced, nor is there a distance between Tom and his Irish relatives. Amy's and Tom's ancestors seem to have never left Ireland. But by immersing themselves so fully in an Ireland of the past, assimilated Irish ethnics distance themselves from their own race and class privilege, which serves to maintain the status quo. In doing so, these recollections of trips to Ireland, like the "No Irish Need Apply" myth, advance a larger racial project.

Many assimilated Irish ethnics foster connections with Ireland during the St. Patrick's Day season. Some actually go to Ireland at this time, but others visit Irish immigrant bars along McLean Avenue in southeast Yonkers to hear the accents and come into contact with Irish people who resemble their ancestors. These sites of hard drinking draw the ire of many assimilated Irish ethnics and the Yonkers Police Department throughout the year, especially during the mid-1990s when the city limited the number of bars in the area. But because hard drinking is more acceptable around St. Patrick's Day, the boundaries between assimilated Irish ethnics and Irish newcomers become less distinct after the public good Paddy is prominently displayed during the Yonkers St. Patrick's Day parade and dinner. Because this day for many assimilated Irish ethnics is all about gesturing the nineteenth-century drinking caricature, hard drinking in Irish immigrant bars is less threatening, perhaps even exciting.

In these Irish immigrant spaces, green shamrocks, corned beef, bagpipers, and Irish step-dancers are conspicuously absent. Unlike their experience with or stories about trips to Ireland, where Irish people are "just like us," some assimilated Irish ethnics tell me that they are met here by Irish immigrants with "uncomfortable stares." Other than these assimilated Irish ethnic voyeurs adorned in green, St. Patrick's Day revelry is conspicuously absent: no green "Who's Your Paddy?" T-shirts, but maybe an immigrant named Paddy wearing an Irish football jersey; no traditional Irish music, but maybe contemporary pop music on the jukebox; no St. Patrick's Day parade on the television, but maybe an Irish football match. Hard drinking, yes, but that is not unusual.

Irish immigrant stares sometimes are accompanied by snickers. On my field visits during the St. Patrick's Day season, I observed many assimilated Irish ethnic voyeurs dressed in green as they entered Irish immigrant establishments. On one occasion, two Irish immigrant men that I had been speaking with noticed the voyeurs right away, pointed in their direction, rolled their eyes, and laughed. While I will examine Irish newcomer reactions to these displays at greater length in the next chapter, I observed similar reactions throughout the night as more green-adorned voyeurs arrived. Unfazed by or perhaps unaware of this reaction, an assimilated Irish ethnic voyeur asked a "native" where he is from in Ireland, only to eagerly share that his great-great-great-grandmother was from Ireland, too. "Really," the native replied, "I don't know where my great-great-great-grandmother is from." Throughout the night, Irish immigrants were asked about where they are from in Ireland. They also were asked to "talk so I can hear your great accent," "sing a song," or recount how "hard it was to grow up in Ireland." With their racial fantasies indulged about an Ireland and Irish people of the past, some assimilated Irish ethnics voiced their puzzlement and disappointment with the Irishness on display here and asked, "Why aren't more people wearing green?"

Indeed, there is an interesting tension between good and bad Paddies during the Yonkers St. Patrick's Day season. Self-consciously good Paddy public displays abound during the parade and are reinforced by narratives of downtrodden Irish immigrants of the past, in the "No Irish Need Apply" myth, in root visits to Ireland, or in less costly trips to Irish immigrant bars on McLean Avenue. These good Paddy encounters with Irishness are offset on this day by bad Paddy digressions in the form of hard drinking. Together they indulge a racial fantasy for Yonkers's assimilated Irish ethnics. But as assimilated Irish ethnic discourse suggests, Irish immigrants who engage in bad Paddy digressions beyond the sanctioned St. Patrick's Day prompt racial anxiety and scrutiny.

Assimilated Irish ethnics often expressed contempt for Irish newcomers based on their everyday interactions in southeast Yonkers. In their discussions of Irish racial benchmarks such as hard work and loyalty, newcomers were linked to the racial transition of the neighborhood. Often they were considered wrongdoers because they failed to maintain the racial exclusivity of the sites long associated with white privilege, namely, segregated neighborhoods, schools, and businesses. Yet many assimilated Irish ethnics engaged with this cohort in bars during the St. Patrick's Day season. In these settings, Irish newcomers have the potential to serve as a direct link with the past; their presence can supplement narratives about Irish downtroddeness in the United States. In other words, assimilated Irish ethnics enjoy contacts with Irish newcomers when they have the capacity to mask white privilege. But at the same time, Irish immigrants are disparaged when they have the capacity to weaken these very same race-based privileges. Assimilated Irish ethnic discourse undoubtedly is shaped by their position as homeowners, which was threatened during the 1980s desegregation controversy in Yonkers. Though they lost the fight against integrated public schools and housing, assimilated Irish ethnic commentary reveals that an everyday battle is currently being waged. Because they are seen as having the capacity to extend the city's closely managed racial diversity beyond public schools and housing, Irish newcomers are both scrutinized and disdained. Irish white flighters, on the other hand, are somewhat different in their treatment of Irish immigrant newcomers. They also disparage new and newer Irish immigrants, but their views are steeped in their own experiences as immigrants who left Ireland during the 1950s and early 1960s. While their discussions are shaped by larger transformations, both in Ireland and in the United States, Irish white flighters also speak of newcomers in ways that evoke race.

Irish White Flighters

Irish white flighters typically participate in ethnic organizations such as Irish county organizations that sponsor yearly dinner dances, as well less formal social gatherings beyond the St. Patrick's Day season. Like the Yonkers St. Patrick's Day parade, Irish county organizations in the United States originated in the nineteenth century and similarly emphasize the good Paddy Irish model. Many of their events begin and end with a prayer, and U.S. flags are prominently displayed to assuage any questions regarding national loyalty at these ethnic events. Like the Yonkers St. Patrick's Day dinner, the Irish county organization dances can be costly, ranging from $75 to $100 a person and upward. Traditional gender roles similarly are displayed at these events, as more public and prominent roles such as giving speeches are given to men, while women typically occupy supporting and often domestic roles by selling raffle tickets and baking soda bread. But unlike the Yonkers St. Patrick's Day parade and dinner, these events are attended largely by Irish immigrants and are shaped by their experience in Ireland and arrival in the United States during the 1950s and early 1960s.

Dancing is paramount, echoing this generation's fondness for dance halls both in Ireland and in New York City, enjoying music that ranges from early rock and roll and country to traditional Irish jigs, reels, and set dances. Pioneer pins also can be found proudly displayed on many lapels, illustrating a lifelong commitment to a pledge made in adolescence to abstain from consuming alcohol. Those who drink at these events tend to do so in moderation; however, these displays typically are gendered as they were when this generation came of age in Ireland. Men usually stand at the bar while women remain seated at tables and chairs to the side. These displays of order, loyalty, family, and faith allow Irish white flighters to perpetuate the good Paddy Irish model, and they correspond to a particular configuration of class and gender. But unlike the Yonkers St. Patrick's Day parade, which takes place in predominantly Black and Latino southwest Yonkers, events associated with Irish white flighers often transpire in New York City or largely white sections of Yonkers. Unlike debates surrounding the Yonkers St. Patrick's Day parade route, there is little concern whether events adhere to a particular racial order. But the importance of white racial homogeneity does punctuate their discourse.

Most Irish white flighters lived in New York City upon their arrival in the United States and moved to Yonkers in the 1970s and early 1980s, lured primarily by affordable homes. Yonkers also offered a short work commute and a respite from New York City's spiraling crime rate and fiscal crisis. But when I asked Irish white flighters to discuss this, they often addressed changing racial demographics. When I asked Theresa, who left Kilkenny in 1959, why she left the Bronx, she explained: "We had no choice. We were the only ones left. It's like it happened overnight. Kevin started at the Mount [a high school] in 1979. By the end of that year, our building was all Black and Spanish, except for us and two older Irish women on the second floor."

Marty, who emigrated from Kerry in 1957, expressed similar reasons for leaving New York City: "I hate to say it, but the niggers and spics ruined the Concourse. Sorry, I'm sorry, I know I'm not being, like they say, politically correct, but it's the *truth* [his emphasis]. They ruined the place when they moved in. You didn't have graffiti, and you didn't have to worry about crime when the Bronx was Irish."

By leaving formerly Irish and increasingly Black and Latino neighborhoods for white sections of Yonkers, Irish white flighters endorsed a particularly homogeneous racial order. Like assimilated Irish ethnics, Irish white flighters would assail Irish newcomers for failing to uphold this particular order and often questioned their racial fitness.

Unlike assimilated Irish ethnics, who come into contact with Irish newcomers typically as residents of the same neighborhood, Irish white flighters often have closer exchanges. Many Irish white flighters and Irish newcomers also share family or occupational ties. Because of regular interactions, Irish white flighters typically offered more detail in their accounts of Irish newcomers, often disparaging them for their failings as immigrants. Many of my Irish white flighter informants hosted new and newer Irish immigrant relatives upon their arrival in the United States. Most recounted experiences with disorderly hard drinking and work absenteeism, behaviors that undoubtedly counter neoliberal values such as thrift and efficiency. Philomena, for example, who immigrated to the United States from Kerry in 1960, did not have kind words for her nieces, who stayed with her family for six months. She recounted:

> When I came here, I stayed with an older aunt who lived on Third Avenue
> [in Manhattan], and I was happy to do the same for my brother's two

girls. They wouldn't last long with my aunt, let me tell you. I found
them both work as nurse's aides, but they wouldn't take the jobs.
They wanted waitressing work instead. I just don't understand that.
In my day, we took would we could get.

Did they get waitressing jobs?

They did, but they didn't last long. They didn't want to work weekends, and
they couldn't get up in time for the early shifts.

Pat, who emigrated from Leitrim in 1961, similarly questioned the
work ethic of Irish newcomers. His impressions, however, stem from
his experience as a contractor in the construction industry. Pat told me,
"I had a load of Irish fellas working for me over the years. There's always
someone missing on a Monday, never a Friday, mind you, when they
get paid, but always on a Monday."

In these examples, missed days of work typically are attributed to disorderly hard drinking, but some of my Irish white flighter informants
attributed this to the immigrant experience in the United States. Mike
and Mary immigrated to New York as a married couple in 1957, after a
brief stay in England. Because they both come from large families, they
hosted many nieces and nephews over the years.

MARY: I don't take a drink myself, and I don't mind people drinking, but
honest to God it would depress you. Out all day Saturday and Sunday, no work on Monday, no job on Tuesday.

Do you think this was a pattern in Ireland?

MARY: No.

MIKE: No, not at all. They never had money to do that at home. That's the
problem. They come over here, make a good wage, maybe too good a
wage. And sure, there's plenty of bars to spend it in.

Like Philomena and Pat, Mike and Mary attributed missed work to
hard drinking. But Mike and Mary also suggest that this trend is part
of the larger experience abroad, rather than a generational difference.
Hard drinking, according to Mike, is located in the prosperity of the
United States rather than in the difficulties of undocumented life. Theresa similarly asserted hard drinking as an Irish immigrant, rather than
Irish American, behavior:

Just drink. It's all they do. You'd think there was nothing else. I guess with all the bars, what can you expect?

Do you think that they drink more than the American-born Irish, of the same age?

Irish Americans drink too. All of my children take a drink. But you don't see them hanging out of bars on the weekend. Every Saturday and Sunday, you see the young Irish ones out there, and I don't mean at night.

Similar to assimilated Irish ethnics, in Irish white flighters' discussions of order, moderate drinking is accepted, but hard drinking is not. Like Mike, Theresa maintains that this is not solely a difference between old and young but a difference between the native- and foreign-born. As discussed in previous chapters, the hard drinking of Irish immigrants created a legacy whereby their descendants drink to excess on St. Patrick's Day but also are more prone to drink-related illnesses. While this is a documented trend among Irish Americans, Irish white flighters and assimilated Irish ethnics both underscore moderate drinking and attribute extreme drinking behavior to immigrants. At the turn of the nineteenth century, Irish Americans were an upwardly mobile group and, as a result, many condemned the hard-drinking behaviors of other Irish Americans that could hinder their group's acceptance in the United States. Contemporary Irish Americans occupy a more privileged position than their immigrant predecessors. The hard-drinking caricature no longer is used, as in the past, to limit Irish access to social, political, or economic resources. But the sentiments of assimilated Irish ethnics and Irish white flighters illustrate how the legacy of becoming good Paddies still compels Irish Americans to police other Irish and assert their regard for order in the United States.

Hard drinking typically animates how Irish newcomers are seen as disorderly, but Irish white flighters also addressed disorderly households. In addition to family and occupational ties, many Irish white flighters and Irish newcomers share the same residence, as the former often own two-family homes. As landlords, Irish white flighters encounter Irish newcomers as tenants. Those in my sample often stressed disorderly residences in their discussions of newcomers, and they usually attributed this trend to their undocumented status. For example, Tom, who left Mayo in 1953, had trouble with his tenants. He explained:

> I was happy at first to see the young Irish when they first started to move onto McLean Avenue. It was nice to hear the accents again, but they have my heart broke. Cigarettes marks on the floor, holes in the walls. They destroyed the place.
>
> *What did you do?*
>
> What could I do? They were illegal. I probably could have reported them, but I couldn't do that.

Philomena and her husband rent out their second home in Yonkers. After a bad experience, they stopped renting to Irish newcomers. Philomena recalled:

> Twice I had renters skip out without paying the rent. Well no more, I tell you. Now I ask for social security numbers.
>
> *Do you find that this solved your problem?*
>
> Well, I don't get the illegals anymore. When they call up, I tell them that I need their social security number to do a credit history. "Ok, thank you," they say and hang up. I don't like doing this, but what else can I do?

I then asked Philomena if she thought that the migration of Irish newcomers enhanced the neighborhood. She responded that "some of them are great people. There are plenty who bought houses and fixed them up. I know there's good and bad in all people, but they give the Irish a bad name." Like many assimilated Irish ethnics, Philomena affirms Irish newcomers associated with private investment in property. But Philomena and Tom diverge from assimilated Irish ethnics because their encounters with Irish newcomers are shaped by their own experience as immigrants. Both are aware of their tenants' undocumented status, and both could react punitively by issuing a complaint to the police. In regard to taking action that could possibly result in deportation, Tom "couldn't do that," while Philomena chooses another alternative, instead screening potential tenants for evidence of legal status.

While Philomena and Tom discussed Irish newcomers in regard to disorderly residences, other Irish white flighters raised questions about disorderly or nontraditional households. When I asked Irish white flighters to discuss the ways that Irish newcomers differ from their own generation, many told me that "they get pregnant without getting married." Nancy and Maureen had much to say regarding this matter. Former neighbors in the same Bronx apartment building after immigrating to the United States in the late 1950s, they now live a few blocks apart in Yonkers.

> NANCY: My niece lived with me when she came here first. She wasn't here long when she started dating a fella and got pregnant. They lived together for a while, never bothered to get married, and then they went their separate ways. I think he moved back to Ireland or maybe England? Anyway, that's how they're different.
>
> *Do you mean different from your generation?*
>
> NANCY: Yes and no. In my day, if you got pregnant, you got married or you went to England. That's just the way it was then. Nowadays they don't seem to care about getting married.
>
> MAUREEN: I know what she means. It's not a big deal anymore in Ireland to be unmarried and pregnant. I'm one of nine children. I have two sisters and two brothers in Ireland, and the rest of us immigrated here. Every one of them [in Ireland] has at least one child who got pregnant, or got a girl pregnant, without being married.
>
> *Wouldn't you say that's a generational difference, that more people in general are having children without being married?*
>
> NANCY: No.
>
> MAUREEN: No (shaking her head).
>
> NANCY: I have four children, and Maureen has three children, all married, all with children. The *Irish* just don't do that over *here* [her emphasis]. But they do it over there. And they go on welfare, and they a get new council house. It's like they are getting rewarded for it.

Like other Irish white flighters, Nancy and Maureen address how newcomers are different from the 1950s immigrant cohort that migrated before them. At the same time they speak to how the Republic of Ireland has changed, especially in regard to unmarried mothers, shifting from a policy of confinement to one of financial assistance.[21] But at the same time, these women read unmarried pregnancy in racialized terms. By stressing what the Irish do not do, alongside the reference to "welfare," Nancy suggests that unmarried Irish mothers are racially unfit. That unmarried mothers in Ireland no longer are marginalized by public policy truly is a significant change since they emigrated. And perhaps there is a tinge of jealously that Irish women are sexually freer and less subject to the scrutiny and sanctions of an earlier generation. By referencing "welfare" and stressing that this is something that the Irish do not do, they make their discomfort with Irish behaviors publicly imagined as nonwhite quite clear. Jim, who emigrated from Dublin in 1953 and joined the New York City Police Department in 1959, used similar language to describe his Irish newcomer tenants:

> A while back one of the girls that rented our basement got pregnant. I guess the Aisling Center helped her. She had the baby in Montifore [a nearby Bronx hospital], I'm sure all of it paid for by the government. Does that sound right to you?
>
> *How do you mean?*
>
> I don't think that the government should pay for people's mistakes, do you?
>
> *What do you think their policy should be?*
>
> I think they make it too easy. When I worked in the Bronx, I saw it all the time. Loads of women, loads of children, not a husband or a job to be found. I never thought I'd see my own doing the same.

Jim, like Nancy and Maureen, came of age in a very different Ireland than exists today. When he states that it is "too easy," perhaps he favors a return to a previous time when unmarried Irish women were sanctioned for their pregnancies. And like Nancy and Maureen, Jim also evokes race to sanction such behaviors in Irish newcomers. He, too, conjures government assistance as well as unmarried and possibly unemployed women in "the Bronx." Evidently he does not approve of inefficient Irish newcomers who engage in behaviors associated with racial ineptitude.

As with their discussion of Irish newcomers who form nontraditional families, Irish white flighters discussed loyalty in terms shaped by their own experience as immigrants. Irish white flighters arrived in the United States under the 1920s quotas, which, unlike the Immigration Act of 1965, gave preferences to countries in northern and western Europe like the Republic of Ireland. While Irish white flighters secured immigrant visas with relative ease, their immigrant life in the United States was not easy. Many Irish immigrant men were drafted in the U.S. military and served in the Korean and Vietnam Wars. Imported Irish products were less available, and most immigrants communicated with family in Ireland by exchanging letters. While the draft has since been suspended, and an array of technological advancements allow immigrants to maintain more regular contact abroad, Irish white flighters often discussed these changes in relation to Irish newcomer disloyalty. Jim, for example, expressed particularly strong convictions:

> When I first came here, I was drafted and I was happy to serve this country. But the young Irish don't seem to want to be American.
> *How so?*
> If you walk around, you'll see Irish flags hanging from windows.
> *But you're Irish. Why does this bother you?*
> But I'm in America. I live here. I earned my living here. I raised my family here. I'll always be proud to be Irish, but I have an American flag outside my house.

Like other Irish white flighers, Jim's own immigrant experience informs how he understands Irish newcomers, who arrived long after the United States suspended its draft. His reference to career and family underscores Jim's longevity in the United States and, by extension, his loyalty to his adopted land. Other Irish white flighters made similar comparisons. Sheila, for example, maintained that technological advancements hinder the acculturation of Irish newcomers:

> Now you can get everything here. I used to have to hide rashers [bacon] and sausages in my case after a trip home. The delis here have everything.
> *Is that a bad thing?*
> No, it's handy, but when we came here, we kind of had to blend in and be American. Now they're all texting and using . . . what do you call it . . . sky?

Skype?

Yes, the Skype. They're on to them all the time at home. When I first came here, there was no phone in my house. You got homesick and you had to stick it out.

Again this sentiment underscores how time has shaped different outcomes for Irish white flighters and Irish newcomers in the United States. With more global flows of goods, such as Irish foods, and advancements in technology including cellular telephones, computers, and the Internet, Sheila maintains that newcomers have an easier experience than immigrants from her era. At the same time, these changes, however useful or "handy," are seen as impediments to acculturation. Echoing sentiments expressed by assimilated Irish ethnics, Irish white flighters evaluate newcomers as consumers and critique choices that privilege Ireland over the United States. Though Ireland has transformed considerably between the migrations of Irish white flighters and Irish newcomers, legal status is the most significant difference between these immigrant cohorts. The undocumented status of Irish newcomers is an additional reason that Irish white flighters deem them as disloyal. Mike, who left Tyrone in 1957, explained:

When we came to the United States, we applied for our visas, and we had to be sponsored. These young ones just jump on a plane. They have no respect for the rules here. They come when they know they're not supposed to be here. It's just not right. The Mexicans are the same way. They just cross the border when they know they aren't supposed to be here.

As with many Irish white flighters, Mike maintains that Irish newcomers have an easier immigrant experience than prior generations. By migrating without a visa, or just "jumping on a plane," they are seen as inefficient and by extension, disloyal to the United States. At the same time, as undocumented immigrants, they are disdained for their proximity to undocumented migrants of color and their supposed racial incompetence.

While Irish white flighters often used generation to explain how more recent Irish arrivals are different, they also used race, especially in their discussion of family and loyalty. In their discussion of faith, however, Irish white flighter discourse most resembles that of assimilated Irish ethnics. Their understanding of faith is shaped by their experiences in Ireland at a time when the Catholic Church exercised considerable control over Irish society.[22] But they also linked religion, Irish newcomers, and neighborhood racial transition. Nancy and Maureen, for exampled, reflected on the poor faith of Irish newcomers:

NANCY: You don't see many of them at mass on a Sunday.

Is it that you don't see young people at mass or young Irish immigrants?

NANCY: I guess you don't see a lot of young people at mass. Usually it's the old ones like us, and the young ones with their parents.

MAUREEN: But it wasn't like that when we were younger. At St. Philip Neri [in the Bronx], you'd see all ages.

Would you say that your children go to mass regularly?

NANCY: No, not really, but they're American.

How do you mean?

NANCY: I don't think the church matters as much to Americans as it does to immigrants. Even the priests are immigrants.

As with order, Irish white flighters contemplate not their failings as younger people but their perceived shortcomings as young people *from Ireland*. As these sentiments suggest, American-born children are not held to the same standards as the Irish-born of a similar age. For Irish white flighters, Irish newcomers, rather than their own American-born children, bear a greater responsibility for upholding religious traditions in the United States. Martin, who emigrated from Kerry in 1957, maintained that there are consequences to the poor participation of newcomers in the local parish. He told me, "We all sent our children to Catholic school, but now you see fewer Irish faces. Before you know it, they'll be saying mass in Spanish. It's like the Bronx all over again." As with many assimilated Irish ethnics, this Irish white flighter links poor Irish newcomer church participation with greater racial diversity. Based on his experience in the Bronx, he forewarns a greater migration of Spanish speakers to Yonkers. While Nancy and Maureen underscore the prevalence of immigrant churchgoers, Martin stresses how an influx in Spanish-speaking churchgoers is not a good transformation.

Based on his experience in the Bronx many decades prior amid changing racial demographics, Martin's comments caution that the same is in
store for Yonkers.

Indeed, assimilated Irish ethnics and Irish white flighters in Yonkers see themselves quite differently from new Irish immigrants of
the early 1990s and the newer Irish who arrived in later years. Both
assimilated Irish ethnics and Irish white flighters speak of Irish newcomers in ways that conform to the good Paddy Irish model. While
distinct histories inform their interpretations, Irish newcomers are
similarly characterized as disorderly, lazy, and disloyal and are disparaged for their approach to family and faith. At the same time,
their discourse is punctuated by our larger neoliberal order, whereby
newcomers are assessed in relation to market-oriented choices like
investment in private property and values like efficiency. For many
assimilated Irish ethnics, the Yonkers desegregation controversy may
be a recent memory, but anxieties over property value have not dissipated. Irish newcomers are read through this lens, and they raise
concerns because they have the potential to make southeast Yonkers more class-inclusive and potentially more racially inclusive.
Though they lost the fight against integrated public schools and
housing, they continue to wage an everyday battle against integrated
neighborhoods.

Irish white flighters, on the other hand, are more likely to interpret
Irish newcomers through their own experience as immigrants. While
they also voice concerns as homeowners, their scrutiny stems from their
own uncertainties as immigrants in the United States. Though they have
spent most of their lives in the United States, the current anti-immigrant climate encourages an emphasis on their own worthiness and an
inclination to weed out detractors. Their histories, nonetheless, intersect with the contemporary present. Our current neoliberal climate,
characterized recently by economic instability in the housing market
and the heightened policing of immigrants, informs and accentuates
differences among the Yonkers Irish. As such, despite sharing the same
ethnic and racial background, both Irish white flighters and assimilated
Irish ethnics question the racial fitness of Irish newcomers and often
place them alongside communities of color and their presumed racial

incompetence. But how do Irish newcomers see themselves? How do they articulate their own relationship to Irish racial benchmarks such as faith and family? How do they see themselves within the larger bipolar racial order in the United States? These are the questions that frame the next chapter.

5

Bad Paddies Talk Back

This chapter highlights the voices of Irish newcomers, both new and newer Irish immigrants in Yonkers, and how they interact with the good Paddy Irish model. As with chapter 4, this chapter begins with the St. Patrick's Day season but does so through the experience of these more recent arrivals to Yonkers. While conditions, both in Ireland and in the United States, have changed since the migration of earlier Irish cohorts to the city, legal status largely sets Irish newcomers apart from their predecessors. As such, these cohorts reveal how being undocumented often makes it difficult to conform to, or even care about, established benchmarks for Irishness in the United States, namely, hard work, order, loyalty, faith, and family. While a precarious legal status encourages indifference toward being a particular kind of Irish person in the United States, their sentiments nonetheless also suggest a greater certainty about America's bipolar racial order.

Many "new" Irish immigrants first immigrated to formerly Irish neighborhoods in the Bronx and Manhattan during the 1980s and later moved to Yonkers beginning in the early 1990s. At the same time, a "diversity" visa program (which will be discussed at greater length in chapter 6) allowed significant numbers of Europeans, and the Irish especially, to

immigrate to the United States. As a result, most new Irish immigrants
were able to change their status and become legal residents of the United
States.[1] Since then, many married, started families, and purchased homes
in Yonkers, and some have obtained U.S. citizenship. With an adjustment
in legal status, many changed jobs. Some Irish men obtained unionized
trade work or started a small business. Some Irish women left service jobs
as waitresses or nannies for office work. Others, who worked as domestic aides, attended college and became nurses. And there are those who
chose to remain working "off the books," especially in home care, to supplement their household income. These changes shape the sentiments
of new Irish immigrants, as they once were undocumented but now are
legal residents of the United States. As a result, they are no longer are
bad Paddies but "good Paddies in transition," as they are not far removed
from their undocumented experience. They tend to be more sympathetic
than assimilated Irish ethnics and Irish white flighers in Yonkers to newer
Irish immigrants, but they also have the resources with which to be hardworking, orderly, loyal, and family-oriented.

While Irish newcomers share experiences as undocumented workers,
the "newer" Irish are different from their immediate predecessors. Unlike
new Irish immigrants who left high inflation and unemployment during
the 1980s, most of the newer Irish left Ireland as its economy started to
expand beginning in the mid-1990s. Many of these migrants come from
rural and working-class backgrounds and were displaced by Ireland's
unprecedented growth, dubbed the Celtic Tiger by contemporaries.[2] Since
the September 11, 2001, attacks, they also have witnessed the enhanced
surveillance of U.S. borders at both the national and local level. They
are more vulnerable than their immediate predecessors to more aggressive policing, as well as the downturns in the U.S. and Irish economies.
Because of these circumstances, they are uncertain about their future.
They are most removed from the good Paddy Irish model, and their sentiments about the United States are apathetic or, at best, ambivalent.

As race plays an important role in how Irish newcomers are perceived
by Irish white flighters and assimilated Irish ethnics, it also shapes
how they see themselves, gravitating toward a specifically U.S. bipolar racial order that disparages blackness associated with African slavery. While Irish immigrants, both then and now, arrive in the United
States with racial knowledge, U.S. racial regimes are still learned, in ways

contemporary Irish immigrants perceive to be novel. At the same time, the language of neoliberalism creeps into their discourse, including racially coded remarks to disparage those who fail to champion supposedly appropriate values and choices. While I examine the sentiments of new and newer Irish immigrants throughout the chapter, the concluding section on race focuses especially on more recent arrivals. Unlike assimilated Irish ethnics born and raised in Yonkers, the Irish white flighters, who have lived longer in the United States than in Ireland, or even the new Irish immigrants, who have resided here for well over two decades, the newer Irish have a relatively short tenure in their adopted land. As a result, they are better positioned to reflect upon their encounters with race. Their sentiments reveal the many ways in which race (and race thinking) is not automatic or natural but learned and, at the same time, a fundamental site of immigrant incorporation within the United States.

St. Patrick's Day in Yonkers: New and Newer Irish

Helen hurried out the door that St. Patrick's Day morning with her children, Shane and Maeve. They were running late, and Helen feared that they would miss the train. They were meeting Gemma and her two children, Cormack and Emily, at the Wakefield train station. Together we would journey into Manhattan and watch the St. Patrick's Day parade on Fifth Avenue. Helen and Gemma are longtime friends who hail from the same town in Tipperary. They once shared an apartment in the Inwood section of Manhattan shortly after they immigrated to the United States in the mid-1980s. When they first arrived in New York, they overstayed their holiday visas and found work in domestic service. Helen attended to the elderly, while Gemma found work as a live-in nanny. They, like most of the new Irish, eventually changed their legal status. In 1991, Helen married Peadar, who now owns his own hardwood floor business. Two years later, Gemma married Tom, who works for the Metropolitan Transit Authority. Both women left the workforce to care for their children, although Gemma also cares for another family's toddler part-time in her home. Both couples purchased homes in southeast Yonkers, where they currently live.

Gemma and Helen adorn their children in attire suited for a St. Patrick's Day parade. Shane wears a green jacket with "Ireland" written across the front, while Maeve wears a green turtleneck. Cormack and Emily wear "Kiss Me I'm Irish" pins, but neither Gemma nor Helen is dressed for the occasion. After we board the crowded train, we have difficulty finding seats, as the cars are filled with surplus passengers who also plan to attend the parade. We stand as more parade enthusiasts board at Woodlawn, the next stop. The crowds do not dissipate when we arrive at Grand Central Terminal; they only seem to grow. Throngs of people dressed in green try to make their way toward the Madison Avenue exit. We walk several blocks north until we find a less crowded side street that brings us closer to Fifth Avenue. For two hours, we cheer and wave as the parade goes by. The children sit under a police barricade for a better view, while Gemma and Helen keep a close eye on the crowd. Around noon, we try to find a place for lunch. Because most of the Irish restaurants in the area are crowded, we opt instead for lunch from one of the food vendors in the basement of Grand Central Terminal. When we board for our return to Yonkers, the train is noticeably less crowded.

Gemma and Helen began to attend New York City's St. Patrick's Day parade after their children were born, typically doing so when weather permits. Although they were not raised with this tradition, they believe the parade is important to share with their children:

HELEN: We never really celebrated St. Patrick's Day at home. We usually
     went to mass, that's about it.
How would you compare it to the parade here?
GEMMA: It's completely mad over here, isn't it? I couldn't get over my first
     St. Patrick's Day here. All the people dressed in green. Everyone
     celebrating being Irish, even if they're not Irish.
HELEN: I was a bit overwhelmed, to tell you the truth. I couldn't get over
     the crowds. My uncle took me to the parade my first year here, and
     that was enough for me until the kids came along.
How did you decide to take them to the parade?
HELEN: I guess it's a day out of the house if the weather's nice.
GEMMA: The kids love to go.
Do you?
HELEN: It's all right. It's a bit plastic Paddy Irish.
GEMMA: It is (pause), but this is what people do over here.

HELEN: I guess so. But it's different for our children with us being Irish. They play Irish sports over here. We take them home to Ireland every year. For us (pause), being Irish is more year-round. We don't need a parade to be Irish. We *are* [her emphasis] Irish.

So why do you take them to the parade?

HELEN: Even though I see my children as Irish, I guess they're really American. This is what they'll probably do when they get older.

Do you go to the parade in Yonkers?

GEMMA: No. It's a bit out of way, isn't it?

HELEN: I'm not too crazy about driving over to Getty Square. What's that they call it? Ghetto Square?

In contrast to many assimilated Irish ethnics in Yonkers, Gemma and Helen are somewhat ambivalent about the St. Patrick's Day parade tradition in the United States. Both were surprised by the magnitude of the parade, while Helen, with her "plastic Paddy" comment, questions the authenticity of this tradition. Despite their reservations, they deem the parade worthy enough to attend for the benefit of their American-born children. At the same time, they do not attend the Yonkers St. Patrick's Day parade. While they are less familiar with this local tradition, they are indeed acquainted with the pejorative moniker for the area. Indeed Getty Square is on the other side of the city, but the area's reputation is a deterrent. Although these women live and raise their families in Yonkers, they prefer the larger parade tradition in New York City. For many new Irish immigrants, Gemma and Helen's experience is typical. The St. Patrick's Day parade is a rather new, somewhat striking tradition. Many attended the parade when they first arrived in the United States and have started to attend more regularly with the arrival of children. The Yonkers parade does not hold the same significance for many new Irish immigrants as it does for many assimilated Irish ethnics, whose families have attended over several generations.

After being in the United States for more than two decades, new Irish immigrants may have the resources to move out of Yonkers, but some have chosen to remain in an ethnic enclave. They maintain a sense of Irishness by living among other Irish immigrants. Like the newer Irish, they also patronize Irish immigrant businesses, watch televised Irish sports matches, and purchase imported Irish products. They also use technology to stay connected to Ireland by way text messaging, Skype, and Facebook. They often obtain news from Ireland by way of the Internet.[3] New Irish immigrants, however, make regular visits to Ireland. And because they are more likely to have American-born children, they interface with more U.S.-based institutions like schools. They are more likely to engage in U.S.-based Irish practices than are newer Irish immigrants, such as attending the St. Patrick's Day parade, but in New York City rather than in Yonkers. And some participate in other adopted traditions, such as decorating their home with shamrocks or even an Irish flag during the St. Patrick's Day season.

In addition to parade enthusiasts, many people travel to New York City on St. Patrick's Day for work rather than leisure. On the same train as Helen, Gemma, and their children are newer Irish immigrants, like Pat and Jackie, who travel to work in one of Manhattan's many Irish bars and restaurants. Pat left Fermanagh for Yonkers in 1998 and has worked as bartender ever since. In 2002, Jackie arrived in Yonkers and soon found work as a waitress. They became friends after working at the same establishment, though they both have changed jobs, moving with the promise of a busier venue and greater earnings. Currently Pat is single lives with two roommates. Jackie also resides in Yonkers and shares an apartment with her boyfriend. They also experience the St. Patrick's Day season quite differently from other Irish cohorts in Yonkers:

> JACKIE: I absolutely dread St. Patrick's Day. One of the beer distributors gives us a countdown calendar for St. Patrick's Day every year. All of us at work use it to countdown until it's all over. We all hate it. It's really worse than New Year's Eve. All amateurs, all loaded.
>
> PAT: I think there's a better atmosphere on St. Patrick's Day, but it's still a hard day to work. You really earn your money that day. You're flat-out [busy], the waitresses are flat-out with food. I know it's St. Patrick's Day, but sometimes I wonder what the fuss is about. It's usually cold out, the bars are always packed, there's no place to sit. People are lining up to pay twenty-five dollars for a pint of Guinness and shot of Jameson's (whiskey) that they'll probably spill.
>
> *What do you think the fuss is about?*
>
> PAT: It's great to see people so proud of being Irish, but it's a bit much, isn't it? I guess everything in America is sort of over-the-top.

JACKIE: I'm running around trying to serve people, but all they want to do is stop and chat when they hear you have an accent.

What do they say?

JACKIE: They love to tell you where their great-grandparents are from. I couldn't give a fuck where they're from. I'm trying to serve food.

How does this compare to other days of the year?

JACKIE: It's definitely busier, but people are always happy to hear your accent.

PAT: Absolutely. I just started at a place in Times Square, and I get it all the time. "Oh, are you from Ireland!" American tourists absolutely love it. I guess they don't have any real Irish out there, wherever they're from. Iowa maybe.

Like Gemma and Helen, Jackie and Pat are not enthusiastic about St. Patrick's Day. They, too, are struck by the scale of the festivities, but for them, this is a day to work, on one of the busiest holidays of the year. While the parade certainly is popular in New York City, the presence of "real" Irish immigrants, like Jackie and Pat, appears to make the experience more meaningful for some parade enthusiasts. While these newer Irish immigrants work because St. Patrick's Day is important within the bar and restaurant industry, most of my newer Irish immigrant informants also work on this day. Some might venture into Manhattan, if they have the day off, but few, if any, attend the local parade in Yonkers. Should they stay longer in the United States, they, like Gemma and Helen, might make this a more regular practice, but it remains to be seen. At any rate, new and newer Irish immigrants, as more recent arrivals to the United States, are less acquainted with U.S.-based traditions such as the St. Patrick's Day parade. At the same time, they experience and understand faith, loyalty, order, hard work, and family in ways that depart from assimilated Irish ethnics and Irish white flighers in Yonkers. Furthermore, their understanding of race is more fluid and has been shaped by their experiences as undocumented immigrants in the United States.

"They Just Don't Want to Be American"

Both assimilated Irish ethnics and Irish white flighters raised questions about the loyalty of undocumented Irish newcomers to the United

States. Irish immigrant displays, by way of imported products and satellite broadcasts of Irish sporting matches, typically are interpreted as an unwillingness to acculturate to the United States. But while more established Irish cohorts question newcomer loyalty, the Irish largely are not seen as a disloyal group in the United States. While nativists doubted Irish American dedication from the middle to late nineteenth century, the relationship between the United States and other parts of the world has changed considerably over the last century. Unlike the Irish, many other immigrant groups arrived (and continue to arrive) as result of U.S. imperialism and have been viewed as either conquests or perpetual enemies, thus significantly compromising their ability to demonstrate loyalty, regardless of their length of time in this country.[4] New Irish immigrants, nonetheless, who obtained legal residency during the 1990s and, in many cases, eventual U.S. citizenship are proud of their adopted country and, because of their former status, are more sympathetic toward current undocumented Irish immigrants. In contrast, the newer, largely undocumented Irish face an uncertain future, punctuated more recently by downturns in both the U.S. and Irish economies. This, in addition to the hard-line monitoring of immigrants at both national and local levels, encourages feelings toward the United States that may be considered hostile at times or ambivalent, at best. Yet, despite these circumstances, some who believe congressional immigration reform will change their undocumented status also believe in the American Dream and upward mobility, however elusive this promise might be.

When they arrived in New York City in 1985, Darragh and Annie both were undocumented and worked at an Irish bar/restaurant in Manhattan, Darragh as a bartender and Annie as a waitress. They met through work, dated, and eventually married. They lived in the United States for nearly ten years before they were able to change their status. In 1991 they moved to Yonkers, where they now own a home and raise three children. I asked them to reflect on their experiences as undocumented immigrants.

> DARRAGH: I understand where people are coming from. They look at this as a legal issue and see it as people breaking the law, but we came here and we worked. We didn't ask the government for anything, and I think most immigrants are the same way. Drive along Yonkers

Avenue any morning. People give out about the Mexican day laborers there. I don't understand why. They're all lining up for *work* [his
emphasis], not welfare.

ANNIE: Exactly, exactly. Instead of deporting immigrants, why don't they
get rid of all the lazy Americans?

*What do you think should be done about the undocumented population in
the United States?*

DARRAGH: They should do what they did for us. Let them be legal, all of
them. Then they'll buy houses and cars. And they'll start businesses.
It will be great for the economy. I really don't understand why it's
such a big deal.

ANNIE: It's because they don't like Mexicans, but America is the land of
immigrants, right? That's what makes this country great. Any one
of our children could be president one day. Where else could that
happen?

Assimilated Irish ethnics often disparage Irish newcomer loyalty by
comparing them to undocumented communities typically imagined
as Mexican border crossers. These new Irish immigrants, however,
forged the same comparisons, but in the context of demonstrating
immigrant loyalty to the United States. Because of their own experience as undocumented immigrants, they advocate for other undocumented, even nonwhite immigrants. When Darragh states that "they
should do what they did for us," he refers to the diversity visa program
that allowed significant numbers of European immigrants to enter
the United States. This program specifically was intended to make the
United States more accessible to white immigrants amid growing anxiety about the changing racial composition of immigrants in recent
decades and the nation at large. Darragh clearly maintains that this
largely race-based program should not be off limits to immigrants of
color. Darragh and Annie locate themselves as part of a larger history
of immigration to the United States, and they praise the American
promise of upward mobility. They also use the language of neoliberalism to praise undocumented immigrants, their values like hard
work, and their choices as consumers. But they do so, nonetheless,
by utilizing race. In their self-description of self-sufficiency, by way
of "not asking the government for anything" and in their contrasting

depictions of day laborers and welfare recipients, they place Irish and Mexican immigrants alongside each other, yet above the publicly imagined Black welfare recipient.[5] While they appear more likely than assimilated Irish ethnics to embrace a less rigid racial hierarchy, Darragh and Annie clearly evoke the bipolar racial order that historically has operated in the United States and disparages those associated with African slavery.

Other new immigrants similarly referenced America's history of immigration to counter claims of Irish disloyalty. In 1988, at the age of eighteen, Sean left Leitrim for New York City and found work as a laborer in the construction industry. He moved to Yonkers in 1992 and legalized his status shortly thereafter. Recently married, Sean is now a union carpenter and homeowner.

> *How did you decide to buy a home in Yonkers?*
> Well, it's very handy for work. You can take the train or the bus to the city [New York]. You can even drive in. I also like being near McLean. With all the Irish there, it's sort of like being at home.
> *Some people have suggested that the very Irish character of the area is too Irish, even un-American. What do you make of that?*
> Oh, I know who you mean. The same people who go mad being Irish on St. Patrick's Day, right? I work with fellas like that. They give out to me to for driving a Nissan and for having a Leitrim sticker on my car. This is New York. There's a Little Italy, there's a Chinatown. I guess you could say that McLean Avenue is a Little Ireland. Those businesses create jobs, and they generate revenue for the city. I think they forget what the area was like before the Irish moved in. We fixed up a lot of houses. We built a lot of bars, but we built nice bars, far nicer than the dives that were there.

By referring to Little Italy and Chinatown, Sean locates McLean Avenue within a larger American history of immigration and ethnic enclaves. At the same time, he references the financial commitment that Irish immigrants have made to the area, to counter any concerns about their loyalty to the United States. Not only did they invest, but they improved the area. In doing so, Sean represents Irish newcomers as more invested and, by extension, more loyal.

On the other hand, newer undocumented immigrants typically do not have access to legal residency or resources such as unionized work, as did their new Irish predecessors. Indeed, they are less certain of their future in the United States. Because of their legal status, some question the legacy of the United States as a nation of upward mobility, and others raise questions about America's loyalty to its residents. Una, for example, left Kerry for Yonkers in 1998 at the age of twenty-four. When she arrived, she first worked as a nanny for a Manhattan family, but now is a homecare aid to the elderly. She told me:

> Sometimes I feel like I'm stuck. That's the only way to describe it. I can't drive a car or travel over here. I can't get a job with benefits. I thought about going back, but things are bad now in Ireland. Even if it wasn't so bad at home, I'm probably too old to go back. I'd probably have to compete with a Polish girl half my age.

In contrast to the new Irish, a newer undocumented migrant like Una stresses the lack of both geographic and economic mobility in the United States. Without access to legal residency, her job prospects are limited largely to unregulated service work. And with the patrolling of national and local borders since the attacks of 9/11, Una finds it difficult to move beyond her ethnic neighborhood. She references other immigrants, but not to justify her place within a larger multicultural United States. In this case, her reference to other immigrants underscores job competition in Ireland. Returning to Ireland to compete for jobs held by eastern European immigrants might signal that her time abroad encouraged downward rather than upward mobility. Instead, Una chooses to remain immobile in the United States rather than return to Ireland without a success story. Tony held a similar outlook. He left Ireland for Yonkers in 1996 and has worked as a painter since his arrival. He explained: "I'm over forty years of age, and I'm still illegal. I can't really go back home with the economy the way that it is. I guess I'll stay. I've put my time into this place (pause). I've given this country the best years of my life. I never thought I'd wind up like this."

Again, in contrast to new Irish immigrants such as Darragh and Annie, Tony, like Una, is uncertain about his future in the United States. Unlike Darragh and Annie's assured narrative of immigrant success,

Tony can only "guess" that he will remain. His decision to stay in the United States appears to be informed more by default than by certitude. While Tony also uses neoliberal language of choice or the "time" he "put into this place," his investment seems almost one-sided. He labored in the United States, or, in his words, gave "the best years" of his life, but his toil did not merit the return that he expected. Indeed, his sentiment calls America's loyalty to him into question. He "put time" into the United States, but his adopted country did not reciprocate.

"Out All Day Saturday and Sunday, No Work on Monday, No Job on Tuesday"

Assimilated Irish ethnics and Irish white flighers often characterized Irish newcomers in Yonkers as lazy. In addition, when they engage in behaviors such as hard drinking, they appear disorderly. New and newer Irish immigrants shed light on the nature of work and on how legal status shapes the relationship between labor and leisure. Tom, for example, left Tyrone for New York in 1986 at the age of nineteen. He currently works for the Metropolitan Transit Authority as a bus driver, but when he first arrived, he labored in construction. His attitudes toward work changed after he became a legal resident of the United States:

> I'd say I was pretty eager to work when I first came to this country. Construction was new to me then, but the novelty definitely wore off. After a while you're doing the same thing every day. You're working for someone else, in a job where it's easy to get hurt, and you have no benefits. I definitely missed my share of days. As soon as I got my green card, I went for a different job completely. Driving a bus isn't the greatest job in the world, but at least I'll have something when I retire. With construction all I had was a sore back.

Other immigrants voiced similar sentiments. Rita, for example, first arrived in New York in 1986 and worked as a home care aid to the elderly. After obtaining a green card, she attended college and became a nurse. She recalled: "I probably wasn't the best worker when I started. I was young and probably a bit immature, but it's hard to see the light at the end of the tunnel when you're in that situation. But I'm a nurse now. I make a decent wage. I set my own hours. I wouldn't dream of missing a day."

Some newer Irish immigrants have not experienced the same upward mobility. Ann and Enda, for example, currently are in positions once held by Rita and Tom. Ann, who left Laois in 2000, works as a home aide, while Enda, who left Kilkenny in the same year, is a construction laborer. In contrast to other undocumented immigrants they work alongside in the construction and bar and restaurant industries, undocumented Irish immigrants receive higher wages and obtain more desirable positions. Even so, as undocumented workers, a precarious legal position makes it difficult, to borrow from Rita, for them "to see the light at the end of the tunnel." In contrast to how they are represented by assimilated Irish ethnics and Irish white flighters, they, like most newer Irish immigrants that I spoke to, assert that they work hard in the United States, even harder than they did in Ireland. Ann described:

> I thought I was a good worker until I came to this country. There's no such thing as vacation, or a sick day, or even just taking the day off.
> *Why do you stay?*
> If I got a green card, I could go back to school and maybe be a nurse.
> *Couldn't you do that in Ireland?*
> I could if I was younger, but not now. Over here, if I decided to go back to school and be a doctor, people would say, "Go for it. You can do it!" But if I tried to do that back home, they'd laugh at me. They'd say I was a fucking eejit [idiot].

While her legal status dictates a more rigid work regimen, the promise of mobility, however elusive, outweighs the reality of undocumented work. For Ann, the realm of work is a contradictory site, one that restricts but also is potentially expansive. Despite the reality of work stagnation, the promise of mobility, both legal and economic, makes her situation more tolerable. Enda, on the other hand, is less optimistic about work and his job prospects: "No, I don't really like my job. I don't think anyone really likes working construction, it's the same thing, day after day, but I guess that's what we do over here. After a while, you just learn to stick it out. Fellas who can, stay, those who can't, leave."

For Enda, construction work is repetitive and monotonous. Instead of offering upward mobility, work merely holds the promise of acclimation. With limited job mobility and an uncertain legal status, some Irish newcomers compensate for limited prospects with hard drinking. But the change of legal status and better opportunities encourage better habits. Both Rita and Tom reflected on this transition:

> RITA: I'm not proud of this, but there were a few Mondays when I went straight from the bar to the subway [to work]. I guess sometimes you just get fed up.
>
> TOM: Sometimes we'd go drinking for days. You might go home and have a bit of a sleep, but you'd be back again in a few hours.
>
> *Would you get in trouble with your boss?*
>
> TOM: No, not really. An Irish boss would let that slide. If I asked for time off for a proper holiday, he'd give out, but if we miss a few days on a tear [extended drinking session], he'd look the other way.
>
> *Would you say that you drank more in the United States than in Ireland?*
>
> TOM: Absolutely. You just didn't have the money like that to drink at home. But some people over here got caught up in it. A few of the boys I worked with are still at the same thing. I dunno. Sometimes America can be a very lonely place.

While it is part of their past, hard drinking clearly played a role in their experience as new arrivals to the United States. As these sentiments suggest, hard drinking, albeit excessive, can be a release from their experience as undocumented immigrants. As discussed in previous chapters, binge drinking certainly has been present in Irish society, as it has in many agricultural societies, and became more commonplace in Ireland after the Great Famine. While immigrants arrived in the United States with this tradition, Irish immigrant drinking in the United States has been interpreted by scholars as a self-conscious form of ethnic expression and is more characteristic of the Irish immigrant experience abroad. While hard drinking does not appear to function as much as an ethnic badge as it did for immigrants past, binging does appear to exist alongside conditions of being an immigrant. While assimilated Irish ethnics and Irish white flighters may exaggerate hard drinking in their representation of Irish newcomers, counselors at the Aisling Community Center confirmed in the local press and during my fieldwork that more recent arrivals struggle with alcohol and drug abuse. Even so, while hard drinking may be deemed disorderly in Yonkers, these representations pale in comparison to national depictions of Mexican immigrants who are firmly associated with drugs, human trafficking, and crime.[6]

While contemporary advancements in communication, transportation, and technology facilitate the immigrant experience in the United States, the undocumented immigrant experience is by no means easy. Newer Irish immigrants more fully relate the relationship between hard drinking and their undocumented status. Unlike new Irish immigrants, they are not removed from their undocumented status; therefore, they are less likely to distance themselves from this practice. Sally, for example, is unapologetic for hard drinking and drinking-related behaviors. She emigrated from Donegal and currently bartends in the area. Sally told me, "I don't see what the trouble is about. People work hard all week. What they do here is their business. If there's a mess, it's our mess. If there's a fight, it's our fight." Other bartenders in the area expressed similar sentiments. Kevin, who emigrated from Louth in 2000, clarified:

> The Irish drink here because they are comfortable here. They don't go to American bars or bars in the city [New York] because you never know who's there next to you. Americans just don't like illegals, no matter what they look like. Who's to say that they won't ask questions if they hear an accent, even if it's an Irish accent? Who's to say they won't make a phone call to INS if they don't like what they hear?

Since 9/11, it is not surprising that these immigrants are defensive about questions regarding their personal lives, when criticisms of their very existence are mounting at both the national and the local level. These sentiments expose the presence of everyday surveillance, but they also demonstrate how bars encourage a more cohesive undocumented Irish community. If there are fights or "messes" among this cohort, they should not, according to Sally, merit the scrutiny of outsiders. Irish immigrant bars also, according to Kevin, have the potential to insulate immigrants from questions regarding their status. When Kevin relates that Irish immigrants do not patronize American bars, he means seemingly Irish bars in the area that are patronized by an American-born, rather than Irish-born, clientele. Irish newcomers patronize immigrant bars to go unnoticed. As these sentiments suggest, some believe that their status could be an issue in establishments with American-born patrons. As with the 1980s new Irish, bars continue to function as community centers, places to network for jobs and housing, to cash checks, and to watch Irish sports. But they are also a buffer against a more intensely anti-immigrant climate.

"They Get Pregnant without Getting Married"

For many Irish newcomers, being undocumented shapes how they understand family, how they maintain ties with relatives in Ireland, and how they form relationships in the United States. For the new Irish who were largely able to legalize their status, they typically met their spouses in the United States and married in Ireland. Those who are parents raise their children with both U.S. and Irish traditions: they may play Irish music or sports but also participate in baseball or ballet. Vacations might involve trips both to the New Jersey shore and to Ireland. Regular contact with family and friends in Ireland is sustained by text messaging, e-mail, Skype, and Facebook. Many stay informed of events in Ireland by using the Internet to read local newspapers or to watch news broadcasts. As discussed in chapter 4, many Irish white flighters maintain that these advancements facilitate an easier immigrant experience in the United States. In contrast, new Irish immigrants stress the increased difficulty of undocumented life and the importance of having obtained legal residency during the 1990s. Rose, who left Kildare in 1989, explained:

> Skype and texting is great, but is just not the same as being there.
> *How so?*
> I really feel bad for the ones here now. When we were illegal, you could drive a car, you could go home. I went back every year. Now you're here or you're there. No more back and forth. You have to make a choice, and you have to stick with it.

Rose also remarked on the importance of bringing her American-born children to Ireland:

There's nothing like being with your family, in the same room. Even if you're just sitting there, drinking tea, saying nothing. It's (pause) more spontaneous, it feels more normal, like it was before I left Ireland. When you text or call, it's like you have to fit everything in. It's more rushed. What's the word I'm looking for? It feels more forced.

Newer undocumented immigrants, on the other hand, have a different experience, as they cannot travel back and forth, which shapes their relationships within the United States. Vicki and Eamon, who immigrated to Yonkers from Cork in the summer of 2001, illustrate why some choose to postpone marriage. Because their future in the United States remains uncertain, so, too, are their wedding plans. I asked Vicki, who had been engaged since 2005, why they did not marry in New York instead of waiting for an undetermined amount of time to travel back to Ireland. She responded, "I suppose we could, but it wouldn't be the same. We both come from big families. They all wouldn't be able to travel here. I want my family with us, even if it means we have to wait. I don't care how long it takes."

Assimilated Irish ethnics and Irish white flighters interpret Irish newcomers differently. The former affirm those who establish families and purchase homes, while the latter, raised with a strict Catholic upbringing, disparage nontraditional households. Vicki and Eamon illustrate why some choose to postpone marriage and family. Irish newcomers choose to not marry not, as Irish white flighters suggest, because of poor family values but because of their strong ties to family. When I interviewed newcomer informants over 2005, many were hopeful that Congress would pass comprehensive immigration reform. Those in long-term relationships at the time also expressed a desire to postpone wedding plans. Others, however, would not be confined by their undocumented status. Noreen, an undocumented mother of three, has lived in the United States since 1999. She discussed her experience as an undocumented immigrant parent:

I'm sure people think we're crazy for having children, but what else can we do? There's nothing for us back home. And there's definitely nothing for them [her children]. I try not to think about it, to tell you the truth.

I'm here fifteen years already, what's fifteen more? By then maybe one of them (the children) can sponsor us (laughs).

During the interview, I asked Noreen to tell me about her American-born children. Unlike the new Irish who often enroll their children in both U.S. and Irish recreational activities, Noreen's sons play only Irish sports. She shed light on this decision: "I don't put the boys in baseball because you just don't know who the other parents are. A lot of Americans don't like illegals. Mexican illegals or Irish illegals. It's all the same to them. They're in Gaelic football because everyone is Irish and no one asks questions."

Historically, the children of immigrants often have acted as "go-betweens," serving to translate the "new world" for their parents. But as Noreen's experience suggests, the children of undocumented immigrants are a potential liability, as they could expose the status of their parents. Child rearing requires interactions with an array of public and private institutions, which could potentially warrant greater scrutiny. Many states have recognized this link and have sought to limit assistance to so-called anchor babies and their undocumented parents.[7] And while some assimilated Irish ethnics maintain that newcomers "just don't want to be American," Noreen reveals the difficulty some face in forging ties to the United States. While undocumented motherhood is by no means easy for immigrants like Noreen, her situation may be better than what other immigrants encounter. As part of a trend that has been called "transnational motherhood," many Latina immigrants, when faced with scant economic prospects and heightened border policing, leave their children behind, only to toil as nannies in American homes.[8]

These newer Irish immigrants reveal that family is indeed important, and their undocumented status shapes their relationships in ways that depart from other Irish cohorts in Yonkers. Some postpone marriage and family, while others do not, even though children add an extra layer of vulnerability to their status.[9] As a result, some forgo family altogether, and their sentiments, like those expressed about work, can be deemed ambivalent at best. Fergal left Mayo for Yonkers in 2002. He works in construction and prefers to remain single because of his legal status. He gave reasons for this decision:

I think having a steady girlfriend would make life more difficult, and I don't mean the way that fellas complain about women. If I get caught, no bother. I might have to leave behind what's in my apartment, but that's it. With a girlfriend, I'd have another person to worry about. I know loads of Irish over here with families. I don't know how they do it. It's just too much of a risk.

While undocumented life encourages Fergal to avoid long-term relationships, others cope by creating an emotional distance from celebratory events. Sally, for example, reflected on the ways that she has changed since coming to the United States:

> I used to love going to weddings. I used to love, and I mean love, Christmas. But I don't really care anymore.
> *Why not?*
> They're just not the same without my family (long pause). I guess I sort of numbed myself. I started to tell myself that it's just another day. I'm sorry, can you turn the recorder off? I don't want to talk about this anymore.

Family, like no other topic, elicited very emotional responses from my newer Irish immigrant informants, and I was asked on more than one occasion to stop recording during the interview. My informants regularly discussed the difficulty of not attending family events, such as weddings, but they also missed other occasions, such as funerals. After the death of a family member, some chose to remain in the United States rather than travel to Ireland, for fear that they would not be able to return. Siobhan, for example, was faced with this difficult decision. She explained, "My brother was killed in a car accident, and I didn't go back for the funeral. I have to live with that for the rest of my life. I chose this place over my brother." Siobhan's experience is not uncommon among the undocumented Irish community in Yonkers. Her response reveals the strain many face and the difficult decisions regarding family that many must contemplate.

"You Don't See Them at Mass on Sunday"

While assimilated Irish ethnics and Irish white flighters understand and experience faith differently from each other, they both interpreted Irish newcomer faith in terms of southeast Yonkers's potentially changing racial demographics. Assimilated Irish ethnics typically addressed this shift in relation to Irish newcomer support for public rather than Catholic schools, while Irish white flighters usually discussed this change in terms of poor church attendance. Much like loyalty, poor newcomer faith does not warrant national scrutiny. While Irish newcomers may be ambivalent Catholics, they are Christians, nonetheless, and are not subject to the same scrutiny as Muslim immigrants, who were targeted and deported after 9/11 for overstaying their visas.[10] Even so, in a significant departure from Irish white flighters, Irish newcomers came of age amid growing criticism of the Catholic Church in Ireland, the sexual abuse of children by priests, and the strict religious administration of Magdalen asylums as well as mother and tot homes. While the Catholic Church in the United States is embroiled in similar controversy, questions about the Catholic Church in Ireland were raised sooner, as were critiques. The Irish government, for example, issued two scathing reports in 2009 detailing abuse in Catholic schools and collusion between the church and police in covering up the sexual abuse of children. At the same time, Prime Minister Enda Kenny condemned the Vatican, rather than local bishops, for covering up cases of child abuse.[11] Not surprisingly, Irish newcomers tend to be more critical of the Catholic Church and are less invested in demonstrating a strong religious faith. For some, the United States is a place where they can be free from religion. Aidan expressed:

> At home we had to go to mass every Sunday. Before I came here, I was working at a factory. I made my own wage, and I gave my mother money every week, but I was still expected to go to mass every week. Over here, no one knows who you are. At home my mother would be mortified if the neighbors didn't see us all at mass.

Like Aidan, other Irish newcomers maintained that their relationship with the Catholic Church changed as a result of their migration to the United States in ways that are both positive and negative. Enda, for example, began to attend mass regularly only after his arrival in the United States. He explained: "My father was a great man for mass. I don't think he ever missed a Sunday in his entire life. When he died in 2004, I didn't go home for the funeral because I was afraid I wouldn't get back in. I don't go every Sunday, but I go most Sundays, out of respect for him."

Caroline, who immigrated to Yonkers in 2001, had a similar experience: "I make an effort to go to mass every Sunday over here. Don't ask me to tell you what the priest said, but when I go, I usually think about my mother. She died years before I came here. Mass has been a way for me to feel close to her."

For these newcomers, church attendance in the United States is a habit cultivated by the loss of a loved one and the reality of undocumented life that makes return visits to Ireland difficult. Here the Catholic Church is an important middle ground between Ireland and the United States. Other newcomers presumed the same but were disappointed by their encounters with the Catholic Church in Yonkers. Martina intended to enroll her sons in a local Catholic school but changed her mind. She recalled:

> I was planning to send the twins to St. Bonaventure, but when I went to sign them up, they asked for tax returns. What am I supposed to say? That I don't have them? That I'm illegal?
> *What did you say?*
> I said I'll be back with them. I never did.

Parish schools typically require proof of income for enrollment, to make sure that parents will be able to afford tuition. Also, such questions help to determine whether Sunday donations will partially offset tuition charges in the local school. Non-Catholic students, for example, typically pay higher tuition than Catholic students, whose parents also are expected to make an envelope contribution every Sunday at mass. As Martina's experience illustrates, requiring applicants to provide proof of income discourages undocumented Irish immigrants from participating in Catholic parish life. Other newcomers also were discouraged by their dealings with a local parish priest in Yonkers. Vicki and Eamon, who decided to postpone their marriage until they could travel to Ireland, welcomed a daughter in 2009. When they started to make arrangements to baptize Sarah, the priest surprised them. Vicki related:

> The priest gave out to us. I nearly died. We're there trying to do the right thing, getting the child christened, and he said that he'd have to think about it because we weren't married. Can you believe that?
> *Do you think you'd be treated differently in Ireland?*
> Absolutely. That would *never* [her emphasis] happen at home.

Others expressed sentiments that the parish was not supportive of undocumented parishioners. Enda, who, as mentioned earlier, regularly attends mass to stay connected with his deceased father, related:

> When there was a lot of organizing for immigration reform [in 2005], the priests didn't say a word about it. What's the name of that priest in Los Angeles?
> *I think it was Cardinal Mahony.*
> He was on the news all the time speaking up for illegals. You didn't see that here. I'm at mass most weekends. Not a word. And no priest was at any of our rallies.

Though immigration politics will be discussed at greater length in chapter 6, Enda reveals how some newcomers feel greater alienation from the Catholic Church in the United States. The Catholic Church *does* support this cohort by way of the Aisling Community Center, and one local parish school did host two rallies for immigration reform. But Enda's experience and the outlooks expressed by other newcomer informants reveal how the undocumented immigrant experience can foster both proximity to and estrangement from the American Catholic Church.

"I Was Never Racist until I Came to This Country"

Assimilated Irish ethnics and Irish white flighers raised questions about Irish immigrant newcomers not only for their disorderly hard drinking but also for their potential to dismantle the neighborhood's racial order, in other words, its white racial homogeneity. How do newcomers navigate a bipolar racial order in the United States that historically equates citizenship with white racialness and disparages the descendants of African slaves? Do they feel compelled to uphold this racial order? And where do they locate themselves and migrants of color they often work alongside? Based on my interviews, Irish newcomers both conform to and depart from the discourse of other Irish cohorts in Yonkers. While Irish white flighers and assimilated Irish ethnics use race to disparage Irish newcomers, members of this more recent cohort tend to make positive connections with immigrants of color. These affirmations, however, often are used to disparage African Americans, which many maintain is a new, but nonetheless justified, outlook.

David Roediger has argued that the stigma of associating Irish immigrants in the nineteenth century with free Blacks, coupled with certain undeniable race-based advantages, encouraged a race consciousness that resulted in a social realignment with their race interests rather than their class interests.[12] What can we make of the undocumented Irish? As examined in previous chapters, they too are stigmatized and compared to communities of color. Though undocumented, they enjoy many race-based advantages in the United States, such as having access to segregated neighborhoods and receiving higher wages for work performed by Latino and Caribbean immigrants, especially in the construction and home care industries. In these same jobs, it literally pays to be Irish. Does this combination of race privilege and race stigma encourage undocumented Irish immigrants to distance themselves from their class interests and align themselves with their race interests? While members of this group realize that they must adopt certain behaviors to "stick it out" in the United States, does that include being racist? The answer is far from clear.

Undocumented Irish immigrants often occupy a literal proximity to Latino immigrants, with whom they share an undocumented status and work alongside in the service economy. Latino immigrants in the United States have an equally complicated trajectory with empire under both U.S. and Spanish regimes, as well as with race, drawing from European, African, and indigenous populations. Unlike Indian, Asian, and West Indian immigrants who regularly are heralded as model minorities in opposition to African Americans, Latino immigrants often are placed in proximity to the latter group. Both Puerto Ricans and African Americans were similarly pathologized during the 1960s under the "culture of poverty." By the 1990s, undocumented Latina immigrant mothers and their so-called anchor babies were racialized in ways to resemble Black welfare queens. More recently, undocumented Latino immigrants have been targeted by states in ways that are similar to the policing of African Americans under Jim Crow laws in the South. On the other hand, because immigrants from Central America and Mexico do not have ties to African chattel slavery in the United States, they still are immigrants with potential. Within this neoliberal climate, Latinos increasingly have been represented in a positive light by politicians, marketers, and writers from across the political spectrum. Nonetheless, Irish immigrant newcomers, in their discussion of Latino coworkers, do not seem as invested in white racial homogeneity as do assimilated Irish ethnics and Irish white flighters in Yonkers.[13]

Irish newcomers often recounted friendly workplace exchanges with their Latino immigrant coworkers. Tim, a thirty-three-year-old carpenter explained, "I've learned a few words of Spanish, and they have a few words of English. Their English is broken, and so is our Spanish, but somehow it just makes sense." I observed a Spanish-English dictionary in an Irish contractor's van, no doubt an additional tool for the work site. In marked contrast to the anti-immigrant rhetoric and calls for making English the national language, many undocumented Irish immigrants were quick to tell me how fast their Latino coworkers learned English. Jackie, mentioned at the beginning of the chapter, recounted her experience in the Irish bar and restaurant industry: "The lads in the kitchen are always asking, 'How to do you say this in English?' Or they will say, 'What does this mean in English?' I've picked up a few words in Spanish, but when I try to practice with them, they say, 'No, say it in English.'" She added that curse words are also a popular exchange: "It's deadly. I taught Juan to say *pog mo thoin* [kiss my ass]. He said it to my boss last week, and all he could do was laugh."

Irish women who work in home care, as nurse's aides or nannies, typically come into contact with West Indian rather than Mexican and Central American immigrants. This exchange is slightly different, shaped by similar histories and familiarity with consumer goods under British colonialism. One Irish nanny I spoke with brings "bags of lucozade and Cadbury's chocolate" to Jamaican nannies who work in the same town. Besides sharing food, these women share information about jobs, undoubtedly much to the chagrin of future employers. The *Irish Echo* and the *Irish Voice* are Irish American newspapers in which many families in the New York metropolitan area look for household help. Surely some use these particular newspapers precisely because they want to hire a white nanny or nurse's aide. West Indian caregivers also use these networks to find work and probably obtain information about these sources through their contacts with Irish nannies.[14] I witnessed similar networks in Yonkers. The Aisling Irish Community Center, for example, posts information about jobs and apartment rentals. Undoubtedly many post notices there precisely because they want to either rent apartments to or employ Irish immigrants. But these efforts to keep both employment and housing in southeast Yonkers racially exclusive are foiled by contacts between Irish and Caribbean workers. On many occasions I observed Caribbean immigrants at the center looking over job announcements.

Some positive work interactions extend beyond the actual workday. I witnessed Irish and Latino laborers cashing checks and sharing drinks in Irish immigrant bars along McLean Avenue. Although I observed this practice before conducting my fieldwork, it had changed somewhat. In the past, the contractor was always an Irish immigrant who would sit at the bar, as would his Irish employees. But Latino immigrants would be seated at tables and chairs to the side, and drinks would be passed over to them. This drinking practice has a long trajectory both in Ireland and in the United States as a way to designate hierarchies typically between men and women. During my fieldwork I observed not only that Latino immigrants sat at the bar alongside their Irish coworkers but that they entered these spaces unescorted by an Irish sponsor. In the past, where some might have found it strange or even threatening to see a group of Latino men enter an Irish immigrant bar (as it would for any group of non-Irish immigrants, including assimilated Irish ethnics but to a lesser degree), I witnessed this new trend on many occasions. This difference is probably possible because some Irish immigrants returned to Ireland during the Celtic Tiger, relaxing the exclusivity of Irish immigrant bar patronage. Irish and Latino laborers share these spaces to cash checks after work or to enjoy a soccer game, as these bars typically televise an array of international matches. Indeed, these interactions are infrequent, but they are less hierarchical than other Irish sites in Yonkers such as the St. Patrick's Day parade, where African American participants, for example, are closely managed.

Siobhan, who chose to remain in the United States after her brother died in Ireland, works for an Irish construction company that employs both Irish and Latino immigrants. During the interview, she described their Christmas party: "The boss took us out for a meal and hired an Irish band and a Spanish deejay for afterward. We were there showing them Irish step-dancing, and they were showing us their dances. It was priceless."

These types of work-based interactions evolved into a few romantic relationships, albeit with mixed results. One Latina immigrant I spoke to had dated an Irish immigrant laborer for more than a year, and they socialized primarily in Irish immigrant bars in the area. "His friends were really nice to me," she recounted, "but the older men in the bar always stared at me." Irish women dating Latino men have a different experience. One Irish woman I spoke with recounted no stares but plenty of comments about her Ecuadorian boyfriend from Irish men, such as "What are you doing with *him*?" Indeed, for Irish men, dating outside their group is less questionable, probably even heralded as a sexual conquest. Similar behaviors from Irish women, however, are less acceptable. This is clear not only to the Irish women I spoke with but to Latino immigrant men as well. One Mexican immigrant who had worked in Irish restaurants in Yonkers, the Bronx, and Manhattan for nearly twenty years explained to me, "You can go to their parties, and you can hang out with them after work, but don't try to date their women." While there are social interactions among Irish and Latino immigrants, clearly there are different standards for men and women.[15]

Many Irish newcomers also discussed positive exchanges in the area's many delis that sell Irish products but are owned and staffed largely by immigrants from the Middle East. As discussed in chapter 4, this was not always the case and was a cause for concern among some assimilated Irish ethnics, who pointed to this change as evidence of a poor work ethic among Irish newcomers. Many regular Irish immigrant customers pointed to their interactions as positive and recounted the generosity of proprietors who give a tin of Irish biscuits or a box of chocolates to their regular Irish patrons around the Christmas holidays. Eileen, a former nanny and now full-time homemaker, underscored these types of exchanges to illustrate how "eclectic" this neighborhood is even though southeast Yonkers is understood to be an Irish enclave. When I asked why she thought immigrants from the Middle East and not Ireland typically sell Irish products, she explained, "The same lad that's there in the morning when I get my coffee is the same lad there late at night. Irish people won't work those kinds of hours for those wages." And here lie the limits to the more positive exchanges among Irish and non-European immigrants.

In many Irish newcomers' accounts of camaraderie with non-Irish coworkers, Latinos especially, their praise typically is coupled with the comment that "they're just like us." Although this expression commonly was used to describe warm, even friendly, exchanges, accounts were punctuated equally with acknowledgments that their nonwhite coworkers are not treated as well and earn less money for the same work. Although many contractors maintain that Latino laborers are preferable to Irish laborers, that they "work harder" and "always show up on a Monday," Latino laborers might be preferable because they are paid less than Irish laborers. Irish contractors I spoke with told me that some Latino laborers are paid as little as $60 a day, although $80 to $100 is more typical, while "no Irish lad will work for less than $150 a day." Though different pay scales exist, workplace relations also are uneven. One Saturday afternoon, for example, I had a very interesting exchange with an Irish immigrant bartender about his Latino coworker who was busing dirty plates from behind the bar.

Have you been working here together very long?
Sean's been here longer than me, since they first opened the place.
Sean? His name is Sean?
No, no, no. His name is Juan, but we all call him Sean. Yeah, all the lads in
    the kitchen speak a few words of Irish. When I go back there looking
    for milk for my tea, I ask for it in Irish and say *bainne*, not *leche*.

Though Irish immigrant accounts of exchanges with Latino immigrants suggest reciprocity, this also illustrates a larger hierarchy in favor of Irish immigrants. Many of my new Irish immigrant informants spoke at great length about racial hierarchies in the United States. Fergal, for example, described his experience in the construction industry:

You'll find all sorts of people on the job . . . Ecuadorians, Mexicans, Jamaicans, West Africans, all pretty decent people.

Has your experience with different people been positive?

I think for the most part, we all want to get the job done right, but the Black fellas couldn't give a shit. Lazy, sloppy, they only get in your way.

When you say Black fellas, do you mean Jamaicans and West Africans?

No, sorry, I mean Black Americans, or what is it you say over here, African Americans? The Jamaican fellas are all right, and the West Africans are great workers. I don't know about the other ones who landed here.

Aidan, who also works in construction, described a similar hierarchy: "You can work with the Jamaicans, but Black Americans are a waste of time. A lot of the Jamaicans are the same as the Irish. They want the same things, to have a nice house and to send their children to college. The Blacks could care less."

Interestingly, "Black" as it is used here by Irish immigrants is not an umbrella term for all immigrants of African descent, but for Americans of African descent who are presumed to adopt poor values and choices. At the same time, Irish immigrants use benchmarks for racial fitness, such as hard work and family, to affirm other immigrants, even those of color. My informants often made comparisons between African Americans and nonwhite immigrants to affirm the possibility of upward mobility in the United States. Recall Darragh and Annie's discussion of loyalty to the United States: "Drive by Yonkers Avenue any morning. People give out about Mexican day laborers there. They're lining up for work, not welfare." Sally the bartender maintained similar sentiments: "Mexicans are the hardest-working people on the planet. They'll mow lawns, work construction, make food, wash dishes. But all you ever hear about over here is how Blacks are discriminated against. If Mexicans can find these jobs, why can't they? They don't want to work."

Interestingly, Sally maintains that African Americas, who have been in the United States longer than the Irish, should accept service jobs currently held by immigrants and positions that the Irish often do not occupy. While Irish and Latino immigrants work alongside each other in the construction industry, Latino immigrants are overrepresented in lower-paying work such as mowing lawns and preparing food. Many Irish newcomers commented that this specific understanding of race, which relegates African Americans to the bottom of the hierarchy, is something they learned in the United States. Siobhan elaborated: "If you said one racist thing to me back in Ireland, I would give you a lecture for an hour. But now I am saying those things. I hate to say it, but it's true. Black people *are* lazy [her emphasis]."

Liam expressed a similar sentiment:

> I was quite shocked actually when I first heard lads at work say "nigger." I thought they were joking to say it so bluntly. But I guess it's easy to fall into it, that you find it's true. There are plenty of jobs here in this country. You can work if you want to.
>
> *Can you tell me a little more about it being easy to fall into?*
>
> Well (pause), work language is a bit rougher, especially when you're working with lads. But you would stick out if you said Black, or what is it they say over here, African American? I'd be laughed at if I said that.
>
> *Did you use that sort of language at home?*
>
> No, but there weren't any Black people when I was in Ireland, not in my town anyway. They're everywhere here, on the subway, in the shops. I'm sorry, but they're useless. They've all got a chip on their shoulder.

I also asked my informants to reflect on Ireland's demographic changes under the Celtic Tiger. Noreen made distinct connections between hierarchies in the United States and Ireland. She told me, "The Polish are sound. They're like the Mexicans here really. They'd work at anything. But the Nigerians are completely different. They're like the Blacks over there. They just sponge off the government." Ann also discussed changes in Irish society along similar lines. Despite the downturn in the Irish economy, she planned to return for good at Christmas 2011:

> *What changes do you expect to find when you return?*
>
> It won't look the same, that's for sure. New roads, I guess, new buildings, and new people.
>
> *What's your sense of that change, of immigration to Ireland?*
>
> I guess it's sort of like here. People don't seem to mind when times are good, but they turn with the economy. The Polish are good workers,

> but I think a lot of them went home. But the Nigerians are still
> around. They have it too good to leave.
>
> *How so?*
>
> They have everything handed to them by the government.

Irrespective of Ireland's own history with difference or racial hierarchies embedded in U.S. films that circulate globally, these Irish immigrants and many others I spoke to acknowledge that they have become more racist since coming to the United States. That newcomers finds themselves making racist remarks is quite telling. Newcomer discourse underscores not only the availability of this rhetoric but its appeal in this neoliberal context, where undocumented migrants face economic and political uncertainty and learn to take up racial rhetoric in ways that are new to them. Irish newcomers also appear to use U.S. racial hierarchies to understand racial change in Ireland. Most of the newer Irish left in the early years of the Celtic Tiger. During their time in the United States, the economy went from boom to bust, but the Republic of Ireland also witnessed a migration of people from eastern Europe and refugees from Africa and Asia. While they typically do not have firsthand experience with these changes, they have their own racial interpretations, shaped no less by racial hierarchies in the United States.

Because of their short tenure, newer undocumented Irish immigrants are better positioned to reflect on their encounters with racial hierarchies and racist sentiment in the United States. As a result, I have chosen to focus on this cohort, yet new Irish immigrants warrant a brief discussion. In chapter 4, I mentioned that many new Irish immigrants send their children to public schools in Yonkers, even though many white ethnic families removed their children after the city's desegregation controversy. For many new Irish families, public education is more affordable than Catholic school education. Yet there are others who, based on negative experiences in Ireland, deliberately decided to place their children in a non-Catholic school setting. While the racial diversity of the Yonkers public school system deterred many whites, as sentiments in the previous chapter suggest, some Irish immigrant families praised the racial diversity in these same settings. Yet new Irish immigrants, who have been here longer than newer Irish arrivals, are more invested in sites that historically have been racially segregated, such as schools and housing. While they point to other nonwhite immigrants to herald diversity in these settings, the presence of African Americans, on the other hand, is seen as a threat.

Darragh and Annie, for example, explained to me, "Our children meet all kinds of people in a public school that they would not meet in a Catholic school." Annie added, "Ciara has all sorts of friends. I think it's good that she just doesn't just have Irish friends." But with the issue of secondary education, diversity is less valued:

Do you think your children also will attend a public high school?

DARRAGH: I'm not sure. We've been talking about that. The schools can be a bit rough at that age. You have students being bused in from Getty Square. I'm not sure if it would be safe.

Do you think you'll move?

ANNIE: We're still trying to decide. Part of it is the schools, but part of it is that the neighborhood is starting to change.

How so?

DARRAGH: Well, during the housing boom, when banks were giving loans away, a few Blacks moved into the area. One or two families are okay, but it could be a sign of things to come.

How so?

DARRAGH: You know how it goes. Your family moved from the Bronx. Once the Blacks and Puerto Ricans move in, it's time to leave.

As these sentiments suggest, Irish newcomers herald diversity between young children. In the local elementary school setting, students of color often are bused from southwest Yonkers to schools in east Yonkers. Interracial exchanges are seen here as less positive when they have the potential to take place between older children or neighbors. Indeed, administrators at the secondary level face an array of challenges, and high schools in Yonkers are not immune to violence. By specifically mentioning Getty Square, however, this new immigrant clearly understands school violence in racialized terms. While he is concerned that public high schools do not adequately manage students, perhaps there also is an underlying concern about the management of racial boundaries. As discussed in chapter 1, in many northern cities where interracial exchanges in work and public facilities were not uncommon, whites rallied to defend more intimate segregated spaces such as home and school. Though it was never publicly articulated, integrated schools and neighborhoods could lead to racially integrated families. This possibility informs Darragh and Annie's outlook regarding integrated public high schools and neighborhoods. In closely supervised interactions between young children, diversity is heralded. Older children, on the other hand, operate with less oversight and have the potential to engage in more intimate exchanges. Sites that invite such relations, such as integrated schools and neighborhoods, are cause for concern.

At the same time, Darragh and Annie's sentiments reveal a desire for closely managed diversity. "One or two families" in an area, a number almost too small to be noticed, is sufficient, but any more are thought to have the potential to seriously alter the white presence in the area. Furthermore, Darragh draws upon narratives of migration to justify his position. Irish white flighters left the Bronx decades ago for many reasons, including upward mobility and suburban affordability, yet the narrative of racial transition has been passed from one generation of immigrants to the next. Stories of neighborhood transition are but one tale more established Irish immigrants relate to help Irish newcomers navigate America's bipolar racial order. Several of my informants also spoke of tips they received from other Irish immigrants about race. McLean Avenue in southeast Yonkers, for example, borders predominantly West Indian immigrant sections of the Bronx and is divided geographically by the Bronx River Parkway. West Indian immigrants might be heralded over African Americans in the context of work, but neighborhood interactions are quite different. Many of my informants told me of how when they first arrived in Yonkers, they were warned "not to turn left" when they exited the train at either the Woodlawn or Wakefield stations because doing so would put them in the "wrong" neighborhood. Una, for example, told me that when she first arrived in the United States, her aunt greeted her and warned her that "there are a lot of darkies over here." When I asked for her reaction at the time, she told me that the encounter seemed "a bit strange," but that she gave her sister a similar warning when she arrived a few years later in the United States. "I didn't say darkies, but I did tell her to stay to mind the Blacks over here." Like their predecessors in the early twentieth century, Irish immigrants continue to educate more recent arrivals in the importance of race, and the value of white racial homogeneity specifically, in the United States.[16] Clearly the sentiments in this chapter suggest that Irish newcomers are worthy students in disparaging peoples associated with African servitude.

* * *

The words of Irish newcomers illustrate how their encounters with Irishness as a race-based tradition in the United States are far more complex than the impressions offered by assimilated Irish ethnics and Irish white flighters in the previous chapter. Characterized as lazy, more recent undocumented Irish arrivals reveal how limited job mobility encourages an ambivalent work ethic and propensity for disorderly hard drinking. This behavior is interpreted largely as a by-product of undocumented life in the United States that has become increasingly precarious in recent years. Local immigrant bars often are scorned by assimilated Irish ethnics and Irish white flighters because they are sites of hard drinking. But Irish newcomers reveal how these establishments foster cohesiveness within the undocumented community. Newcomers also shed light on how undocumented life shapes family relationships and encourages parents to limit contact with U.S. institutions, such as recreational sports but also the Catholic school system. Often seen as deficient in regard to family and faith, newcomers maintain strong ties to family in Ireland, while others adopt new religious practices to reinforce these bonds. Furthermore, sentiments about the United States reveal a degree of ambivalence. As undocumented workers, Irish newcomers maintain that they give up job satisfaction, family, and security, and in doing so, they yield more than they receive from their adopted land.

Yet in some ways, Irish newcomers appear to be more yielding in regard to white racial homogeneity, in comparison to other Irish cohorts in Yonkers. Newcomers often are disparaged for their proximity to communities of color and their supposed racial deficiency. Yet they challenge negative depictions of their Latino counterparts, but through the lens of America's bipolar racial order and the language of neoliberalism. Latino and Caribbean immigrants are praised for their choices and values, only to discredit African Americans. Newcomers maintain that this outlook is novel, shaped undoubtedly by their interactions with other Irish cohorts and the larger neoliberal climate of aggressive privatization and policing that mandates an uncertain and unstable everyday existence. While newcomers draw a new and firm line between themselves and the descendants of African slaves, how firm is the line drawn around themselves and other undocumented migrants of color? What happens to these local race and class dynamics on a larger, national stage? With contentious debates over immigration reform in the backdrop, do Irish newcomers still maintain that Latino immigrants are "just like us"?

When Irish newcomers must articulate a public Irish identity to petition the U.S. government for a change in legal status, they must present a decidedly good Paddy, racially exclusive face.

6

Paddy and Paddiette Go to Washington

Race and Transnational Immigration Politics

Contemporary immigration politics is among the most complex and volatile sites of identity and belonging in the United States. As with urban redevelopment policies, immigration politics are as contradictory as ever in this current neoliberal climate. This is perhaps best illustrated by the Secure Communities Program, which was established in 2008 to assist with the deportation of dangerous criminals. Many local police departments have conducted fingerprint checks with the Department of Homeland Security. While the program is supposed to operate nationwide, there is considerable confusion regarding whether participation is mandatory, in addition to controversy surrounding the deportation of nonviolent offenders. As a result, the states of New York, Illinois, and Massachusetts have withdrawn from the program.[1]

Much of this uncertainty stems from the priorities of the executive branch being at odds with state and local authorities. As Philip Kretsedemas has shown in his examination of neoliberal immigration governance, our most recent presidents, irrespective of political affiliation, have pursued free-market agendas predicated upon the mobility of capital, goods, and services, but also people. While the number of temporary work visas has expanded in recent years, most immigrants arrive in the United States with no path to legal residency. As a result, approximately 40 percent of the undocumented population is composed of people who overstay student, worker, or tourist visas. In response, state and local governments have enacted their own laws to restrict the movement of undocumented workers, while some states are calling to end birthright citizenship for children of the undocumented. But this confusion and aggressive policing are not limited to local governments or conservative policymakers concerned with border security. The current administration has deported record numbers of immigrants, while at the same time President Obama issued an executive order to partially regularize the status of undocumented immigrants brought to the United States as children.[2]

How do the undocumented Irish navigate contemporary and increasingly contradictory immigration politics? Do they form alliances with other undocumented, largely nonwhite immigrant groups with whom they work in the construction, homecare, and restaurant industries? Or do they stress their white racialness and presumed fitness for citizenship and distance themselves from publicly imagined Mexican "illegal aliens"? This chapter examines how Irish newcomers turn to race in this progressively more fractious neoliberal climate and considers previous Irish encounters with immigration reform in the United States. I first trace how Irish Americans mobilized when Congress enacted significant changes to U.S. immigration law in the 1920s and 1960s. I then consider the Irish Immigration Reform Movement (IIRM) and the Irish Lobby for Immigration Reform (ILIR), two political lobbies organized in 1987 and 2005, respectively, on behalf of legalizing undocumented Irish immigrants in the United States. Race plays a vital role in the relationship between each lobby and the U.S. government. In previous chapters, I discussed how undocumented, working-class Irish immigrants are not, and cannot be, invested in the race-conscious and class-dependent values of hard work, loyalty, and family associated with being Irish in the United States. When green cards are at stake, however, I show through my ethnographic analysis of ILIR events such as fundraisers and political rallies both in Yonkers and in Washington, DC, how undocumented Irish immigrants are made, and make themselves, into good Paddies. I also trace how, when efforts to "legalize the Irish" by way of comprehensive immigration reform unraveled in Congress over the summer of 2007, the ILIR sought a bilateral trade agreement between the United States and the Republic of Ireland, where immigration politics were marred equally by race. Ultimately, this chapter considers the salience of race to transnational immigration politics. Efforts to "legalize the Irish" largely have been cast aside in both Ireland and the United States, and thus the undocumented Irish are relegated to a political limbo in which their legal status remains unresolved.

Legalize the Irish

Immigration politics certainly is not new to Irish Americans, who have mobilized in the wake of major changes to U.S. immigration law. During the 1920s, Congress made the unprecedented move to reduce immigration to the United States and established quotas that significantly favored immigrants, albeit in smaller numbers, from northern and western Europe. While limits on European immigration were unprecedented at the time, legal restrictions informed by race, class, and gender were not. Chinese and Japanese immigrants were barred from entering the United States in 1882 and 1907, respectively, while immigrants from India were excluded beginning in 1917 as part of a larger ban on the "Asiatic Pacific Zone." Furthermore, the Supreme Court ruled that Asian immigrants were ineligible for U.S. citizenship. Filipino migrants, who filled the labor void resulting from these restrictions, were accorded somewhat better treatment as nationals of the United States but were subject, nonetheless, to local antimiscegenation laws. The head tax initially legislated in 1882 and raised in the years that followed limited working-class and working-poor immigrant access to the United States, as did the literacy test enacted by Congress in 1917 (over three presidential vetoes). The "likely to become a public charge" (LPC) clause of 1891 similarly excluded those likely to be poor, and some custom officials interpreted this provision to exclude single women. The Page Act of 1875, though intended to prevent the entry of prostitutes, largely was used to keep Chinese women from entering the United States, undoubtedly a device to prevent the establishment of long-term Chinese American communities. American citizens also were subject to restrictions as women experienced the termination of their citizenship upon marriage to a foreign national. While the new 1920s laws often are thought of as an aberration in the history of our "nation of immigrants," they were a culmination of restrictions over four decades.[3]

Intended as a temporary measure, the Emergency Quota Act of 1921 limited the number of immigrants to 3 percent of the foreign-born population counted in the census of 1910. Congress revised this formula in 1924 so that arriving immigrants would reflect 2 percent of the number of immigrants present in 1890. In the larger context of labor unrest after World War I, the Red Scare, and the "one-hundred percent Americanism" campaign waged by the Ku Klux Klan, Congress implemented these formulas specifically to reduce Catholic and Jewish immigration from southern and eastern European nations, as they had sent rather small populations to the United States by 1890. The Immigration Act of 1924 additionally restructured immigration quotas so that incoming immigrants would instead reflect the "national origins" of the United States. In doing so, Congress suggested that only persons of British descent were true Americans. Though this component of the 1924 law was supposed to go into effect in 1927, the controversy incited by the national origins formula delayed its implementation until 1929. Eugenicist Harry H. McLaughlin's 1924 report for the House Committee on Immigration and Naturalization, which claimed Ireland as the "chief source of defectives" in the United States, undoubtedly dismayed many Irish Americans. Yet much of McLaughlin's evidence was contradictory. With disproportionately larger numbers of "imbeciles," the Irish were at the same time underrepresented in his statistics for crime and "feeblemindedness." Not surprisingly, Irish Americans challenged the methodology used to determine the national origins formula. Michael O'Brien, historian for the American Irish Historical Society, questioned the validity of using surnames from the 1790 census to determine quotas for Ireland, and used marriage, birth, land, and military records to demonstrate how the Irish were underrepresented in the count.[4]

At the same time, Irish Americans questioned the fairness of the national origins formula and the second-class citizenship it appeared to convey to people of non-British descent. In an address to members of the American Irish Historical Society in 1897, Edward F. McSweeney condemned the large quota reserved for Great Britain, or, in his words, "giving less than 2½ percent of the population of the world almost 50 percent of the quotas." McSweeney voiced opposition to national origins–based system due to its "DISCRIMINATION solely on religious grounds . . . because it would reduce immigration from countries predominantly Catholic and Jewish." His concern for other immigrant groups reflected interethnic alliances that Irish Americans forged in organizations such as the Knights of Columbus and the National Welfare Catholic Council, which mobilized in opposition to anti-Catholic rhetoric and legislation during that era.[5] McSweeney's primary concern, and that of Irish Americans at large, was not how national origins quotas affected other groups but how it specifically affected the Irish. Joseph Carey, president of the American Irish Republic League, more clearly articulated Irish American sentiment. In his 1927 testimony before Congress, Carey maintained that the federal government should keep the 1890 formula in place rather than transition to national origins. Whether using a quota formula based on national origins or a percentage of the foreign-born population in 1890, southern and eastern European nations still would be allotted small quotas, as significant numbers of their emigrants were not present in the United States at either juncture. National origins, however, signaled a significant decline in numbers for the Republic of Ireland, as significantly more Irish immigrants were present in 1890 than in the century prior. While Irish Americans may have voiced objections to formulas that targeted nations that were "predominantly Catholic and Jewish," they nonetheless were willing to support hierarchies that favored the Republic of Ireland over these very same countries. And no one, Jeanne Petit has pointed out, protested the exclusion of Asians and Africans from the quotas. While the 1920s immigration quotas certainly codified a hierarchy among Europeans in the United States, placing the Irish very close to the top, they also drew a circle around Europe, proscribing the United States as a "white man's country."[6]

Racial hierarchies encoded by the 1920s immigration quotas were reinforced, moreover, in the decades that followed. During the Great Depression, the LPC clause was applied vigorously to Mexicans, even though the Western Hemisphere largely was exempt from the quota system and migrants presumably could enter the United States more freely. The larger political economy of the Great Depression deterred new arrivals and encouraged 450,000 mostly European immigrants to leave the United States. Mexican migrants, on the other hand, and many of their American-born children, were repatriated to Mexico, assisted by local, state, and federal authorities.[7] But with labor shortages during World War II, the United States reversed this policy by way of the bracero program. With the program in place well after the war, American businesses enjoyed a steady supply of temporary workers who could not unionize, gain permanent residency, or, by extension, qualify for U.S. citizenship. Though World War II also prompted the repeal of the Chinese Exclusion Act, Congress only allotted a small quota to China, and the Cold War that soon followed merely affirmed European primacy. Those fleeing Communist regimes in eastern Europe were able to enter the United States as political refugees, while "almost without exception," Rachel Buff writes, nonwhite people from developing countries were not. The McCarran-Walter Act of 1952, which expanded immigration restrictions to include "subversives" (as well as homosexuals), also upheld the system of national origins. At the same time, this law imposed quotas on former British colonies in the Caribbean, undoubtedly a device to halt the movement of Black migrants. Voicing his opposition to this law, President Truman maintained that "the idea behind this discriminatory policy was, to put it baldly, that Americans with English or Irish names were better people and citizens than Americans with Italian or Greek or Polish names." Despite his resistance, and the efforts of various ethnic, religious, and civil rights groups to repeal national origins, Congress passed the McCarran-Walter Act over Truman's veto.[8] Not surprisingly, Irish Americans largely were absent from this debate because national origins, albeit hierarchical, placed them in a privileged position over other groups. But when U.S. law no longer guaranteed this privilege, Irish Americans would soon mobilize.

Though President Truman appointed a special Commission on Immigration and Naturalization, which recommended the abolition of national origins quotas in 1953, efforts to enact new legislation failed, and they continued to fail under the Eisenhower administration. But with the election of John F. Kennedy in 1960 and the growing civil rights movement, support for a new global system, favoring skills and family ties over national origins, began to take shape in Congress. With Kennedy's assassination in 1963, his successor, Lyndon B. Johnson, championed immigration reform. Though some feared a reduction in European immigration, supporters maintained that an overhaul would not upset the existing demographics of the United States. Senator Ted Kennedy (D-MA), a major proponent of the change, explained that "the ethnic mix of this country will not be upset . . . will not inundate America with immigrants from any one country or area or the most populated and economically deprived nations of Africa and Asia." Many in Congress believed that the new system largely would benefit European nations, since Asian and African people had few immediate relatives in the United States. Others assumed that large numbers of Europeans were ready and qualified to come to the United States, but the reality was that most were not likely to meet the new restrictions. Instead, many Asian immigrants who had been in the United States legally since the World War II era used the 1965 law to build a base for continued migration, a trend that lawmakers did not foresee. If they did, members of Congress surely would have placed limits as they did for the Western Hemisphere, a "compromise," Bill Ong Hing explains, for abolishing the national origins system. In other words, since white immigrants from Europe no longer were guaranteed entry to the United States, immigrants from Canada, but also from Mexico, Central America, the Caribbean, and Latin America, would be subject to restrictions for the first time.[9] Nevertheless, the Immigration and Nationality Act, or Hart-Cellar Act, of 1965 passed both houses of Congress with large cross-party majorities.

But with the shift from an immigration system based on national origins to one based on family ties and skill, immigrants from the Republic of Ireland and from other nations in northern and western Europe no longer were guaranteed entry to the United States. Irish Americans soon mobilized to recoup the special advantage they enjoyed under the 1920s immigration legislation. In 1967, the American Irish Immigration Committee (AIIC) formed in New York City to lobby Congress for a "special" Irish immigration quota. The AIIC drew from several Irish American organizations, such as the Ancient Order of Hibernians (AOH), Irish county societies, and the Gaelic Athletic Association (GAA), which also began to mobilize in support of the growing Catholic rights movement in Northern Ireland. That year, Congressman William Ryan (D-NY) introduced legislation that would provide additional visas for nations, such as the Republic of Ireland, that had "suffered" under the new 1965 law. Because his bill did not get out of committee,

Ryan introduced another bill two years later, which would have created an annual immigration floor for all nations. Based on an average of
annual immigration to United States between 1956 and 1965, 75 percent
of this figure would constitute each nation's annual floor. In the case of
the Republic of Ireland, approximately 5,300 immigrants would be permitted to enter the United States every year.[10]

Seventy-five members of Congress cosponsored this bill, and many
emphasized the "inadvertent" and "unintended" impact of the 1965
law, specifically in regard to the Irish. Despite immigration law changes
in 1965, the impact of earlier 1920s legislation resonated in Congress.
The descendants of European immigrants from northern and western
Europe, who disproportionately benefited from the 1920s national origins system, were well represented. The largely Irish American members of Congress who endorsed this legislation justified their support
on the grounds that the Irish were uniquely positioned to warrant
special treatment. While the Irish were the first immigrant group
to threaten the largely white, Anglo-Saxon American majority in the
nineteenth century, members of Congress justified the proposal on the
grounds that the Irish were a singularly special group, "the foundation
of the country," a "delightful addition" worthy of special treatment, who
gave the United States its "special luster." Asians and Mexicans with
equally long histories in the United States were noticeably absent from
this narrative, as were enslaved Africans. And unlike Ted Kennedy, who
assured members of Congress during the 1965 immigration debates
that "deprived nations from Asia and Africa" would not inundate the
United States, in this round poor Irish immigrants were represented in
an especially positive light. According to Congressman Dominick Daniels (D-NJ), "Because Ireland is a poor country and so many of its most
energetic sons and daughters do immigrate, I would like to see these
young people come to our shores."[11]

In his congressional testimony, John P. Collins, national chairman of
the AIIC, raised questions about the fairness of the 1965 act. The "American Irish," he explained, made "no protest" when the United States
sought to "correct discrimination against other nations." The new law,
according to Collins, "has now saddled Irishmen—and quite possibly
other nationalities—with an inequitable and unfair immigration policy." Collins clearly equated immigrant exclusion under 1920s legislation

with European treatment under the new 1965 law. While the 1920s quotas significantly restricted southern and eastern European immigrants and excluded Asian immigrants outright, to Collins, this injustice was equal to what the Irish now encountered. While Irish immigrants were not barred outright, as the Chinese had been, and their nation was not intentionally targeted, as countries like Italy and Russia had been, the inequality was that the Irish would now have to contend with immigrants from other nations for visas. Irish immigrants would now have to compete in a first come, first served global system in which they no longer were guaranteed entry as they previously had been in a largely race-based system. At the same time, the AIIC president raised objections to the 1965 law in terms that were neoliberal and racially coded. In his testimony, Collins maintained that unlike many nations of the world, Ireland was "never" the recipient of "substantial" foreign aid. Foreshadowing immigration debates in later years, the Republic of Ireland and, by extension, its people were represented as uniquely self-sufficient, while the unspoken but understood nations of Asia and Africa were presumed to be dependent on U.S. government aid. Interestingly, Collins appeared to have a memory lapse regarding the Marshall Plan, which gave substantial U.S. support to European nations, including the Republic of Ireland, after World War II. Nonetheless, despite efforts of the AIIC, this legislation and similar bills sponsored in the early 1970s failed to become law. Some members of Congress feared that an annual immigration floor would present a "backdoor" reinstatement of the national origins system.[12] Like Irish Americans during the 1920s debates, the AIIC could acknowledge the unfairness of racial and ethnic hierarchies but supported them, nonetheless, when they specifically benefited the Irish. That Irish Americans would represent themselves as a superior ethnic group and demand preferential treatment was not limited to the immigration debates of the 1920s and 1960s but also informed immigration legislation during the 1980s and 1990s.

Despite the shift from national origins to a family- and skills-based quota system, the 1965 immigration law upheld the principle of numerical limits enacted in the 1920s legislation. By focusing on the supply, rather than the demand, for labor in the United States, Congress produced a stream of undocumented immigrants with its earliest restriction laws. With Chinese Exclusion in 1882, the LPC clause in 1891, and the literacy test in 1917, Chinese and European immigrants, who had been denied entry, began to enter the United States unlawfully. They soon were joined by Mexicans, who found a heightened police presence along the U.S. southern border in the early decades of the twentieth century.[13] With a steady demand for cheap labor and numerical limits on the Western Hemisphere in place for the first time, the number of undocumented immigrants from this region began to grow after 1965. In response, Congress established the Select Commission on Immigration Policy in 1978 to study this growing "problem." Though the commission recommended employer sanctions and amnesty for undocumented immigrants in 1981, legislation would not be passed until 1986. The larger neoliberal order punctuated popular discourse as U.S. immigration policy and undocumented populations often were represented as lacking the efficiency necessary for an aggressively privatized society; undocumented immigrants typically were cast as a drain on government resources, and the U.S. border with Mexico was depicted as out of control. Undocumented immigrants, however, were marked not by race or ethnicity but by their choices, as "illegal aliens" who entered the United States without authorization. Despite this color-blind approach, immigration rhetoric undoubtedly was color-coded, as illegals always were thought to be Mexican, and the border always was understood to mean southern, even though students, workers, and tourists who overstay their visas constitute a considerable proportion of the undocumented population.[14] This language, nonetheless, would shape how the Irish placed themselves in the growing debate about illegal immigration.

The 1986 Immigration Reform and Control Act (IRCA) often is thought of as a compromise between businesses, restrictionists, and immigrant activists. The law was unprecedented for giving undocumented immigrants the ability to change their status and for imposing penalties on businesses that hired illegal migrants. At the same time, while IRCA allowed 300,000 additional agricultural guest workers into the United States, it also provided for stricter border enforcement.[15] While efforts to secure a "special" Irish visa program failed in the late 1960s and early 1970s, Irish American lobbying efforts were successful at this juncture, at a time when increasing numbers of undocumented Irish immigrants began to arrive in the United States. As discussed in previous chapters, large numbers of young Irish citizens left Ireland during the 1980s, fleeing high unemployment and inflation. Ireland's economic "boom" during the 1960s and 1970s produced few emigrants who could later sponsor family members in the 1980s. Changes ushered in by the Immigration Act of 1965, giving preferences to family unification and job skills, ensured that most of those Irish who arrived in the United States were undocumented migrants who overstayed ninety-day tourist visas. In this context, the Irish Immigration Reform Movement (IIRM) was established in 1987 by Patrick Hurley and Sean Minihane, two undocumented immigrants from County Cork, to "legalize the Irish." IIRM publicity was assisted by County Louth native Niall O'Dowd, who had founded the *Irish America Magazine* two years prior. O'Dowd later would launch the *Irish Voice*, a weekly Irish American newspaper aimed at exposing the difficulties faced by the "new Irish" of the 1980s.[16] The IIRM would work with established Irish American organizations, including the Ancient Order of Hibernians, Irish county societies, and the Irish Labor Council, in their lobbying efforts.

Though its broader goal was to win amnesty for all undocumented immigrants in the United States, the IIRM hoped to secure special visas for European immigrants "disadvantaged" by changes in U.S. immigration legislation. The IIRM claims that the Immigration Act of 1965 "discriminated" against European immigrants obscured the ways in which the law also hurt non-European immigrant groups, and how the legislation it replaced overwhelmingly favored European immigrants. The 1965 law also imposed quotas on the Western Hemisphere for the first time, restricting immigration from the Caribbean, Latin America, and Mexico especially, and thus the Irish, and Europeans more generally, were not the only ones to face difficulties in legally migrating to the United States. Despite immigration law changes in 1965, the impact of earlier legislation continued to resonate in Congress during debates over immigration reform. As in the 1960s and 1970s, the descendants of European immigrants from northern and western Europe, who disproportionately benefited from the aforementioned 1920s national origins quotas, continued to be well represented in Congress. That many members of Congress at the time could claim Irish ancestry and represented states with large Irish American populations, including Speaker of the House Tip O'Neill (D-MA), Senator Ted Kennedy (D-MA), Senator Daniel Moynihan (D-NY), Congressman Bruce Morrison (D-CT), and

Congressman Brian Donnelly (D-MA), gave the IIRM an advantage over larger lobbies that represented non-European immigrants.

In the early stages of debate over IRCA, Congressman Brian Donnelly generated an amendment that would have specifically aided undocumented Irish immigrants. This addition undoubtedly sparked controversy in favoring a relatively small, white immigrant group. Because Donnelly could not muster enough support for his amendment, he withdrew his support from the entire bill. But other, more powerful members of Congress were working to help the undocumented Irish. Speaker Tip O'Neill suspected that Donnelly played a role in the bill's initial failure and called him to the bench. Donnelly explained to O'Neill that he voted against the bill because "they are refusing to include my amendment." Donnelly recounted O'Neill's response that "everyone thinks I am dressing you down Brian. . . . I'm going to stare at you and look very stern. But don't worry, we'll look after the Irish."[17] Clearly, with promises to "look after the Irish," the IIRM had special allies in Congress. Donnelly, however, successfully sponsored a provision to IRCA that established the first lottery program, which was aimed at countries "adversely affected" by the Immigration Act of 1965. This stipulation made 5,000 NP5, or "diversity," visas available for each of the fiscal years 1987 and 1988, to thirty-six countries that had experienced a decline in immigration after enactment of the 1965 law. At a time when immigration was overwhelmingly more global and less white than in previous decades, these so-called diversity visas allowed largely European immigrants to enter a largely Eurocentric nation. Amendments to this law in 1988 made 40,000 visas available over the next three years, of which 40 percent were allocated to the Irish. Amendments in 1988 also included broadly defined "Berman visas," which extended 10,000 visas for 1990 and 1991; the Irish were less successful and received only 1 percent of these visas. The Morrison visas, which were an extension of the Donnelly program, allocated 40,000 visas between 1992 and 1994, of which 40 percent again were reserved for the Irish.[18] During immigration debates of the 1920s, Irish Americans objected to Great Britain's treatment under the national origins system, as this nation contained a small percentage of the world's population but received a majority of the national origins quota. But now when the Irish, who constituted less than 1 percent of the world's population, received a near majority, Irish

Americans deemed the Morrison and Donnelly visa programs to be "only right." They were, in fact, anything but fair. While the IIRM maintained that these programs offered a corrective to the "injustices" of the 1965 act, they clearly were a continuation of the race-based advantages that Irish immigrants, including the undocumented, continued to enjoy under U.S. immigration law.

The Immigration Act of 1990 nonetheless made "diversity visas" a permanent program. Beginning in 1995, Congress made available a pool of 55,000 visas to nations from which the number of immigrants had been less than 50,000 over the previous five years. These visas, also known as "Schumer visas," were named after Brooklyn congressman Chuck Schumer (D-NY), who sponsored the legislation. Although none of these visas were reserved especially for the Irish, Schumer was considered an ally to the undocumented Irish because he helped pass a 1994 law that allowed citizens of Ireland to visit the United States for ninety days without first obtaining a tourist visa from a U.S. consulate. The Visa Waiver Program was established in 1986 with the purpose of eliminating barriers to business or tourist travel to the United States. That the Republic of Ireland was now part of this largely European program had many important consequences. Now the Irish could readily enter the United States, and many undoubtedly did so, fully intending to overstay their tourist visas. More important, this program solidified public perceptions of the undocumented Irish as harmless tourists and more fully associated lawless border crossing with Mexican migrants. This boost for the Irish undoubtedly garnered support from New York's Irish American community in Schumer's successful election to the U.S. Senate in 1998.[19]

Ray O'Hanlon estimates that due to these four programs, 72,000 visas were awarded to the Irish by 1997.[20] Undoubtedly this feat was possible because of the Irish American presence in Congress and the numbers game played by the IIRM. Although "500,000 was uttered within earshot of journalists on a few occasions," IIRM estimates of the undocumented Irish in the United States ranged anywhere from 100,000 to 200,000.[21] Historian Linda Dowling Almeida argues, however, that the number of undocumented Irish during the 1980s probably was closer to 50,000. Even if the larger estimates were correct, the number of undocumented Irish paled in comparison to the total number of undocumented immigrants in the United States at the time, which was estimated at between 3 and 8 million. Indeed, exaggerated estimates were necessary to justify the allotment of visas in their favor, which were not fully utilized. Almeida notes that in 1994, the last year visas were available under the Morrison program, 22,524 were obtainable because the target for the previous two years had not been claimed. Almeida suggests that this can be explained by a number of factors: that the number of illegal Irish was much lower than claimed, that the undocumented in the United States were shut out by applicants in Ireland, and/or that many Irish did not apply for these visas because they did not have long-term plans to stay in the United States.[22] Indeed, if the Irish did not need a great number of visas, that a significant allotment was set aside further underscores the favored status of a small lobby, representing a small number of undocumented immigrants.

While close connections with Irish American politicians were important, shared heritage alone did not result in the legislation necessary for these visa programs. As white Europeans, the Irish surely were looked upon favorably by members of Congress and the nation at large, undoubtedly drawing the ire of other immigrant groups who were equally disaffected by the Immigration Act of 1965 but were not allotted a significant portion of diversity visas. The slogan "Legalize the Irish," though possibly a tactic to make the Irish more visible in a national debate that focused largely on Latino newcomers, also can be interpreted as a way that the Irish subtly distanced their lobby from other immigrant lobbies, and thus secured preferential treatment under new visa programs. Legislation was passed that benefited not only the Irish as a group but also specifically one of the IIRM's leaders, Patrick Hurley. Born in New Zealand and raised in Ireland, Hurley carried an Irish passport, but New Zealand was not a country "disadvantaged" by the 1965 immigration law. He did not want to apply for a Donnelly visa because he feared he would not be permitted to return to the United States once the truth about his place of birth emerged. Hurley instead obtained a Morrison visa because Brian Donnelly added a clause to the 1990 Immigration Act which stated that any person who had applied for a visa, had been accepted for an interview, but only after that had been found ineligible, would now be eligible. According to journalist Ray O'Hanlon, "Jokes are made to this day about the Hurley Act."[23]

The presence of the Irish in the national debate over immigration reform was no laughing matter for other immigrants who did not receive a special allotment of diversity visas or for some of the IIRM's supporters. Many older Irish immigrants and Irish Americans who worked to "legalize the Irish" referred to ILIR members as "brash" and "aggressive."[24] Congressman Bruce Morrison, who sponsored legislation on their behalf, described their "us and them attitude." He recalled: "I told the IIRM that their presentation had a racial tone, that it was strategically flawed. There were enough anti-immigration advocates against everybody and the IIRM needed support from pro-immigration groups. I told them that there were only two sides to the immigration debate, for it and against it."[25] Even though Morrison criticized the "racial tone" of the IIRM, the allotment of special diversity visas to the Irish indicated that race nonetheless could be a valuable tool for legalizing the Irish.

While the "racial tone" certainly aided the IIRM, race was never referenced explicitly but emerged in racially coded ways, as it had in past debates over immigration reform. Informational pamphlets expressed that unlike "most undocumented aliens," the Irish feel that "because of the great contribution to the U.S., they have an inherent right to immigrate legally to the U.S." And during a 1987 congressional hearing, the IIRM referenced an article in the *Wall Street Journal* that extolled Irish immigrants for leaving behind a "complete" and "generous" welfare state to "risk" defying U.S. immigration laws.[26] Clearly the IIRM sought to represent the self-sufficient, market-oriented Irish against Black welfare recipients and Mexican aliens. While the identities of these racialized peoples were presumed and unspoken, Irish identity was hypervisible in this discourse yet equally color-coded. The emphasis in public discourse, that this group was *Irish*, was a reminder of their race. Because undocumented immigrants were (and continue to be) demonized as unlawful Mexican border crossers, emphasis on the Irishness of this undocumented group was a proxy for their white racialness. Only at this specific juncture, when undocumented immigrants were underscored as white, could they be represented as "risk" takers and worthy of special treatment under U.S. immigration law.

Though the Irish enjoyed favorable treatment under the law until the early 1990s, an array of anti-immigrant measures soon followed, falling squarely on undocumented communities of color. In 1994,

California voters approved Proposition 187, which would have denied all public services to undocumented immigrants and their children had it not been declared unconstitutional by federal courts. That same year, the Immigration and Naturalization Service (INS) began to aggressively police the U.S.-Mexico border by way of Operation Gatekeeper. In 1996, Congress passed the Illegal Immigration Reform and Immigrant Responsibility Act (IIRAIRA), which instituted three- and ten-year bans on undocumented immigrants looking to reenter the United States. At the same time, the Welfare Reform Act placed limits on public assistance and restricted immigrant access to Supplemental Security Income and public housing. These laws were possible because of the rhetoric that fused immigrants, irrespective of legal status, with other groups racialized as lacking the self-sufficiency necessary for a market-oriented society. At this time, alarm over immigrants invading the U.S. border with Mexico shifted to alarm over immigrant mothers giving birth to so-called anchor babies, presumably draining resources from public hospitals and later schools. In other words, immigrants, illegal and legal alike, were thought to be vehicles for welfare dependency. As such, programs like welfare, intended to minimize inequality, were cut. Lisa Newton notes that members of Congress often told immigration narratives to rationalize the restrictions achieved by these laws. Positive self-representations of Europeans and their contributions abounded during congressional debates of the 1990s. As a result, congressional discourse created an "us" versus "them" divide between supposedly good and bad immigrants. Such constructions undoubtedly would assist Irish American organizations that would lobby again for immigration reform in later years.[27] While the Donnelly and Morrison visas assisted the new Irish of the 1980s, they did not help the newer Irish displaced by the supposed growth of the Celtic Tiger, who continued to arrive in the United States in the years that followed. Their chance for legalization would lie largely in the Schumer visa program, which typically draws more than 6 million applicants for 50,000 visas.[28] New attempts to "legalize the Irish" would be grounded in coalitions between Democrats and Republicans, as well as with other immigrant lobbies, largely because the numbers of undocumented Irish were much smaller than those of the 1980s, which could dilute their power as a single lobby. Nonetheless, renewed efforts to "legalize the

Irish" would continue to be shaped by race politics, as well as changes both in Ireland and in the United States.

Efforts to change the legal status of newer undocumented Irish immigrants were revived after the national crackdown on illegal immigration after the attacks on September 11, 2001. Calls across the United States for a zero tolerance approach to immigration trickled down to the local level, including states such as New York, where the Department of Motor Vehicles announced in 2004 that licenses with invalid social security numbers would be suspended. This restriction on driver's licenses had a profound impact on the undocumented Irish community; small independent contractors could no longer travel to work, and parents could no longer drive their U.S.-born children to school. With a precarious legal status now compounded, some undocumented people returned to Ireland.[29]

This new difficulty faced by undocumented Irish immigrants after 9/11 was highlighted in many newspaper articles, including a series in the *Irish Voice* titled "A Life Undocumented." These stories, however, often prompted more anger than sympathy. On any given week, hostile letters to the editor graced the pages of both the *Irish Echo* and the *Irish Voice* with titles such as "Keep America American," "Illegals Are Lawbreakers," and "Keep Illegals Out." Most of these letters were penned by self-identified "proud Irish Americans" who underscored how their parents or grandparents came to the United States legally. By the end of 2005, the *Irish Voice* exposed Christine Owad, a lawyer who had defrauded 150 Irish immigrants in a green card scam.[30] In that same year, two immigration bills had been introduced in Congress. In May 2005, the Secure America and Orderly Immigration Act, or the McCain-Kennedy Bill, was proposed in the Senate, and the Border Protection, Anti-Terrorism and Illegal Immigration and Control Act, or the Sensenbrenner Bill, passed the House of Representatives in December 2005. The former was presented as comprehensive immigration reform that would secure U.S. borders and provide a path to citizenship for the nation's undocumented. At the same time, the later bill would have made illegal immigration a felony and would have criminalized anyone who aided an undocumented immigrant.[31]

In the broader context of these developments, the Irish Lobby for Immigration Reform formed in December 2005. The ILIR emerged under the leadership of Chairman Niall O'Dowd, editor of both *Irish America* magazine and the *Irish Voice* newspaper, who previously worked with the IIRM. Ciaran Staunton, a Manhattan bar/restaurant owner who helped found the IIRM's Boston branch, would serve as the ILIR's vice-chairman. That this lobbying effort emerged under a different name signaled a break with the IIRM. The ILIR vowed to work alongside other immigrant lobbies under the Coalition for Comprehensive Immigration Reform (CCIR) and would be bipartisan, fostering relationships with prominent senators such as Ted Kennedy (D-MA), Chuck Schumer (D-NY), and Hillary Clinton (D-NY), but also John McCain (R-AZ). Despite the change in name, their slogan continued to be "Legalize the Irish."

The new year ushered in a busy schedule for the ILIR, including lobbying trips to Washington, DC, in March, local fund-raisers, and a Yonkers rally for John McCain. Nationwide protests against criminalizing undocumented immigrants and the subsequent backlash during the spring of 2006 resulted in an equally busy summer in which the ILIR lobbied the halls of Congress yet again and attended congressional hearings on immigration reform. Their hopes for comprehensive immigration reform were raised in November of that year when Democrats took control of Congress. The ILIR held another Yonkers rally, but this time for Chuck Schumer, in December 2006 and made another lobbying trip to Washington, DC, in March 2007. The exposure of another green card scam and an Irish smuggling ring could not weaken the momentum of the ILIR.[32]

As with the IIRM, race politics in the United States undoubtedly assisted the ILIR. For a small lobby representing a small number of undocumented immigrants, the ILIR made front-page news in the *New York Times* and garnered support from several prominent members of Congress, much to the ire of other immigrant lobbies. Senator Chuck Schumer first spoke about immigration reform at an event sponsored by the Queens branch of the ILIR in February 2006, after declining invitations from other lobbies. A Latino immigrant rally held in Washington, DC, in March 2006 drew 40,000 supporters but only one senator, Richard Durbin, who did not speak. At the same time, an ILIR rally that drew 3,000 supporters included three well-known senators: Kennedy, Clinton, and McCain. John Carlos Ruiz, an immigration activist, was "heartbroken" over the inconsistent treatment. "The immigrants of color for these senators are not important," he explained.[33]

The ILIR, however, attributed support for its cause to hard work. "It may be politically incorrect to point out who is doing the heavy lifting and who is not, but that does not make it true," said ILIR chairman Niall O'Dowd.[34] In the midst of a color-blind approach to inequality in the United States, whereby race is presumed not to matter, it is unsurprising that the ILIR failed to acknowledge the salience of race to its lobbying efforts. The following two anonymous postings on the lobby's blog, however, were more telling:

> Why not just enforce our laws and give a fair number of green cards to the Irish instead of giving Mexico the majority of green cards and allowing them to break our law. . . . The entire population of Ireland is smaller than the entire Hispanic illegal Alien population in the USA. I say enforce our laws and instead of giving the majority of green cards to Mexico give Ireland more.

> The number of illegal Irish citizens here in the US is quite small and they all speak the English language, tend to have at least some education and they don't commit other crimes. . . . If we have amnesty I think Irish citizens are deserving but im not so sure about the rest of the world. . . . So Legalize the Irish, but just them :)[35]

Although the importance of race was not acknowledged publicly, it informed not only these postings but also the confidence with which ILIR members spoke at local meetings about the possibility of having "something slipped in" to the immigration legislation taking shape in Congress, akin to the Morrison and Donnelly visas. After all, the IIRM had secured special visas for the Irish in earlier years. Why wouldn't the ILIR expect the same?

Whiteness alone, however, could not help the undocumented Irish in the United States. Whether they were making a public case for Irish immigrants and comprehensive immigration reform, or a private plea for special Irish visas behind closed doors, the undocumented would have to adhere to the model of Irishness well established in the United States. They would have to appear orderly and loyal to the United States, as well as hardworking and family-oriented, when petitioning the U.S. government to change their legal status. Though the realities of undocumented life complicate how well Irish immigrants can adhere to this model, drawing the ire of other Irish in Yonkers and the city at large, the ILIR would go to great lengths to shape undocumented Irish immigrants into good Paddies (and Paddiettes).

All the Paddies and the Paddiettes

Prior to an ILIR lobbying trip to Washington, DC, I met some of my informants at a local Irish immigrant establishment on McLean Avenue. The bar was particularly crowded for a weeknight. Part of the draw was Cray and Dempsey, a duo from Dublin who had just performed one of their more popular songs, "We're Irish (and We're Rockin')":

> Ulster Munster Leinster and Connacht[36]
> The bus is outside we're all getting on it
> We'll drink with the worst and we'll march with the best
> Legalize the Paddies and the Paddiettes

When it is time for the chorus, the whole crowd sings along:

> We're Irish, we're Irish and we're Rockin'
> We're Irish, we're Irish and we're Rockin'
> All we wanna do is Rock 'n Roll
> All we wanna do is Rock 'n Roll
> All we wanna do is Rock 'n Roll
> Cause we're Irish,
> We're Irish and we're Rockin'
> We're Irish and we're Rockin'[37]

When this song was played live, however, Cray and Dempsey instead sang, "All we wanna do is fuck and drink," to wild applause from the audience. Despite the great buzz in the crowd about the upcoming rally, an ILIR organizer warned us, "Listen lads. Don't forget, if you're going to Washington don't wear your football jerseys and absolutely no drinking. If you think you can go from the bar to the bus, think again." This

was not the only time I witnessed concerns over certain Irish immigrant behaviors such as hard drinking or clothing that might identify
them as foreigners and hurt their efforts to secure green cards.

Cahill, a former undocumented new Irish immigrant who has been
in the United States for nearly twenty years, described an ILIR fund-
raiser held in a local bar: "It was meant to be like *The Dating Game*,
three bachelors and one bachelorette who asked the questions. All the
bachelors were loaded. And they were asked questions like 'How big is
your cock?' What if members of Congress saw this?"

Cahill also raised concerns over the planning of another ILIR fund-
raiser, "Cultchie of the Year." A "cultchie" typically refers to someone
from a rural area and often is used in a derogatory way by Dublin
natives to refer to anyone from outside of Ireland's capital. At the fund-
raiser, five representatives from local bars, dressed in rubber boots
and poking fun at "cultchie life," competed for the title. In mocking a
rural stereotype in Ireland, this event was markedly different from the
St. Patrick's Day season, when assimilated Irish ethnics evoke the U.S.-
based drinking caricature of the Irish. "Don't worry," Cahill was told by
another ILIR supporter, "it's just us here." Indeed, the word was out that
they would have to be good Paddies during public visits to the Capitol. But when they were in Irish immigrant spaces, such as this bar on
McLean Avenue, they were free to let their bad Paddies out.

Not all Irish immigrants embraced the good Paddy role prescribed
for them at ILIR-related events in which they might come into contact
with more assimilated Irish ethnics. I traveled with about twenty members of the ILIR to a fund-raising event sponsored by a U.S.-based Irish
ethnic organization in upstate New York. The event included many
U.S.-based constructions of Irish ethnicity: the Irish national anthem
was sung in English, and bagpipers were present, each adorned with
a small American flag. The speeches given by ILIR supporters underscored loyalty both to the United States and to family, clearly an appeal
to U.S.-based constructions of Irishness. The crowd was told of the
undocumented Irish carpenter who ran to Ground Zero immediately
after the World Trade Center attacks on September, 11, 2001, and was
injured while assisting the recovery efforts. They also were told of an
undocumented nurse who could not be with her family in Ireland after
a sibling was killed in a car accident for fear of being banned upon

her return to the United States. Together, these stories constructed the undocumented Irish as exceptionally loyal to the United States, putting their adopted country above personal safety and family, which drew wild applause from the largely American-born audience. Despite this very good Paddy display, as the night wore on, many drinks were enjoyed, the crowd thinned, and the bad Irish Paddy slipped out. One Irish immigrant marched up to the stage where a small band had been playing, whispered to one of the musicians, and then announced over the microphone, "Now I'm gonna sing it the way you want to hear it." She then sang the Irish national anthem in Irish, as is the custom in Ireland.

Washington, DC

On my first lobbying trip to Washington, DC, I met Sharon and Paul on a particularly dark and cold early March morning. Sharon and Paul are an undocumented married couple who have lived in Yonkers for more than ten years. They delayed starting a family because of their legal status. "Maybe we should start a family," Paul had quipped the first time I met the couple. "At least one of us would be legal, and the child could sponsor us in twenty-one years." Along the way we passed other ILIR supporters getting breakfast at local delis. We waited outside a public school before we were directed to board the buses. Once on the bus, we were given an overview of the day's events by Tommy, our bus leader. Each bus (there were others leaving from Queens, Boston, and Philadelphia) would break up into groups, with each group assigned a list of congressional members to visit on behalf of comprehensive immigration reform. Tommy handed out white T-shirts with green letters that read, "Legalize the Irish." "You *have* to wear these," Tony added before giving the bus a few lobbying tips: do not drink, and wish everyone a happy St. Patrick's Day. "A happy St. Patrick's Day," Paul exclaimed behind me. "I'm not wishing anyone a fucking happy St. Patrick's Day!" A few snickers could be heard in response to Tommy's recommendation. "Lads," Tommy replied, "I know it sounds a bit silly, but it really helps."

Ann, our other bus leader, was walking down the aisle with a sign-in-sheet. "Oh, you're American?" she asked me. "We are asking people with citizenship to do the talking." She handed me a lobby packet, which included a map of the United States with the percentage of residents in each state claiming Irish ancestry and a color handout with the pictures of Presidents John F. Kennedy and Ronald Reagan under the heading "No Irish Need Apply?" Among the points on this flyer were the following:

> Ronald Reagan or John F. Kennedy's Irish ancestors or relatives could not come to America legally today.
> Without Immigration Reform the Irish Will Stop Coming to America. Already great Irish communities across the United States are in jeopardy.
> We have fought the wars (record number of Medals of Honor), built the cities, created the school system and built the Catholic Church. We have always stood tall for the country we love.

As first discussed in chapter 2, many in the United States believe that businesses have discriminated against the Irish by way of "No Irish Need Apply" signs, yet questions have been raised about the historical accuracy of this treatment. The use of the slogan here, nonetheless, serves to underscore Irish victimization under the Immigration Act of 1965, while the references to Presidents Kennedy and Reagan are a bipartisan appeal to Democrats and Republicans alike. Emphasis on military service,[38] as well as on building cities, schools, and churches, is an appeal to U.S.-based constructions of the Irish as loyal, religious, hardworking, and family-oriented, but it also is alarmist, playing upon U.S. racial anxieties. If the "Irish stop coming to America," then there will be fewer *white* people in the United States. This logic dictates that legalized Irish immigrants could serve as a buffer against the hordes of Latino immigrants demonized in popular discourses about immigration. At the same time, by emphasizing how long the Irish have been in the United States, the ILIR, like its predecessors, subtly distances itself from Latino and Asian immigrants and, by extension, their lobbies, framing them both as new and as different from earlier waves of European immigrants.

Other "talking tips" in the packet were less subtle in distancing the Irish from other presumably racially deficient groups. One bullet point, "Other than overstaying their visas, Irish people are by and large law abiding," clearly positions the undocumented Irish as tourists and apart from border-crossing Mexicans. Another states, "Most Irish people who can pay taxes. Zero percent are on welfare," and surely is meant to set the Irish apart from the unspoken Black welfare recipient. In addition to these talking points, we were warned not once but twice again that "alcohol consumption is banned for the day" and "please do not visit the local bar/restaurants."

Our group of six, Paul, Sharon, and I, as well as three of their friends, Brian, Alan, and Brendan, took turns reading the lobby packet before we arrived in Washington, DC, and headed to our assigned congressional buildings. Unable to locate one of offices, Paul asked a congressional aide for directions. "Thanks," he said, "and have a happy St. Patrick's Day," which was met with giggles from our group. As we reached our destination, we were welcomed into a conference room by a staff member. Another contingent of ILIR supporters already were there, explaining why they supported comprehensive immigration reform. One undocumented women explained, "We have elderly parents that we cannot visit. We have missed many christenings and weddings. The borders have been closed since 9/11." Brian from our group quickly added, "We speak English. And the Irish have never collected welfare." Clearly the "talking points" worked. This was one of the few office visits where we actually spoke with a staff member; in most cases we just left behind some ILIR literature. On several occasions staff members enthusiastically shared where their Irish ancestors were from in Ireland and asked if we had any extra "Legalize the Irish" T-shirts. As we made our way from our congressional office visits to the scheduled afternoon rally, we were stopped often and questioned by passersby:

PASSERBY: What do you mean "Legalize the Irish"? What did the Irish do
   that's illegal?
BRENDAN: We don't have green cards.
PASSERBY: What a shame. The Irish built this country. My great-grand-
   mother came from Kerry.

Indeed, it is interesting how differently undocumented Irish immigrants are received. In Washington, DC, the presence of Irish immigrants, albeit undocumented, allows Irish Americans to forge a connection with their Irish heritage. In Yonkers, on the other hand, other Irish Americans, such as assimilated Irish ethnics and Irish white flighters, who come into contact with this same cohort often speak of Irish newcomers in disparaging terms, in ways that highlight how they fall short of the good Paddy Irish model. This model for Irishness, which is difficult for many undocumented Irish to meet on an everyday lived basis, is a representation, nonetheless, that is projected in public appeals to the U.S. government.

Get *Up!*

ILIR rallies in Washington, DC, took place in a hotel and were well attended by politicians from both Ireland and the United States. Attending members of Congress included Representatives Anthony Weiner (D-NY), Elliot Engel (D-NY), and Senators Clinton, Kennedy, and McCain. On my first trip, Cray and Dempsey played music before the rally, and they too had their good Paddy faces on. Here they sang the cleaner version, with the words "All we wanna do is Rock 'n Roll." The rally itself officially began with the broadcast of a popular soccer anthem recording, which prompted the crowd to chant, "ole, ole, ole ole" as invited politicians entered the room to wild applause.

When speaking to the crowd, many of the elected officials emphasized either their Irish or immigrant ancestry and their family's upward mobility. Chuck Schumer, on the other hand, who is Jewish, called attention to his Irish American brother-in-law and the Irish surnames of his staff members. Overall, the political speeches typically underscored Irish hard work, loyalty, and upward mobility. The following points drew loud applause:

> Where else but in the United States could an uneducated immigrant have a grandson that would serve in Congress?
> The Irish have won more Medals of Honor than any other group.
> The Irish are here the longest, work the hardest, and are the best at teaching lessons to other groups.

Family equally is underscored. In an *Irish Voice* editorial, Niall O'Dowd described the "star" at one Washington rally:

The star of the show for me was not the politicians like Senator Edward
Kennedy and Hillary Clinton who came to the rally to show their support. Rather it was a cute young fellow named Darragh. I saw him in the
crowd as cute as a button, about six months old nestled in his mother's
arms and wearing a Legalize the Irish t-shirt. I invited him up on the
stage and told his story as his mother told me. They wanted him to grow
up in America. They loved this country and wanted him and them to be
part of it forever. He was what their future was about, and they wanted
him to grow up to be president.[39]

Because the Irish in the United States are so thoroughly associated
with the race-conscious and class-dependent values of hard work, loyalty, and family, undocumented Irish immigrants, regardless of how their
everyday lives detract from this model, must put on a good Paddy face
when petitioning the U.S. government. After the rally, however, many
enthusiastically took off this mask. The bar outside the conference room
was packed with ILIR supporters, and many clearly felt comfortable
imbibing now that the rally was over, despite repeated warnings to the
contrary throughout the day. A nearby liquor store was equally crowded
with ILIR supporters buying provisions for the return trip to New York.
During the bus ride home, some began to smoke cigarettes, much to
the displeasure of our bus driver, who threatened to call the police. Her
warnings were ignored, as were stern cautions from bus leaders, such
as "You can't smoke on the bus and expect green cards!" The bad Irish
Paddy could be kept hidden on this day, but only for so long.

The ILIR held similar rallies in Yonkers in honor of Senators John
McCain and Chuck Schumer in April and December 2007, respectively. They also began with the soccer anthem recording and showcased speeches from local politicians. At the McCain rally, both Irish
and U.S. flags were distributed to members of the audience, but by the
time of the Schumer rally, only American flags were present, perhaps a
response to the backlash against foreign flag-waving at immigrant protests that spring.[40] So as to clearly express ILIR gratitude for these guest
speakers, we were prompted by an ILIR leader to "get *up!*" This ILIR
supporter mouthed these words while signaling us with furious hand
movements to stand, in case the gesture was not fully clear. We were
prompted so often to give standing ovations that one audience member

Figure 6.1. An ILIR rally in Washington, DC. Photo by author.

behind me exclaimed in protest, "For fuck sake!" Another member of the audience caught my attention by remaining seated, despite furious directives from the front of the room. When I looked over, she rolled her eyes and laughed at the prompted ovations.

The ILIR tried to create a public good Paddy image for the undocumented Irish in a variety of ways, from invoking U.S.-based Irish traditions such as the "No Irish Need Apply" myth and "Happy St. Patrick's Day" greetings, to invocations of U.S.-based constructions of the Irish as particularly hardworking and loyal to the United States in talking points during their lobby trips. The undocumented Irish are so loyal that they were literally jumping out of their seats when U.S. politicians visited Yonkers. This construction of the Irish only was underscored by how members of Congress and their staff, as well as passersby, treated members of the ILIR when they visited the Capitol. While some immigrant newcomers were frustrated by having to wear the good Paddy Irish mask, they wore it, nonetheless, because green cards were at stake.

The highlight of these Yonkers rallies occurred when a non-Irish immigrant in the audience approached the microphone set up at the back of the room with a question for John McCain. He identified himself as an immigrant from El Salvador (the local paper reported the next day that he was a math teacher who fled his native land twenty years prior)[41] and thanked Senator McCain for his efforts on immigration reform. Without any prompting, the entire audience jumped to their feet, turned around to face the speaker, and cheered loudly. Around me people were saying, "Fair play to him," expressing their support of his comment. This spirit of solidarity from Irish immigrants toward non-Irish immigrants, however, often was at odds with the tactics and rhetoric employed by the ILIR.

We're All in the Same Boat

Though the ILIR participated with other immigrant organizations in rallies, both in Washington, DC, and in New York City, these efforts at interethnic solidarity sparked critiques from both ends of the political spectrum. *New York Times* reporter Lawrence Downes attended the Schumer rally in December 2006 and commented:

> When you hear the chairman of the Irish Lobby for Immigration Reform, Niall O'Dowd, vow to fight "to get what is rightfully ours"—more visas for the Irish—you can't help wondering how quickly such words would get a Latino banished to the militant fringe. "We Are America" is the Latinos' and Asians' cry. The well-organized Irish don't feel the need to say that. Their slogan, on T-shirts and the Irish Lobby's Web site, is blunt: "Legalize the Irish."[42]

While their privileged position among immigrant lobbies is criticized here, the ILIR is at the same time publicly attacked for associating with other immigrant groups, regardless of how tenuous the affiliation may in fact be. Patrick Hurley, founding member of the IIRM, publicly criticized the ILIR, both as president of the County Cork Association and through online postings:

> There is no such a thing as the generic immigrant group. Each one is different. Some, like the Irish, speak English, enjoy a high standard of education, are very well motivated and assimilate effortlessly. Others, not

so. ILIR, by merging the undocumented Irish into the monolithic block of illegal aliens, who may not share some, or, indeed, all of these characteristics, has severely diluted these natural advantages in the public's perception.[43]

In addition, letters unsympathetic to the undocumented Irish in the Irish American press did not disappear but only became more heated as the ILIR campaigned for comprehensive immigration reform throughout 2006–2007.[44] Given these criticisms of the ILIR, and its hope that special Irish visas might be "slipped into" comprehensive immigration legislation, the ILIR undoubtedly was pleased with media coverage that suggested otherwise. This moment came after an ILIR rally in San Francisco, whereby an Irish immigrant was quoted as saying, "We're all in the same boat" to describe the relationship among different undocumented immigrant groups.[45]

While the ILIR also would stress publicly the shared experience of the Irish and other immigrant groups, many of my informants resisted this narrative and instead emphasized the privileged position of the Irish in the national debate over immigration reform. Most stressed how other undocumented immigrants, especially from Mexico and Central America, experience migration to the United States quite differently from the Irish. Paul, mentioned earlier in the chapter, explained:

> We think the Irish have it bad. I work with Peruvians. One guy's brother took two months to get here, and it cost him $10,000. Another guy was a schoolteacher back home, but what he makes in a month there, he makes in a week here. We came over here on a plane by our own choice. They are here because they have to be here.

Jackie shared similar sentiments about undocumented Latino immigrants:

> My boyfriend works with a lad from Mexico. He and his wife were smuggled here. They were eventually brought to Queens, where they were held and told that their family had to come up with more money in order to be let go. Their captor left, and they escaped. The Irish have it bad, but we don't have it bad like that. It doesn't make sense to go through that.

Not only are circumstances of their migration different, but many Irish acknowledged how other immigrant groups cannot pursue the same lobbying tactics as the ILIR. Sally, the bartender mentioned in chapter 5, reflected on one of the ILIR's lobbying trips to Washington, DC:

> I would like to think that the Mexicans would get the same reception lobbying in Washington as us, but the reality is that security would probably have them out the door if they went into offices the way we did. On May Day, some of our guys didn't come in. I don't know if that's the best way to go about protesting. The ILIR was so organized and professional with T-shirts, approaching senators, and the like. Their way was kind of like, "Fuck you. We're not going to work, now see how you're going to get on without us." I guess they can't lobby the same way the ILIR did.

Surely the demonization of Latino immigrants in popular discourse encouraged the ILIR to keep a careful distance, but this sentiment was not fully embraced by all supporters. Jack, through contacts made at rallies with other immigrant groups, received an invitation to a vigil hosted by a Latino immigrant lobby in southwest Yonkers. Although he was told by ILIR leaders "not to be bothered with these sorts of things," a small group of ILIR supporters and I traveled to southwest Yonkers. Jack explained his decision, "I'm going anyway. We're all in the same boat."

We arrived wearing our "Legalize the Irish" T-shirts before the vigil, which was held in a church parking lot and attended by approximately a hundred people, mostly Latino immigrants and a few local politicians. Our contingent was noticed right away. A local news reporter came up to us almost immediately with a cameraperson and asked Jack for an interview. While Jack was talking to the reporter, a white male passerby in his thirties stopped members of the ILIR and asked, "What's this? Legalize the Mexicans?" "Shut the fuck up," an ILIR supporter fumed in response. Jack was then asked by organizers of the vigil to say a few words. He was introduced as "Brother Jack" and spoke of common struggle, which simultaneously was translated into Spanish and met with enthusiastic applause from the crowd. After the vigil ended and we made our way back to southeast Yonkers, everyone commented on how warmly we were received. While I certainly agreed, I could not help but wonder how a Latino immigrant contingent would be received if they showed up, unannounced, at one of ILIR rallies in Washington, DC.

The spirit of solidarity expressed by many undocumented Irish immigrants began to unravel when comprehensive immigration legislation failed to pass the Senate in June 2007. With undocumented immigration off the congressional table as well as having "something slipped in" for the Irish, the ILIR put its efforts into "Plan B," that is, changing the status of the undocumented Irish in the United States by way of a trade agreement with the Republic of Ireland.[46] After the failure of comprehensive immigration reform, some undocumented Irish immigrants remained optimistic. Paul explained to me, "I've been here over ten years without a green card. What's a few more years?" Others were less hopeful. Enda lamented: "We tried to do the right thing by working with other groups. We should have gone for a special deal all along. That bill failed in the Senate because of the fucking Mexicans."

Others were less angry but nonetheless also underscored the role of race in the bill's defeat. Noreen, for example, expressed that "the bill failed because of white America. On all the radio and television shows people were calling in to say that the defeat was a great thing for white Americans." After the bill's failure, I spoke again with Sally, who worked with Latino immigrants in the bar and restaurant industry and initially sympathized with their shared plight.

> *If the Irish are able to legalize their status because of a trade agreement, how*
> *will you explain that to your undocumented, non-Irish coworkers?*
> Things are different now. It's every man for himself. That what this country
>   is about. I can't say that I deserve a visa more than someone else, but
>   I am not going to say no to one if they give it to me because I'm Irish.

Spirits were raised when Governor Eliot Spitzer unveiled a plan to allow undocumented immigrants to apply for driver's licenses in New York State, which he soon rescinded amid hostile opposition.[47] Disappointment in this legislative failure was compounded when an ILIR supporter was arrested and deported in the fall of 2007. This event unleashed panic such as I had never witnessed before among the undocumented Irish community. Countless people I spoke with expressed that they now were afraid of being deported, even though

European visa violators are apprehended at much lower rates than their proportion of the undocumented population. To make matters worse, many Irish Americans wrote angry letters to the *Irish Voice*, outraged at the sympathetic portrayal of the deportation in the press.[48] While race may have shaped how some treated the Irish in the debate over immigration reform, these letters underscore how race had not changed the minds of many Irish Americans. In the larger, national anti-immigrant climate, members of Congress would rather do nothing than change the legal status of undocumented immigrants. In this context, it is not difficult to comprehend how many undocumented Irish immigrants would support their own self-interest should doing so secure a change in their legal status. But at the same time, negotiating a trade agreement between Ireland and the United States would not be easy.

Immigration Politics: Irish Style

Both the IIRM and the ILIR worked with the Irish government to help legalize the undocumented Irish in the United States. With the collapse of congressional proposals over the summer of 2007, a special trade agreement between the United States and the Republic of Ireland, whereby visas could be exchanged, seemed to be the only option. Commitment from the Irish government, therefore, was crucial. The ILIR hired former congressman Bruce Morrison, who had sponsored special visas for the Irish in earlier years, to help lobby the U.S. government. Because Ireland's economy had not yet faltered, the Irish government was in a unique position to negotiate with the United States. Because of generous tax subsidies from the Irish government, U.S. corporations had prospered in Ireland during the Celtic Tiger, while the U.S. military was permitted to refuel at Shannon Airport despite opposition to the Iraq War from Irish citizens and members of the European Union. At this time, the Irish government could present a trade agreement as something that the United States "owed" Ireland.[49] But the Republic of Ireland had contentious immigration politics of its own.

Two years after economists dubbed Ireland's unprecedented economic growth the Celtic Tiger, the nation witnessed a profound shift in its demographics. Beginning in 1996, more people immigrated to, than emigrated from, the Republic of Ireland. While approximately 50 percent of the in-migration included return migrants, European immigrants from member and nonmember states in the European Union, as well as asylum seekers from Africa and eastern Europe, also sustained this influx. The unprecedented migration of people to Ireland, however, obscured how young people continued to migrate from Ireland, irrespective of the nation's purported growth, albeit in smaller numbers than during the economically troubled 1980s. On average, 31,000 people a year left Ireland between 1990 and 2003, while yearly emigration rates later hovered closer to 21,000. Piaras Mac Einri notes that approximately 44,600 people left Ireland for the United States between 1995 and 2004, after special visa programs for the Irish in the United States expired. This ensured that those in this flow who overstayed their tourist visas would be undocumented immigrants.[50]

Despite Ireland's long history of emigration, the immigration of people into Ireland was marked by a rise in racism. Popular discourse treated racism in Ireland as a relatively new phenomenon in a primarily racially homogeneous and Christian society. This homogeneity, Irish scholars have argued, is largely mythical and stems from efforts to forge a nation free of British rule in the early twentieth century.[51] Irish scholars not only have traced a trajectory of multiculturalism in Ireland but also have underscored a history of racism largely before the Celtic Tiger toward the nation's Travelers, an indigenous, nomadic group, long the dominant "other" in the construction of Irish identity. The Celtic Tiger, Ronit Lentin and Robbie McVeigh have argued, merely prompted new articulations of Irish racism, including mob attacks, discrimination in housing, and government policy on immigration.[52]

During the Celtic Tiger, the Republic of Ireland created a two-tiered system for migrants from non-EU countries. The Working Visa/Work Authorization (WV/WA) program administered by the Department of Foreign Affairs targeted high-skilled workers, while another program overseen by the Department of Enterprise, Trade and Employment (DETE) recruited low-skilled workers. Sponsored by prospective employers, the latter did not have access to free medical, education, and other social welfare programs. These programs, especially DETE, which limited migrant rights and encouraged a short-term stay in Ireland, were directed, moreover, at largely white, Christian nations via government-sponsored job fairs beginning in 2000. Potential migrants from

Asia and Africa could not enter Ireland through this system, and most usually did so by applying for asylum.[53]

The Republic of Ireland historically accepted small numbers of asylum seekers and refugees from nations that included Hungary, Vietnam, Chile, Iran, and Bosnia. In recent decades, however, Ireland witnessed a significant increase in asylum applications, from 39 in 1992 to 11,634 in 2002. While the number of asylum seekers increased during the Celtic Tiger, the number who were actually granted refugee status remained low. By the end of 2005, 6,814 persons had been granted full refugee status since 2000, in comparison to the 48,632 applications processed since then.[54] Those who seek asylum in Ireland are not permitted to work while their application is being processed. Those who arrived before 2000 received full welfare assistance, but those arriving after that year were on "dispersal and direct provision," which means they received less assistance and were housed in youth hostels and mobile homes throughout the country, so as to prevent the formation of large-scale communities.[55] Many often left this system and worked in the underground economy, prompting constructions of the "asylum seeker" in popular discourse. Much like "illegal aliens" in the United States who are presumed to be Mexican, asylum seekers in Ireland are presumed to be African. And much like U.S. discourse during the 1990s about anchor baby–bearing immigrant women, the childbearing of asylum-seeking women, who supposedly were "breeding like rabbits," entered public discourse in Ireland at the same time. Although asylum seekers constituted less than 10 percent of all migrants who entered Ireland, immigration and asylum often were conflated and created a "moral panic" about the overrun by Black migrants. In its wake, refused asylum seekers usually were deported while migrants who overstayed work visas were not. At the same time, Black Irish women faced growing hostility by way of physical attacks.[56]

In response to these changing demographics and the supposed crisis posed by female asylum seekers, the Irish government changed its citizenship laws, which had been among the most liberal in Europe. Anyone with a grandparent born in Ireland can be an Irish citizen, and prior to this point, anyone born in Ireland, irrespective of parental origin, could be an Irish citizen. Under a 2004 referendum, however, voters overwhelmingly struck down the latter provision. And much like U.S. immigration reform discourse, market-oriented efficiency anchored much of the debate. Immigrant mothers again were represented as a drain on government resources, and Irish immigration policy was castigated as "hopelessly inefficient." By shifting the definition of Irish citizenship from birth to blood, the third Irish generation living abroad can claim Irish citizenship, while scores of children born and raised in Ireland to legally resident parents cannot, unless they apply for naturalization. To borrow from Ronit Lentin and Robbie McVeigh, "Being Irish in Ireland became white for the first time." Much like the American 1920s national origins quotas in this regard, the referendum attempted to "freeze" the composition of the Irish population in time by limiting access to citizenship for new ethnic and racial groups.[57]

This transformation in Irish society largely shaped how the Irish government and the ILIR approached the issue of undocumented Irish immigrants in the United States. The very acknowledgment of Irish immigrants in the United States would challenge the purported growth of the Celtic Tiger long heralded by Irish politicians and underscore the growing inequality that had been unleashed in its wake. At the same time, support for undocumented Irish immigrants abroad could be used to advocate for asylum seekers in Ireland, who increasingly were referred to as "illegal aliens."[58] Thus the ILIR and the Irish government approached "legalizing the Irish" in the United States rather cautiously.

The ILIR responded to these challenges by launching a pro-ILIR lobby in Ireland called Families and Friends of the Undocumented, which held a Dublin rally in April 2007.[59] A lobby in Ireland could put more direct pressure on the Irish government. But its separate existence in Ireland also could provide a cover for ILIR maneuverings in the United States, where there was little or no discussion of a trade agreement in the Irish American press or on the organization's own website, as such talk might draw the ire of other immigrant groups in the United States who would not be able to secure a similar agreement. Despite these efforts to stay hidden, criticisms of the ILIR's "Plan B" eventually reached both the Irish and the Irish American press.[60]

So as not to jeopardize badly needed support from the Irish government, Families and Friends of the Undocumented was careful not to criticize government policies that created an undocumented immigration population both in the United States and in Ireland. Instead, the organization framed legalizing the Irish in the United States as a way to support Irish families, arguing that undocumented Irish immigrants in the United States should be legalized so they would no longer have to miss important events in Ireland such as weddings, christenings, and funerals. Many of my informants, on the other hand, were less willing to tiptoe around Irish government policies and framed their presence in the United States in terms of economic displacement. Ann explained:

> The Celtic Tiger never hit my town. I worked for a French company before I came here. This French owner was able to come to Ireland and was given a grant for ten years and was free to leave when it was over, and that's exactly what he did. The company closed, I lost my job, and now I'm here.

Aidan expressed similar sentiments. He told me:

> I know a lot of people are talking about the Celtic Tiger, but I didn't see that when I was living there. Me and the girlfriend were both working in Cork. She was bartending, and I was laboring. By the end of the week we were always broke. We just couldn't put any money aside. I always have extra money in my pocket over here.

Undoubtedly shaped by Ireland's own contentious immigration politics, many Irish citizens were indifferent to the undocumented Irish in the United States, as sympathy would require a reconsideration of asylum seekers. Furthermore, developments in Ireland suggested that a bilateral trade agreement would do little for the undocumented Irish. Reports of a possible trade agreement between the United States and the Republic of Ireland maintained that it could be used to mark the successful conclusion of the Northern Ireland peace process, and visa preferences could be given to those disadvantaged by years of sectarian strife. Although the ILIR hoped for clauses that would change the status of the undocumented in the United States, by fall 2007, Ireland's minister of foreign affairs, Dermot Ahern, suggested otherwise. He explained, "There are a number of other suggestions in relation to bilateral arrangements, which might not necessarily assist [the] undocumented which might make it even more difficult for [the] undocumented in a way." Indeed, Ahern was correct. In December 2011, Senator Charles Schumer introduced legislation that would allow 10,500 high-skilled Irish immigrants to enter the United States, as part of the E-3 temporary worker program that currently is open to Australian nationals. Senator Scott Brown (R-MA) soon introduced similar legislation. While country-specific programs for high-skilled workers are not unusual, positive support for these bills was remarkable, given the hostile climate surrounding immigration since the downturn of the U.S. economy. In light of this specifically Irish visa program, it appeared that bipartisan support for legislation was possible only when it pertained to white immigrants. Though proponents hoped to have a vote before St. Patrick's Day the following spring, no significant action was taken until after the 2012 elections. One immigration bill before Congress includes Senator Schumer's plan to extend 10,500 temporary work visas to the Irish, but to high school graduates, even though E-3 visas are typically set aside for the highly skilled.[61]

* * *

Efforts to "legalize the Irish" on both sides of the Atlantic were marred equally by the politics of race. In some ways, the experience of the undocumented Irish in the United States first appeared to transcend race. Since the post-9/11 crackdown on illegal immigration, restrictions on driver's licenses and an openly hostile anti-immigrant climate, as reflected in the Irish American press, make it difficult for undocumented Irish immigrants to remain in the United States. In addition, they too are vulnerable to green card scams and deportation proceedings. Race, nonetheless, ultimately shaped how the undocumented Irish attempted to change their legal status. Because undocumented immigrants more generally are largely demonized in popular discourse as Mexican border jumpers, lobbies organized on behalf of the Irish created a careful distance from these and other immigrants communities of color. Both the IIRM and the ILIR stressed the racial fitness of the undocumented Irish when petitioning the U.S. government precisely because race politics work, as the Morrison and Donnelly visas have shown. These efforts ultimately encouraged undocumented Irish immigrants to abandon their solidarity with other undocumented immigrants in favor of a more race-conscious agenda.

With the failure of comprehensive immigration reform in Congress during the summer of 2007, undocumented Irish immigrants turned to their own government, hoping that the Republic of Ireland could obtain a bilateral trade agreement. But this shift was shaped equally by race. Although other nations like Mexico give tax subsidies to U.S. corporations, under the Celtic Tiger, the Irish were better positioned to negotiate a bilateral trade agreement precisely because the Irish as a group are thoroughly associated in the United States with the race- and class-coded values of hard work, loyalty, and family. Nonetheless, because the undocumented Irish too closely resembled working-class communities of color in the United States, they made themselves into good Paddies as their status too closely resembled that of Ireland's Black "illegal aliens." In their quest for legalization, the undocumented Irish distanced themselves from racialized others both in Ireland and in the United States, but to no avail.

In the wake of severe economic recessions, both in the Republic of Ireland and in the United States, the future remains uncertain for the undocumented Irish. Though Congress began to consider comprehensive immigration reform after the 2012 elections, immigration strategies in Ireland have changed. Since the economic downturn, those lured from eastern Europe to Ireland by the Celtic Tiger have started to leave, as have scores of young Irish men and women. The Irish Economic and Social Research Council estimates that as many as 200,000 will leave Ireland by 2015. Most, however, are making their way to Australia and Canada because the United States offers few paths to permanent legal residency. With emigration a grim reality once again, the Irish government is trying to secure E-3 visas for Irish citizens, yet it remains uncertain whether they could change the status of those living in the United States illegally. If anything, these visas are more likely to benefit the Irish government because they will provide a safety valve for the nation's growing numbers of unemployed. Overshadowed during both Ireland's boom and bust, the undocumented Irish in the United States remain in a legal limbo. Some, undoubtedly frustrated by this uncertainty, have returned to Ireland despite the poor economic climate. Others remain, buoyed by the numbers of Irish who have begun to arrive in Yonkers since the collapse of the Celtic Tiger.[62] Will the "Celtic Tiger Irish" bring new life to the ILIR? Although it changed its leadership in 2009, this organization is unlikely to change its tactics. With immigration politics as contentious and divisive as they were in 2007, it is likely that they will reach for race once again, with a tone that reflects this current climate—aggressive, vitriolic, and unapologetic.

CONCLUSION

To Belong

Because the U.S. Congress failed to pass comprehensive immigration reform in 2007, some undocumented newcomers in Yonkers returned to Ireland. Caroline, who worked as an undocumented waitress for eleven years, is one of my informants who returned that winter. She e-mailed me with her first impressions of how Ireland changed since she left: "I cannot get over the changes to my village. New cars and new houses are everywhere. And the number of foreigners working in the shops, even in my local pub! I couldn't have imagined this ten years ago." I cannot help but wonder how Caroline will interpret the presence of foreigners in her village and in Ireland more generally, in light of her experience in the United States, whereby race is a fundamental component of belonging. Undocumented Irish newcomers, like Caroline, who did not embody the good Paddy Irish model for hard work, loyalty, order, religious faith, and family were subject every day to scrutiny by other Irish Americans and the city of Yonkers at large. Because they could not demonstrate their racial fitness according to these standards, they did so by adhering to America's bipolar racial order, disparaging the descendants of African slaves. And when they petitioned the U.S. government to change their legal status between 2005 and 2007, Irish newcomers distanced themselves from other "illegal" aliens, typically imagined as Mexican border jumpers. Though they often expressed warm sentiments about Latino immigrants, with whom they work in the construction and service industries, many abandoned this outlook. Because class solidarity failed to secure comprehensive immigration reform, some questioned whether a more assertive race-based strategy would have been more effective. Ultimately, without access to the secure legal and economic resources that had been available to their predecessors, these Irish newcomers staked their claim in the United States by adopting and defending a racist ideology.

Some return migrants, like Caroline, also were amazed by Ireland's shifting economic terrain. In an *Irish Voice* article, one returning couple lamented how difficult it was to obtain well-paying work in the Republic of Ireland. Self-employed in the United States, they found work in Ireland in low-paying, dead-end service sector jobs, a transition they described as "going from the top of the barrel to the bottom."[1] Under the purported growth of the Celtic Tiger, it was increasingly difficult for members of Ireland's working class to make ends meet. For return migrants, however, it was even more challenging because they could not receive government assistance. In an effort to prevent "welfare tourism" from new European member states, the Republic of Ireland began to require Habitual Residence Condition (HRC). To qualify for social welfare payments, applicants must prove that they have been habitually present in Ireland. Although the flood of "welfare tourists" never materialized, return migrants in Ireland have been affected by this change.[2] In a nation with a long history of emigration, stories undoubtedly abound about Irish success abroad. What did it mean for members of this generation to return less successful than when they left Ireland? Did they disparage Ireland's new immigrants to compensate for their own marginalization? As in the United States, the recent Irish recession unleashed more anti-immigrant sentiment. While scholars have considered how return migrants brought entrepreneurial skills back to Ireland, did the migrants also carry a more racist point of view?[3]

And while U.S. racial regimes may have traveled to Ireland, both in the past and in recent years, are Irish racial hierarchies making their way to the United States?[4] Since the demise of the Celtic Tiger beginning in 2007, both migrants and Irish citizens are leaving the Republic of Ireland. While most are making their way to Australia and Canada, some have arrived in the city of Yonkers, New York. How will this latest cohort be received by the Yonkers Irish? Unlike previous generations of Irish immigrants, these "Celtic Tiger" migrants came of age in an era of unprecedented prosperity. Will this help or hinder their acculturation to the United States? Will they be good or bad Paddies? With access to higher education and high-end consumer goods, will they be able to demonstrate a propensity for hard work? Will their expanded use of alcohol and other drugs in Celtic Tiger Ireland encourage disorderly behaviors in the United States? And will their encounters with migrants in Ireland shape how they treat other immigrants in the United States?

It remains to be seen how this cohort will interact with Irishness as a race-based tradition, and answers to these questions fall beyond the scope of my work. This project, nonetheless, has attempted to foster a more critical examination of being Irish in the United States. Indeed, race is difficult to comprehend especially for white groups like the Irish, whose racial membership is presumed. As such, I have offered terms such as racial expectations and racial hazing so we can begin to grasp how marginalized groups articulate a race-conscious identity in the United States. By locating Irishness within the context of nine-teenth-century British colonialism and U.S. racial slavery, we can see how this socially constructed identity emerged from encounters with exclusion. My attention to different generations of Irish immigrants in Yonkers is offered not as an exhaustive survey but as an illumination of race as an uneven and differentiated process. Though each Irish cohort has been socialized, and continues to be socialized, around race, Irish newcomers are less enmeshed in Irishness as a race-based tradition in the United States. Moreover, at this neoliberal juncture whereby race is presumed not to matter, my study demonstrates how racial boundaries are drawn and defended in terms that range from the racially explicit to the racially coded. At the same time, by looking more closely at everyday interactions among the Yonkers Irish, at local Irish bar poli-tics and national lobbying efforts toward comprehensive immigration reform, we can begin to see how seemingly benign traits such as family, faith, order, hard work, and loyalty can be burdensome. Attention to the way Irishness evolved over time in the United States—intersecting with race, class, and gender, how it excludes homosexuals and people of color, how it maintains unequal relations between men and women, and how it monitors members of its working class—challenges us to reimagine what Irishness in the United States *could* be.

New and newer Irish immigrants articulated their own understanding of Irishness in 2012 when the city of Yonkers witnessed two St. Patrick's Day parades. In early March, the long-established parade transpired in southwest Yonkers, but later that month, a new adaptation also emerged on McLean Avenue in southeast Yonkers. Organized by the McLean Avenue Merchants Association, the parade itself was a literal departure from the more traditional event.[5] For years there have been discussions of moving the time-honored St. Patrick's Day parade to southeast Yonkers, but organizers have refused in the name of tradition. Rather than conform, Irish newcomers invented their own St. Patrick's Day celebration. While the separate parade was a deliberate dismissal of St. Patrick's Day convention in Yonkers, in many ways the new parade conformed to the good Paddy Irish model.

The St. Patrick's Day parade on McLean Avenue in southeast Yonkers began with a mass at St. Barnabas. Parade organizers asked a local judge to preside as grand marshal while most parade aides were local clergy members, and like the grand marshal they largely were male. Both U.S. and Irish flags were displayed prominently at mass. Parade organizers hosted fund-raisers to support the festivities, as the city provided no financial assistance. In the weeks leading up to the parade, as I discussed it with new and newer Irish immigrants, I was told to spread the word that drinking-related problems would not be tolerated. One local bar owner informed me that the police had circulated a very clear warning: if there was any trouble, the parade would "never happen again." Public drinking, however, was tolerated as spectators consumed alcoholic beverages from plastic cups that were purchased in nearby drinking establishments. Pipe bands, Emerald societies, and Irish county organizations participated in the parade, as did an array of Irish step-dancing schools. Members of a roller derby team even skated along McLean Avenue. Parade participants walked more than they marched, as rigorous parade instructions were noticeably absent. Passersby included both the American- and Irish-born of all ages. While the parade clearly was Irish Catholic, it was decidedly multicultural. A local Lutheran minister and Italian American business owners were honored as aides. Indeed, the inclusion of non-Irish and non-Catholic honorees was an attempt to reflect the composition of the neighborhood, which itself was stressed in promotional literature for the parade. "Meet Me at McLean," a phrase that adorned parade flyers, stressed the locality of the event. Indeed, the parade's location was a convenience because many onlookers could walk, rather than drive, to the event, as they would have to for the celebration in southwest Yonkers. While the new parade was self-consciously multicultural, that it occurred in a largely white neighborhood surely appealed to parade participants and onlookers alike.

What the future holds for this Yonkers neighborhood is unclear. The McLean Avenue section of southeast Yonkers is a profoundly transnational space, where flows of people, capital, goods, and ideologies intersect. Assimilated Irish ethnics, with deep ties to the city, might make "roots visits" to Ireland or to mass-produced Guinness pubs, so as to connect with their nineteenth-century past. They may live on the same street as Irish white flighters who enjoyed a U.S. political economy in which they could immigrate and secure employment with relative ease. Both Irish cohorts might be served food and beverages in the area by Irish newcomers who are not as fortunate as their predecessors. They leave an Ireland largely transformed by U.S. corporate investment and American styles of consumption, and they arrive in a city increasingly dependent on these vehicles of supposed growth. These flows will become only more intense as the fiscal austerity imposed on the Republic of Ireland will prompt more young people to leave, rather than shoulder the cost of aggressive privatization and corporate recklessness. They will arrive, however, in a space that is more likely to embrace Irish goods and services over people who fail to uphold Irish racial expectations. As they leave an increasingly fractious Republic of Ireland and arrive in a nation similarly fraught with growing inequality and an increasingly anti-immigrant climate, they will reach for race. Racial ideologies continue to travel across the Atlantic, as they did throughout the nineteenth century. Both then and now, in a context where it is difficult for not only these immigrants, but Americans at large to stake a claim to the United States socially, economically, and politically, they will disparage others in racially coded ways in an attempt to belong, replicating the very inequality that neoliberalism promises to diminish.

NOTES TO INTRODUCTION

1. *United States v. Nickelset al.*, 18 F. 242 (S.D.N.Y., 1993); "Irish Family Describes Anger over Beating," *New York Times*, May 8, 1993, B26; "Irish Charged in Yonkers Fracas," *Irish Echo*, January 17, 1996, 1; "Irish Trio Charged in Brawl with Yonkers Police, Brutality Allegations Rise Again," *Irish Voice*, January 17, 1996, 3.

2. Mary C. Waters, *Ethnic Options: Choosing Identities in America* (Berkeley: University of California Press, 1990), 17–18. Because of this disparity, when I refer to people by race, I use "white" instead of "White," and "Black" instead of "black."

3. Scholarly examinations of this topic include Richard Stivers, *A Hair of the Dog: Irish Drinking and the American Stereotype* (University Park: Pennsylvania State University Press, 1977); Monica McGoldrick, ed., "Irish Families," *Ethnicity and Family Therapy*, 3rd ed. (New York: Guildford Press, 2005), 595–615. For debates among Irish Americans over drinking on St. Patrick's Day, see "Irish Americans Attack Beer-Ad Images," *Wall Street Journal*, March 16, 1992, B4; "Ethnic Clichés Evoke Anger in Irish Eyes," *New York Times*, March 12, 1995, http://www.nytimes.com/1995/03/12/nyregion/on-sunday-ethnic-cliches-evoke-anger-in-irish-eyes.html; "In the Absence of Challenges, Irish Stereotypes Persist," *Irish Echo*, January 8, 2003, 16; "What Exactly Is Anti-Irish?," *Irish Voice*, July 19, 2006, 11; "Family Guy Calls Irish 'Drunks,'" *Irish Voice*, April 25, 2007, 6; "Family Guy Follies," *Irish Voice*, April 25, 2007, 14; "Glee Show with Damian McGinty Is a Disgrace," *Irish Voice*, http://www.irishcentral.com/story/news/people_and_politics/glee-show-with-leprechaun-damien-mcginty-a-disgrace-producer-ryan-murphy-owes-fellow-irish-an-apology-133060398.html.

4. Linda Dowling Almeida has referred to the 1980s Irish as the "new" Irish. See *Irish Immigrants in New York City* (Indianapolis: Indiana University Press, 2001). Sara Brady has referred to more recent Irish arrivals as the "newer" Irish, in "Newer Irish in New York: Technology and the Experience of Immigration," *Foilsiu* 1, no. 1 (Spring 2001): 95–106. Additional studies of the new Irish migration include Mary P. Corcoran, *Irish Illegals: Transients between Societies* (Westport, CT: Greenwood Press, 1993); A. P. Lobo and J. J. Salvo, "Resurgent Irish Immigration to the US in the 1980s and 1990s: A Socio-demographic Profile," *International Migration* 36, no. 2 (1998): 258–277. For a discussion of the continued, albeit smaller, migration from Ireland, see Brendan Bartley and Rob

Kitchin, "Ireland in the Twenty-First Century," in *Understanding Contemporary Ireland*, ed. Brendan Bartley and Rob Kitchin (Dublin: Pluto Press, 2007), 1–26. According to Bartley and Kitchin, on average, 31,000 people per year left Ireland between 1990 and 2003. Piaras Mac Einri notes that approximately 44,600 left Ireland for the United States between 1995 and 2004. See Piaras Mac Einri, "Immigration: Labour Migrants, Asylum Seekers and Refugees," in Bartley and Kitchin, *Understanding Contemporary Ireland*, 236–248; "Lost in Yonkers (and the North Bronx Too!): Influx of New Residents and Businesses Creates Booming Irish Mecca," *Irish Voice*, September 24, 1996, 22; "Dublin on the Thruway," *New York Times*, August 25, 2002, WC1.

5. The city of Yonkers is one of many urban communities struggling with the impact of deindustrialization. See Barry Bluestone, *The Deindustrialization of America: Plant Closings, Community Abandonment and the Dismantling of Basic Industries* (New York: Basic Books, 1982); John H. Mollenkopf and Manuel Castells, eds., *Dual City: Restructuring New York* (New York: Russell Sage Foundation, 1991); Thomas J. Sugrue, *The Origins of the Urban Crisis: Race and Inequality in Postwar Detroit* (Princeton: Princeton University Press, 1996); Robert Self, *American Babylon: Race and the Struggle for Postwar Oakland* (Princeton: Princeton University Press, 2003). Also see Saskia Sassen, *The Global City: New York, London, Tokyo* (Princeton: Princeton University Press, 1991); Sassen, *Globalization and Its Discontents* (New York: New Press, 1998).

6. My understanding of neoliberalism is that it involves in large part the dismantling of the New Deal consensus between government, business, and big unions during the 1960s in favor of a rearticulation of classical liberalism's vision of free markets in ways that have advanced the upward distribution of various resources. See Lisa Duggan, *The Twilight of Equality? Neoliberalism, Cultural Politics and the Attack on Democracy* (Boston: Beacon Press, 2003), x–xiii; David Harvey, *A Brief History of Neoliberalism* (New York: Oxford University Press, 2005). For "zero tolerance" policing, see Andrea McArdle and Tanya Erzen, eds., *Zero Tolerance: Quality of Life and the New Police Brutality in New York City* (New York: NYU Press, 2001).

7. Peter Marcuse, "Abandonment, Gentrification and Displacement: The Linkages in New York City," in *Gentrification of the City*, ed. Neil Smith and Peter Williams (Boston: Allen and Unwin, 1986); Mike Davis, *City of Quartz: Excavating the Future of Los Angeles* (New York: Verso, 1990); Janet Abu-Lughod, *From East Village to Urban Village: The Battle for New York's Lower East Side* (Cambridge: Blackwell Press, 1994); Neil Smith, *The New Urban Frontier: Gentrification and the Revanchist City* (New York: Routledge, 1996); Arlene Davila, *Barrio Dreams: Puerto Ricans, Latinos and the Neoliberal City* (Berkeley: University of California Press, 2004); Derek Hyra, *The New Urban Renewal: The Economic Transformation of Harlem and Bronzville* (Chicago: University of Chicago Press, 2008).

8. Aihwa Ong, *Buddha Is Hiding: Refugees, Citizenship and the New America* (Berkeley: University of California Press, 2003), 11; Mary Waters, *Black Identities: West*

Indian Immigrant Dreams and American Realities (New York: Russell Sage Foundation, 1999); Milton Vickerman, *Crosscurrents: West Indian Immigrants and Race* (New York: Oxford University Press, 1999); Nicholas De Genova, *Working the Boundaries: Race, Space and "Illegality" in Mexican Chicago* (Durham, NC: Duke University Press, 2005); Beth Frankel Merenstein, *Immigrants and Modern Racism: Reproducing Inequality* (London: Lynne Rienner, 2008); Lorrin Thomas, *Puerto Rican Citizen: History and Political Identity in Twentieth-Century New York City* (Chicago: University of Chicago Press, 2010); Eichiro Azuma, *Between Two Empires: Race, History and Transnationalism in Japanese America* (New York: Oxford University Press, 2005); Antonio Tiongson, Edgardo Gutierrez, and Ricardo Gutierrez, eds., *Positively No Filipinos Allowed: Building Communities and Discourse* (Philadelphia: Temple University Press, 2006).

9. Michael K. Brown, Martin Carnoy, Elliot Currie, Troy Duster, David B. Oppenheimer, Marjorie M. Schultz, and David Wellman, *Whitewashing Race: The Myth of a Color-Blind Society* (Berkeley: University of California Press, 2003); Eduardo Bonilla-Silva, *Racism without Racists: Color-Blind Racism and the Persistence of Racial Inequality in America*, 3rd ed. (New York: Rowman and Littlefield, 2009); Moon Kie-Jung, Joao Helion Costa Vargas, and Eduardo Bonilla-Silva, eds. *The State of White Supremacy: Racism, Governance and the United States* (Stanford: Stanford University Press, 2010); Duggan, *The Twilight of Equality?*

10. A racial project is defined as "simultaneously an interpretation, representation, or explanation of racial dynamics, and an effort to reorganize and redistribute resources along particular racial lines." Michael Omi and Howard Winant, *Racial Formation in the United States, from the 1960s to the 1990s*, 2nd ed. (New York: Routledge, 1994).

11. Brown et al., *Whitewashing Race*, 5; Imani Perry, *More Beautiful and More Terrible: The Embrace and Transcendence of Racial Inequality in the United States* (New York: NYU Press, 2011).

12. Hasia Diner, *Erin's Daughters in America: Irish Immigrant Women in the Nineteenth Century* (Baltimore: Johns Hopkins University Press, 1983); Hasia Diner, *Hungering for America: Italian, Irish and Jewish Foodways in the Age of Migration* (Cambridge: Harvard University Press, 2001); Timothy Meagher, *Inventing Irish America: Generation, Class and Ethnic Identity in a New England City, 1880–1928* (Notre Dame, IN: University of Notre Dame Press, 2001); Kerby Miller, *Emigrants and Exiles: Ireland and the Irish Exodus to North America* (New York: Oxford University Press, 1985). For a sociological case study of assimilated Irish Americans, see Reginald Byron, *Irish America* (New York: Oxford University Press, 1999).

13. David Roediger, *The Wages of Whiteness: Race and the Making of the Working Class*, 2nd ed. (New York: Verso, 1999); Noel Ignatiev, *How the Irish Became White* (New York: Routledge, 1995). For critiques of whiteness, see *Journal of American Ethnic History* 18, no. 4 (Summer 1999), for an extended debate; Peter Kolchin, "Whiteness Studies: The New History of Race in America," *Journal of American History* 89, no. 1 (June 2002): 154–173; Eric Arnesen, "Whiteness and

the Historians' Imagination," *International Labor and Working-Class History*, no. 60 (Fall 2001): 1–92. Arnesen argues that scholars are reading whiteness into accounts of nineteenth-century immigration. Roediger maintains that ethnicity is a relatively new term, one he suggests scholars of European immigration read into the history of their subjects. See Roediger, *Working towards Whiteness: How America's Immigrants Became White: The Strange Journey from Ellis Island to the Suburbs* (New York: Basic Books, 2005); Roediger, "Whiteness and Its Complications," *Chronicle of Higher Education* 52, no. 45 (July 2006): B6–B8; Ronald H. Bayor, "Another Look at Whiteness: The Persistence of Ethnicity in American Life," *Journal of American Ethnic History* 20, no. 1 (Fall 2009): 13–30. Scholars of Irish American history also have raised questions about this approach. See Kevin Kenny, "Race, Violence and Anti-Irish Sentiment in the Nineteenth Century," in *Making the Irish American*, ed. J. J. Lee and Marion R. Casey (New York: NYU Press, 2006), 364–378; Timothy J. Meagher, "Firemen on the Stairs: Communal Loyalties in the Making of Irish America," in Lee and Casey, *Making the Irish American*, 609–648.

Other studies that examine "whiteness" and immigration include Neil Foley, *The White Scourge: Mexicans, Blacks and Poor Whites in Texas Cotton Culture* (Berkeley: University of California Press, 1997); Karen Brodkin, *How Jews Became White Folks and What That Says about Race in America* (New Brunswick, NJ: Rutgers University Press, 1998); Matthew Frye Jacobson, *Whiteness of a Different Color: European Immigrants and the Alchemy of Race* (Cambridge: Harvard University Press, 1998); Thomas Guglielmo, *White on Arrival: Italians, Race, Color, and Power in Chicago, 1890–1945* (New York: Oxford University Press, 2004); Roediger, *Working towards Whiteness*; Eric L. Goldstein, *The Price of Whiteness: Jews, Race and American Identity* (Princeton: Princeton University Press, 2007); Arlene Davila, *Latino Spin: Public Image and the Whitewashing of Race* (New York: NYU Press, 2008); Sarah Gualtieri, *Between Arab and White: Race and Ethnicity in the Early Syrian American Diaspora* (Berkeley: University of California Press, 2009); John Tehranian, *Whitewashed: America's Invisible Middle Eastern Minority* (New York: NYU Press, 2008). Scholars have begun to explore the salience of race to white working-class immigrant women; see Jennifer Guglielmo, *Living the Revolution: Italian Women's Resistance and Radicalism in New York City, 1880–1945* (Chapel Hill: University of North Carolina Press, 2010).

14. Ann Laura Stoler, *Carnal Knowledge and Imperial Power: Race and the Intimate in Colonial Rule* (Berkeley: University of California Press, 2002), 6. Also see her earlier work, *Race and the Education of Desire: Foucault's History of Sexuality and the Colonial Order of Things* (Durham, NC: Duke University Press, 1995); Anne McClintock, *Imperial Leather: Race, Gender and Sexuality in the Colonial Context* (New York: Routledge, 1995); Jane Carey, Leigh Boucher, and Katherine Ellinghaus, "Re-orienting Whiteness: A New Agenda for the Field," in *Re-orienting Whiteness*, ed. Leigh Boucher, Jane Carey, and Katherine Ellinghaus (New York: Palgrave Macmillan, 2009), 1–16.

15. Diane Negra, "The Irish in Us: Irishness, Performativity and Popular Culture," in *The Irish in Us: Irishness, Performativity and Popular Culture*, ed. Diane Negra (Durham, NC: Duke University Press, 2006), 1–19; Negra, "Irishness, Innocence and American Identity Politics before and after September 11, 2001," in Negra, *The Irish in Us*, 354–372; Catherine Eagan, "Still Black and Proud: Irish America and Racial Politics of Hibernophilia," in Negra, *The Irish in Us*, 84–109; Lauren Onkey, *Blackness and Transatlantic Irish Identity: Celtic Soul Brothers* (New York: Routledge, 2010); Eithne Luibheid, "Irish Immigrants in the United States' Racial System," in *Location and Dislocation in Contemporary Irish Society: Emigration and Irish Identities*, ed. Jim MacLaughlin (Notre Dame, IN: University of Notre Dame Press, 1997), 253–274.

16. John Hartigan Jr., *Racial Situations: Class Predicaments of Whiteness in Detroit* (Princeton: Princeton University Press, 1999); Hartigan, *Odd Tribes: Toward a Cultural Analysis of White People* (Durham, NC: Duke University Press, 2005); Mike Hill, ed., *Whiteness: A Critical Reader* (New York: NYU Press, 1997); Matt Wray and Annalee Newitz, eds., *White Trash: Race and Class in America* (New York: Routledge, 1997); Matt Wray, *Not Quite White: White Trash and the Boundaries of Whiteness* (Durham, NC: Duke University Press, 2006).

17. Paul DiMaggio, John Evans, and Bethany Bryson, "Have Americans' Social Attitudes Become More Polarized?," *American Journal of Sociology* 102 (1996): 690–755; Lawrence Bobo, James R. Kluegel, and Ryan A. Smith, "Laissez-Faire Racism: The Crystallization of a Kinder, Gentler, Anti-Black Ideology," in *Racial Attitudes in the 1990s: Continuity and Change*, ed. Steven A. Tuch and Jack K. Martin (Westport, CT: Praeger, 1997), 15–44; Maria Krysan, "Privacy and the Expression of White Racial Attitudes: A Comparison across Three Contexts," *Public Opinion Quarterly* 62 (1998): 506–544; Nina Eliasoph, "Everyday Racism in a Culture of Political Avoidance: Civil Society, Speech and Taboo," *Social Problems* 46, no. 4 (1999): 479–502; Eduardo Bonilla-Silva and Tyrone A. Forman, "I'm Not a Racist But . . . Mapping White College Students' Racial Ideology in the USA," *Discourse and Society* 11, no. 1 (January 2000): 50–85; Melanie E. L. Bush and Joe R. Feagin, *Breaking the Code of Good Intentions: Everyday Forms of Whiteness* (New York: Rowman and Littlefield, 2004); Kristen Myers, *Racetalk: Racism Hiding in Plain Sight* (New York: Rowman and Littlefield, 2005), 27; Leslie Houts Picca and Joe R. Feagin, *Two-Faced Racism: Whites in the Backstage and Frontstage* (New York: Routledge, 2007); Bonilla-Silva, *Racism without Racists*.

18. I initially conducted fieldwork between March 2006 and September 2007. I returned to the field in the spring of 2008 and again in 2010 during the "St. Patrick's Day season," and from summer 2010 to early spring 2011. My sample includes 12 assimilated Irish ethnics, 12 Irish white flighters, 12 new Irish immigrants, and 20 newer Irish immigrants. This sample included equal numbers of men and women, and the interviews were conducted in sites convenient to my informants, either in their home or in a semipublic space such as a coffee shop

or local bar. The interviews were taped and lasted anywhere between one and two hours.

19. In March 2006, the U.S. House of Representatives passed H.R. 4437, which would have made illegal immigration a felony and criminalize those who provide aid to undocumented workers. Because this and many other congressional bills failed to become law, many states have passed their own immigration legislation. Arizona and Alabama have passed the most controversial of these laws, while other states have debated whether to cancel citizenship for children born in the United States to illegal immigrants. See "Arizona Lawmakers Push New Round of Immigration Restrictions," *New York Times*, February 24, 2011, A16; "In Alabama a Harsh Bill for Residents Here Illegally," *New York Times*, June 3, 2001, A10; "Birthright Citizenship Looms as Next Immigration Battle," *New York Times*, January 5, 2011, A1.

20. Lisa Lowe, *Immigrant Acts: On Asian American Cultural Politics* (Durham, NC: Duke University Press, 1996); Nyan Shah, *Contagious Divides: Epidemics and Race in San Francisco's Chinatown* (Berkeley: University of California Press, 2001); Michelle Mitchell, *Righteous Propagation: African Americans and the Politics of Racial Destiny after Reconstruction* (Chapel Hill: University of North Carolina Press, 2004); Claudio Saunt, *Black, White and Indian: Race and the Unmaking of an American Family* (New York: Oxford University Press, 2005); Pablo Mitchell, *Coyote Nation: Sexuality, Race and Conquest in Modernizing New Mexico, 1880–1920* (Chicago: University of Chicago Press, 2005); Tiya Miles, *Ties That Bind: The Story of an Afro Cherokee Family in Slavery and Freedom* (Berkeley: University of California Press, 2006); Natalia Molina, *Fit to Be Citizens: Public Health and Race in Los Angeles, 1879–1939*(Berkeley: University of California Press, 2006); Ann Laura Stoler, *Haunted by Empire: Geographies of Intimacy in North America* (Durham, NC: Duke University Press, 2006).

NOTES TO CHAPTER 1

1. "Rackets Cripple Yonkers," *New York Times*, December 10, 1969, 10; "Yonkers Inquiry Told of Profits," *New York Times*, December 12, 1969, 66; "Charges Shock Yonkers," *New York Times*, December 21, 1969, 57; "Yonkers: Another Newark," *New York Times,* December 24, 1969, 24.

2. "Usual Civic Fights Subside as Yonkers Hopes for $3.1 Billion Project," *New York Times*, February 27, 2006, B1.

3. Kevin Kruse and Thomas Sugrue, eds., *The New Suburban History* (Chicago: University of Chicago Press, 2006).

4. *Yonkers Historical Bulletin*, October 1954, 4.

5. Charles Allison, *The History of Yonkers, Westchester County, New York* (1896; reprint, Harrison, NY: Harbor Hills Books, 1984).

6. *Landmarks Lost and Found: An Introduction to the Architecture and History of Yonkers* (Yonkers, NY: Yonkers Planning Bureau, 1986), 9.

7. *Yonkers Historical Bulletin*, October 1958, 7.

8. Quoted in Kenneth T. Jackson, *Crabgrass Frontier: The Suburbanization of the United States* (New York: Oxford University Press, 1985), 36.

9. "Yonkers Census over the Years," Yonkers Vertical File (YFV): Yonkers Population, Local History Collection (LHC), Riverfront Library, Yonkers, New York.

10. Quoted in Thomas Shelley, *Slovaks on the Hudson: Most Holy Trinity Church, Yonkers and the Slovak Catholics of the Archdiocese of New York, 1894–2000* (Washington, DC: Catholic University Press, 2002), 2.

11. Ibid., 22.

12. The city of Yonkers, in conjunction with New York State, announced plans in 2005 to uncover the Saw Mill River as part of a larger redevelopment plan for downtown Yonkers. See "Yonkers Plans to Uncover River Running through It," *New York Times*, January 6, 2005, B5; "Yonkers Begins to Uncover Saw Mill," *Journal News*, December 16, 2010, 20A; "Restored River a Boon to Yonkers," *New York Times*, August 9, 2012, http://www.nytimes.com/2012/08/12/realestate/westchester-in-the-region-restored-river-a-boon-to-yonkers.html.

13. Eddie Dee, *Getty Square: The Village and Other Yonkers Memories* (Yonkers, NY: Yonkers Historical Society, 2005).

14. Shelley, *Slovaks on the Hudson*, 135–136.

15. Bruce D. Haynes, *Red Lines, Black Spaces: The Politics of Race and Space in a Black Middle-Class Suburb* (New Haven: Yale University Press, 2001), 10.

16. Harold A. Esannason and Vinnie Bagwell, eds., *A Study of African American Life in Yonkers from the Turn of the Century: An Overview* (Elmsford, NY: Harold A. Esannason, 1993); "Yonkers Jewry," *Yonkers Historical Society Newsletter*, Spring 1996, 6.

17. J. Kendrick Noble, "Where Have All the Great Ones Gone? The Spacious Victorian Mansions of North Broadway," *Yonkers Historical Bulletin*, January 1970, 7–13; "Forgotten Westchester, Birthplace of Golf," *Westchester Magazine*, September 2005, 30.

18. "An Interesting Neighbor," *New York Times*, April 22, 1894, 24; "Queen City of the Hudson," *New York Times*, May 27, 1894, 17; "Yonkers, the City of Homes," *New York Times*, June 3, 1894, 25; "Yonkers Has Many Charms," *New York Times*, June 10, 1894, 17; Jackson, *Crabgrass Frontier*, 166; Barbara Troetel, "Suburban Transportation Redefined: America's First Parkway," in *Westchester: The American Suburb*, ed. Roger Panetta (New York: Fordham University Press), 247–290.

19. *Yonkers Historian*, Winter 2004, 4.

20. Gray Williams, "Westchester County: Historic Suburban Neighborhoods," in Panetta, *Westchester*, 179–246.

21. Haynes, *Red Lines, Black Spaces*, 37; Andrew Wiese, *Places of Their Own: African American Suburbanization in the 20th Century* (Chicago: University of Chicago Press, 2003).

22. *New York: A Guide to the Empire State* (New York: Writers Program of the Works Progress Administration, 1940), 371.

23. Shelley, *Slovaks on the Hudson*, 162.

24. "Black Heritage Spans Nearly Thirty Years," *Herald Statesman*, April 7, 1980, YVF: Ethnic Groups-1980's, LHC; "Yonkers Proud of Its Riverfront," *Herald Statesman*, March 17, 1966, YVF: Yonkers Business: Refined Sugar, LCH.

25. James C. Cobb, *The Selling of the South: The Southern Crusade for Industrial Development, 1936–1980* (Baton Rouge: Louisiana State University Press, 1982).

26. Tami J. Friedman, "Communities in Competition: Capital Migration and Plant Relocation in the United States Carpet Industry, 1929–1975" (PhD diss., Columbia University, 2001), 278.

27. Ibid., 289.

28. Harry Taubin, "Small Manufacturer Suggests Otis Should Not Demand City's Favors," *Herald Statesman*, March 2, 1955, YVF: Business and Industry-Otis, LHC.

29. Sharon Zukin, "The Mill and the Mall: Power and Homogeneity in Westchester County," in *Landscapes of Power: From Detroit to Disney World* (Berkeley: University of California Press, 1991), 135–178; "Yonkers Woos Jobs but Ends Up Jilted," *New York Times*, August 21, 1983, E6.

30. Bartholomew F. Bland, "Market in the Meadows: The Development and Impact of Westchester's Cross County Shopping Center," in Panetta, *Westchester*, 291–326.

31. Herbert Salisbury, "Changing Economy Jars Yonkers, Unprepared for Swift Transition," *New York Times*, April 18, 1955, 1; Salisbury, "Yonkers Business Takes a New Turn," *New York Times*, April 19, 1955, 21; Salisbury, "Schools Are Clue to Yonkers' Pain," *New York Times*, April 20, 1955, 30; Salisbury, "Choice of Future Is Up to Yonkers," *New York Times*, April 21, 1955, 25.

32. Jackson, *Crabgrass Frontier*, 203–205.

33. Friedman, "Communities in Competition," 280; "Annual Report: City of Yonkers," *Herald Statesman*, August 15, 1959, YVF: Yonkers Population, LHC.

34. In addition to Jackson, see Arnold R. Hirsch, *Making the Second Ghetto: Race and Housing in Chicago, 1940–1960* (Chicago: University of Chicago Press, 1998); Douglas Massey and Nancy Denton, *American Apartheid: Segregation and the Making of the Underclass* (Cambridge: Harvard University Press, 1998).

35. Kenneth L. Kusmer and Joe W. Trotter, eds., *African American Urban History since World War II* (Chicago: University of Chicago Press, 2009); Virginia Sanchez Korrol, "Building New York Community, 1945–1965: A Historical Interpretation," in *Boricuas in Gotham: Puerto Ricans in the Making of Modern New York*, ed. Gabriel Haslip-Viera, Angelo Falcon, and Felix Matos Rodriguez (Princeton: Markus Wiener, 2005), 1–20; Lorrin Thomas, *Puerto Rican Citizen: Historical and Political Identity in Twentieth Century New York City* (Chicago: University of Chicago Press, 2010).

36. Department of Commerce, Bureau of the Census, *Population and Housing Statistics Census Tracts, Yonkers New York, 1940*, YVF: Yonkers Population, LHC; Yonkers City Planning Board, *Neighborhood Analysis, 1964*, YVF: Yonkers Population, LHC.

37. "Diagnosis of Yonkers Ailments," *Herald Statesman,* August 14, 1964, YVF: Social Welfare, LHC; "Staff, Space, Time Shortages Cramp Welfare Operation," *Herald Statesman,* August 18, 1968, YVF: Social Welfare, LHC; "Spanish Barrier Hurts City's Welfare Efforts," *Herald Statesman,* April 27, 1966, YVF: Social Welfare, LHC.

38. Frances Fox Piven and Richard A. Cloward, *Regulating the Poor: The Functions of Public Welfare* (New York: Vintage, 1993); Kenneth Neubeck and Noel Cazenave, *Welfare Racism: Playing the Race Card against America's Poor* (New York: Routledge, 2001); Ellen Reese, *Backlash against Welfare Mothers: Past and Present* (Berkeley: University of California Press, 2005).

39. Larry R. Jackson and William A. Johnson, *Protest by the Poor: The Welfare Rights Movement in New York City* (Lexington, MA: Lexington Books, 1974); "Mothers End 30 Hour Sit-In at Welfare Office," *Herald Statesman,* June 3, 1967, YVF: Social Welfare, LHC.

40. Let me underscore that the ghettoization of Getty Square was due to larger structural factors such as the deindustrialization of the local economy and employment discrimination. For other studies with similar interpretations, see Thomas J. Sugrue, *The Origins of the Urban Crisis: Race and Inequality in Postwar Detroit* (Princeton: Princeton University Press, 1996); Robert Self, *American Babylon: Race and the Struggle for Postwar Oakland* (Princeton: Princeton University Press, 2003).

41. "Renewal Could Save the Life of the Flats," *Herald Statesman,* November 1, 1965, YVF: Urban Renewal, LHC; "State Sets Hearing in Yonkers Rent Case," *Herald Statesman,* June 8, 1968, YVF: Yonkers Housing, 1960's, LHC.

42. Oscar Lewis, *Five Families: Mexican Case Studies in the Culture of Poverty* (New York: Basic Books, 1959); Lewis, *La Vida: A Puerto Rican Family in the Culture of Poverty* (New York: Random House, 1966); Douglas S. Massey and Robert J. Sampson, "Moynihan Redux: Legacies and Lessons," *Annals of the American Academy of Political and Social Science* 621, no. 1 (January 2009): 6–27; Thomas Cripps, *Making Movies Black: The Hollywood Message Movie from World War II to the Civil Rights Era* (New York: Oxford University Press, 1993).

43. "Blacks Move towards Unity," *Herald Statesman,* April 6, 1980, YVF: Yonkers Black History, LHC.

44. I do not want to suggest in my comparison of postindustrial New York City and Yonkers that the restructuring of the former was in any way more equitable than the latter; it simply was more diversified. John H. Mollenkopf and Manuel Castells, eds., *Dual City: Restructuring New York* (New York: Russell Sage Foundation, 1991); Saskia Sassen, *Globalization and Its Discontents* (New York: New Press, 1998); Miriam Greenberg, *Branding New York: How a City in Crisis Was Sold to the World* (New York: Routledge, 2008).

45. Bland, "Market in the Meadows," 317.

46. "Yonkers Default Is Diverted Again," *New York Times,* December 13, 1975, 16; "Yonkers Powers Reduced by State," *New York Times,* June 29, 1976, 20.

47. Andrew Hacker, *The New Yorkers: A Profile of an American Metropolis* (New York: Mason Charter, 1975), 22; "We're the State's Fourth Largest," *Herald Statesman*, September 2, 1970, YVF: Yonkers Population, LHC.

48. Vincent J. Cannato, *The Ungovernable City: John Lindsay and His Struggle to Save New York* (New York: Basic Books, 2001), 525–526.

49. Joe Austin, *Taking the Train: How Graffiti Art Became an Urban Crisis in New York City* (New York: Columbia University Press, 2001); Charles R. Morris, *The Cost of Good Intentions: New York City and the Liberal Experiment, 1960–1975* (New York: Norton, 1980); Evelyn Gonzalez, *The Bronx* (New York: Columbia University Press, 2004). In postwar New York City, working-class people were less likely to own their homes than in other parts of the country; see Joshua B. Freeman, *Working Class New York: Life and Labor since World War II* (New York: Free Press, 2000), 30.

50. Ronald H. Bayor, *Neighbors in Conflict: The Irish, Germans, Jews and Italians of New York City, 1929–1941* (Urbana: University of Illinois Press, 1988).

51. Joshua Zeitz, *White Ethnic New York: Jews, Catholics and the Shaping of Postwar Politics* (Chapel Hill: University of North Carolina Press, 2007); Nathan Kantrowitz, *Ethnic and Racial Segregation in the New York Metropolis: Residential Patterns among White Ethnic Groups, Blacks and Puerto Ricans* (New York: Praeger, 1973).

52. "Changing Economy Jars Yonkers, Unprepared for Swift Transition," *New York Times*, April 18, 1955, 1; George Lipsitz, *The Possessive Investment in Whiteness: How White People Profit from Identity Politics* (Philadelphia: Temple University Press, 1998).

53. Quoted in Jackson, *Crabgrass Frontier*, 224.

54. "Sledgehammer Sounds Sad Note for Pioneer Families on the Hill," *Herald Statesman*, April 20, 1939, YVF: Ethnic Groups, LHC.

55. Eddie Dee, "The Concrete Kingdom," *Yonkers History*, Winter 2001, 1.

56. "Cottage Place Space Seekers File at Rate of Two a Minute," *Herald Statesman*, August 16, 1948, YVF: Yonkers Housing, LHC; "Tenants in Public Housing Here Are Required to Swear They Don't Belong to These Groups," *Herald Statesman*, December 23, 1952, YVF: Yonkers Housing, LHC; "More Aids Sought to Handle Applications for Cottage Place," *Herald Statesman*, October 21, 1948, YVF: Yonkers Housing, LHC; Piven and Cloward, *Regulating the Poor*; Rhonda Y. Williams, *The Politics of Public Housing: Black Women's Struggles against Inequality* (New York: Oxford University Press, 2004); Nicholas Dagen Bloom, *Public Housing That Worked: New York in the Twentieth Century* (Philadelphia: University of Pennsylvania Press, 2008).

57. "Reverend J. C. Hoggard First Negro to Serve on Major City Board," *Herald Statesman*, March 9, 1945, YVF: Yonkers Housing, LHC; "St. Nick Site Rejected by 10–3 Vote," *Herald Statesman*, June 7, 1956, YVF: Yonkers Housing, LHC.

58. Jill Quandango, *The Color of Welfare: How Racism Undermined the War on Poverty* (New York: Oxford University Press, 1994); Samuel Zipp, *Manhattan*

Projects: The Rise and Fall of Urban Renewal in Cold War New York (New York: Oxford University Press, 2010).

59. "Yes! The People Want Renewal!" *Herald Statesman*, March 15, 1965, YVF: Urban Renewal, LHC; "Renewal Could Rescue Fading Lamartine Heights," *Herald Statesman*, January 3, 1966, YVF: Urban Renewal, LHC.

60. "Yonkers' Good Urban Record Falls Behind," *Herald Statesman*, January 10, 1969, YVF: Urban Renewal, LHC.

61. "Special Patrol for MHA," *Herald Statesman*, August 17, 1968, YVF: Urban Renewal, LHC.

62. *U.S. and Yonkers Branch of NAACP v. Yonkers Board of Education et al.*, 655 F. Supp. 1577 (S.D.N.Y., 1986), 21, LHC.

63. "Five Public Housing Sites Debated at Hearing Here," *Herald Statesman*, April 30, 1958, YVF: Yonkers Housing, LHC; "Applicants for Public Housing Might Form Pressure Groups," *Herald Statesman*, March 22, 1957, YVF: Yonkers Housing, LHC.

64. Haynes, *Red Lines, Black Spaces*, 105–107; "Pro Negro Groups Win Council Delay on Ridgeview Land," *Herald Statesman*, May 9, 1956, YVF: Yonkers Housing, LCH.

65. "Yes! The People Want Removal"; "Low Rent Housing Out in Slum Clearance," *Herald Statesman*, May 14, 1957, YVF: Yonkers Housing, LHC; "Rights Commission Wants Council to Fight Housing Discrimination," *Herald Statesman*, April 27, 1965, YVF: Yonkers Housing, LHC.

66. "Urban Renewal Too Secret," *Herald Statesman*, December 22, 1966, YVF: Urban Renewal, LHC; "Didn't Know All Zoning, Says Austin," *Herald Statesman*, January 10, 1967, YVF: Urban Renewal, LHC.

67. "O'Rourke Says Some Trying to Thwart Model Cities Here," *Herald Statesman*, April 19, 1968, YVF: Urban Renewal, LHC.

68. Quandango, *Color of Welfare*, 102–105.

69. "Candidates Zero In on Scattered Housing," *Herald Statesman*, July 8, 1968, YVF: Urban Renewal, LHC; "Low Cost Housing Site Dead," *Herald Statesman*, January 25, 1970, YVF: Urban Renewal, LHC; "Anger Flares at URA," *Herald Statesman*, February 17, 1972, YVF: Urban Renewal, LHC.

70. "City Voice Sought in Welfare Placements," *Herald Statesman*, March 25, 1975, YVF: Social Welfare, LHC; "Welfare Limit Sought," *Herald Statesman*, April 9, 1975, Page YVF: Social Welfare, LHC.

71. Michael N. Danielson, *The Politics of Exclusion* (New York: Columbia University Press, 1976), 307–321.

72. "County Sued over Lack of Affordable Homes," *New York Times*, February 4, 2007, M5; "Judge Faults Westchester County on Desegregation Efforts," *New York Times*, February 26, 2009, A24; "Monitor Again Finds Westchester's Housing Desegregation Plan Inadequate," *New York Times*, July 9, 2010, A10.

73. *U.S. and Yonkers Branch of NAACP v. Yonkers Board of Education et al.*, 3.

74. Ibid., 46–47.

75. Peter Schuck, "Residential Neighborhoods: Subsidizing and Mandating Diversity," in *Diversity in America: Keeping Government at a Safe Distance* (Cambridge: Belknap Press of Harvard University Press, 2003), 203–260.

76. Oscar Newman, *Defensible Space: Crime Prevention through Urban Design* (New York: Macmillan, 1972).

77. "Time for Yonkers to Get On with It," *Herald Statesman*, December 30, 1987, YVF: Yonkers Housing 1980–1988, LHC; "Council Backs Housing Order in Yonkers," *New York Times*, January 29, 1988, YVF: Yonkers Housing 1980–1988, LHC.

78. "He's a Hypocrite: Yonkers Residents Stage Protest at Judge Sand's Home," *Herald Statesman*, May 8, 1988, YVF: Yonkers Housing 1980–1988; "A Matter of Economics or Race," *Herald Statesman*, August 14, 1988, YVF: Yonkers Housing 1980–1988, LHC; "Another Saturday, Another Rally at a Housing Site," *Herald Statesman*, May 12, 1991, YVF: Yonkers Housing 1980–1988, LHC.

79. Jack O'Toole, "Yonkers Case Rooted in Class Not Race," *Herald Statesman*, August 16, 1988, 24.

80. Jonathan Rieder, *Canarsie: The Jews and Italians of Brooklyn against Liberalism* (Cambridge: Harvard University Press, 1985); Ronald Formisano, *Boston against Busing: Race, Class, Ethnicity in the 1960s and 1970s* (Chapel Hill: University of North Carolina Press, 1991); Steven J. L. Taylor, *Desegregation in Boston and Buffalo: The Influence of Local Leaders* (Albany: State University of New York Press, 1998); Howell S. Baum, *Brown in Baltimore: School Desegregation and the Limits of Liberalism* (Ithaca: Cornell University Press, 2010). Also see Hirsch, *Making the Second Ghetto*; Sugrue, *Origins of the Urban Crisis*.

81. Kevin M. Kruse, *White Flight: Atlanta and the Making of Modern Conservatism* (Princeton: Princeton University Press, 2005); David M. P. Freund, *Colored Property: State Policy, White Racial Politics in Suburban America* (Chicago: University of Chicago Press, 2007).

82. "A Matter of Economics or Race"; "Residents Vent Anger over Housing Plan," *New York Times*, August 17, 1988, YVF: Yonkers Housing 1980–1988; Mary Silvestri, "Track Record Awful in Yonkers Housing," *Herald Statesman*, August 17, 1988, 19A; "The Talk of Yonkers," *New York Times*, November 27, 1985, B5; "Civic Groups Vow to Press Housing Fight in Yonkers," *New York Times*, June 19, 1988, WC1; "Yonkers Residents React with Anger," *New York Times*, August 4, 1988, B4; "Neighborhood Groups Wield Influential Role," *New York Times*, August 21, 1988, WC1.

83. Alan Bratter, "Decision Puts City in Peril of Crime," *Herald Statesman*, August 11, 1988, 21A; Helen Emrich, "Yonkers Should Have Its Own Tea Party," *Herald Statesman*, August 23, 1988, 15A; Anna D'Esposito, "Sand Is King in Yonkers Fable," *Herald Statesman*, September 23, 1988, 3AA.

84. Steven Streitfeld, "Sand Would Correct Injustices of the Past," *Herald Statesman*, August 12, 1988, 15; "As Blacks in Yonkers See It, Time To Say You're Wrong," *Herald Statesman*, August 11, 1988, YVF: Yonkers Housing 1980–1988, LHC;

Martin Kilson quoted in "Scholars: Leadership Void Costly," *Herald Statesman*, August 14, 1988, YVF: Yonkers Housing 1980–1988, LHC.

85. "Yonkers: The Legacy of Contempt," *Herald Statesman*, December 18, 1988, YVF: Yonkers Housing 1988, LHC; "Desegregation Parties Angered by KKK Fliers Flooding East Side," *Herald Statesman*, February 13, 1988, YVF: Yonkers Housing 1988, LHC.

86. "Many Minorities Are Blasé, but Many Others Are Bitter," *Herald Statesman*, August 5, 1988, YVF: Yonkers Housing 1980–1988, LHC.

87. "He's a Hypocrite"; "Yonkers Is Fighting for Survival," *Herald Statesman*, June 6, 1988, YVF: Yonkers Housing 1980–1988, LHC.

88. "Profile: Edward J. Fagan, Jr.," *New York Times*, August 31, 1988, YVF: Yonkers Housing 1988, LHC.

89. "Yonkers Residents React with Anger, Anxiety and Some Support for Judge," *New York Times*, August 5, 1988, YVF: Yonkers Housing 1980–1988, LHC; "A Matter of Economics or Race"; "Yonkers Anguish: Black and White in Two Worlds," *New York Times*, December 22, 1987, YVF: Yonkers Housing, 1980–1988, LHC; "Yonkers Legacy: 38 Distinct Neighborhoods," *New York Times*, September 13, 1988, YVF: Yonkers Housing 1988, LHC.

90. "People Probably Have the Wrong Idea about Us," *Herald Statesman*, August 8, 1988, YVF: Yonkers Housing 1980–1988, LHC.

91. "Housing Construction Starts without Fanfare in Yonkers," *New York Times*, April 13, 1988, YVF: Yonkers Housing 1988, LHC; John Zakian quoted in "In Big Factory, Small Businesses Prosper," *New York Times*, August 26, 1990, WC23. Kawasaki Heavy Industries, for example, occupied a former Otis Elevator plant in 1987.

92. "Braveheart of Yonkers," *New York Times*, July 30, 2000, WC1.

93. Schuck, "Residential Neighborhoods," 258–259.

94. "Yonkers Grilled on Desegregation Efforts," *New York Times*, October 6, 2000, B1; "Court Spurns Yonkers Appeal," *Journal News*, December 4, 2001, 1A.

95. Xavier de Souza Briggs, Joe T. Darden, and Angela Aidala, "In the Wake of Desegregation: Early Impacts of Scattered-Site Public Housing on Neighborhoods in Yonkers, New York," *Journal of the American Planning Association 65*, no. 1 (Winter 1999): 27–50; Lisa Belkin, *Show Me a Hero: The Story of an Urban Tragedy and of the Housing Revolution That Is Changing America's Neighborhoods* (New York: Little, Brown, 1999); Xavier de Sousa Briggs, "Brown Kids in White Suburbs: Housing Mobility, Neighborhood Effects and the Social Ties of Poor Youth" (PhD diss., Columbia University, 1996).

96. Quoted in Belkin, *Show Me a Hero*, 321.

97. "Accord Is Reached in School Bias Suit Involving Yonkers," *New York Times*, January 9, 2002, A1; "Yonkers Calmly Closes Case on Desegregation 20 Years Later," *Journal News*, May 2, 2007, 5A; "After 27 Years, Yonkers Housing Desegregation Battle Ends Quietly in Manhattan Court," *New York Times*, May 2, 2007, B5.

98. "Neither Separate Nor Equal: Yonkers Integrates Its Schools, to Little Effect,"
    New York Times, December 28, 1995, B1.After the desegregation controversy,
    Yonkers witnessed its first population decline in decades, from 195,351 in 1980
    to 188,082 in 1990; http://www.cityofyonkers.com/Index.aspx?page=217.In 2000,
    nearly 16 percent of the city's population lived in poverty. U.S. Census Bureau,
    "2000 State and County Quick Facts, Yonkers, New York," http://quickfacts.
    census.gov/qfd/states/36/3684000.html; U.S. Census Bureau, "2000 Profile
    of Selected Economic Characteristics, Yonkers, New York," http://factfinder.
    census.gov/servlet/QTTable?_bm=y&-qr_name=DEC_2000_SF3_U_DP3&-ds_
    name=DEC_2000_SF3_U&-_lang=en&-_sse=on&-geo_id=16000US3684000;
    Fernanda Santos, "Usual Civic Fights Subside as Yonkers Hopes for $3.1 Billion
    Project," *New York Times*, Februay 27, 2006, B1.
99. Yonkers has the highest number of foreign-born residents in Westchester
    County. Migrants, largely from the Dominican Republic, Mexico, Jamaica, and
    Ireland, have helped bring Yonkers's population back to presegregation levels.
    Westchester County Department of Planning, *The Newest to Westchester: Immi-
    gration Trends* (White Plains, NY: Westchester County Department of Planning,
    2006).

NOTES TO CHAPTER 2

1. Tom Flynn, *St. Patrick's Day and the Irish Community in Yonkers* (Yonkers, NY:
   Sharing Community, 2005), 1–2, 19, 24, 78–86.
2. Harry Dunkak, *Freedom, Culture, Labor: The Irish of Early Westchester County,
   New York* (New Rochelle, NY: Iona College Press, 1994); Kevin Kenny, *The
   American Irish: A History* (Essex, UK: Pearson, 2000), 45; Paul A. Gilje, "The
   Development of an Irish American Community in New York City before the
   Great Migration," in *The New York Irish*, ed. Ronald Bayor and Timothy Mea-
   gher (Baltimore: John Hopkins University Press, 1996), 70–83. These Yonkers
   census statistics are from Thomas Shelley, *Slovaks on the Hudson: Most Holy
   Trinity Church, Yonkers and the Slovak Catholics of the Archdiocese of New York,
   1894–2000* (Washington, DC: Catholic University Press, 2002), 10. According
   to Hasia Diner, 133,730 of New York City's residents were born in Ireland, 26
   percent of the city's total population. See Diner, "The Most Irish City in the
   Union: The Era of the Great Migration, 1844–1877," in Bayor and Meagher, *The
   New York Irish*, 91.
3. Michael Omi and Howard Winant, *Racial Formation in the United States from the
   1960's to the 1990's*, 2nd ed. (New York: Routledge, 1994).
4. Nicholas Canny, *Making Ireland British, 1580–1650* (Oxford: Oxford University
   Press, 2003); Padraig Lenihan, *Consolidating Conquest, 1603–1727* (New York:
   Longman, 2008); Richard Lebow, *White Britain and Black Ireland: The Influence
   of Stereotypes on Colonial Policy* (Philadelphia: ISHI, 1976), 75. There is a debate
   over whether Ireland can be thought of as a colony or, since the creation of the

Irish Free State, as postcolonial. See Kevin Kenny, ed., *Ireland and the British Empire* (Oxford: Oxford University Press, 2004).

5. Eric Arnesen, "Whiteness and the Historians' Imagination," *International Labor and Working-Class History*, no. 60 (Fall 2001): 1–92; David Roediger, *Working towards Whiteness: How America's Immigrants Became White: The Strange Journey from Ellis Island to the Suburbs* (New York: Basic Books, 2005); Barbara Fields, "Ideology and Race in American History," in *Region, Race and Reconstruction: Essays in Honor of C. Vann Woodward*, ed. J. Morgan Kousser and James M. McPherson (New York: Oxford University Press, 1982), 143–177; Barbara Fields, "Slavery, Race and Ideology in the USA," *New Left Review* 181 (1990): 95–118.

6. Benedict Anderson, *Imagined Communities: Reflections on the Origins and Spread of Nationalism* (New York: Verso, 1991); Edward Said, *Orientalism* (New York: Pantheon, 1978); Ann Laura Stoler, *Carnal Knowledge and Imperial Power: Race and the Intimate in Colonial Rule* (Berkeley: University of California Press, 2002), 6. Also see her earlier work, *Race and the Education of Desire: Foucault's History of Sexuality and the Colonial Order of Things* (Durham, NC: Duke University Press, 1995), as well as *Haunted by Empire: Geographies of Intimacy in North American History* (Durham, NC: Duke University Press, 2006); Anne McClintock, *Imperial Leather: Race, Gender and Sexuality in Colonial Contest* (New York: Routledge, 1995).

7. L. P. Curtis, *Apes and Angels: The Irishman in Victorian Caricature*, rev. ed. (Washington, DC: Smithsonian Institution Press, 1997), 18; William H.A. Williams, *Tourism, Landscape and the Irish Character: British Travel Writers in Pre-Famine Ireland* (Madison: University of Wisconsin Press, 2008).

8. Curtis calls this the Celtic Jekyll and Hyde in *Apes and Angels.*

9. Michael C. Coleman, *American Indians, the Irish and Government Schooling: A Comparative Study* (Lincoln: University of Nebraska Press, 2007), 94, 107, 124.

10. L. P. Curtis, *Anglo-Saxons and Celts: A Study of Anti-Irish Prejudice in Victorian England* (Berkeley: University of California Press, 1968), 51; Lebow, 45; Curtis, *Apes and Angels*, xxii; Michael de Nie, *The Eternal Paddy: Irish Identity and the British Press, 1798–1882* (Madison: University of Wisconsin Press, 2004).

11. Theodore Allen, *The Invention of the White Race* (New York: Verso, 1994); Ronald Takaki, *A Different Mirror: A History of Multicultural America* (New York: Back Bay Books, 1994); Luke Gibbons, "Race against Time: Racial Discourse and Irish History," *Oxford Literary Review* 13 (Winter 1991): 95–117; McClintock, *Imperial Leather.*

12. Kerby Miller, "'Revenge for Skibbereen': The Great Famine and Irish Emigration, 1856–1855," in *Emigrants and Exiles: Ireland and the Irish Exodus to North America* (New York: Oxford University Press, 1985), 66–78; Hasia Diner, *Hungering for America: Italian, Irish, and Jewish Foodways in the Age of Migration* (Cambridge: Harvard University Press, 2001), 114.

13. Hasia Diner, *Erin's Daughters in America: Irish Immigrant Women in the Nine-teenth Century* (Baltimore: Johns Hopkins University Press, 1983), 9–11, 30.

14. For studies of U.S. middle-class domesticity, see Mary P. Ryan, *Cradle of the Middle-Class: The Family in Oneida County, New York, 1780–1865* (Cambridge: Cambridge University Press, 1983); Carol Smith-Rosenberg, *Disorderly Conduct: Visions of Gender in Victorian America* (New York: Oxford University Press, 1985); Stephanie Coontz, *The Social Origins of Private Life: A History of American Families, 1600–1900* (New York: Verso, 1988). At the turn of the nineteenth century, the "modern" American household was underscored as both white and heterosexual. See Lisa Duggan, *Sapphic Slashers: Sex, Violence and American Modernity* (Durham, NC: Duke University Press, 2000).

15. Bruce Dorsey, *Reforming Men and Women: Gender in the Antebellum City* (Ithaca: Cornell University Press, 2002); Elaine Franz Parsons, *Manhood Lost: Fallen Drunkards and Redeeming Women in the Nineteenth-Century United States* (Baltimore: Johns Hopkins University Press, 2003); Linda Gordon, *The Great Arizona Orphan Abduction* (Cambridge: Harvard University Press, 1999); Coleman, *American Indians, the Irish and Government Schooling;* Grace Elizabeth Hale, *Making Whiteness: The Culture of Segregation in the South, 1890–1940* (New York: Vintage, 1998); Pablo Mitchell, *Coyote Nation: Sexuality, Race and Conquest in Modernizing New Mexico, 1880–1920* (Chicago: University of Chicago Press, 2005); Matt Wray, *Not Quite White: White Trash and the Boundaries of Whiteness* (Durham, NC: Duke University Press, 2006); Philip Reilly, *The Surgical Solution: A History of Involuntary Sterilization in the United States* (Baltimore: Johns Hopkins University Press, 1991); Alexandra Minna Stern, *Eugenic Nation: Faults and Frontiers of Better Breeding in Modern America* (Berkeley: University of California Press, 2005); Nyan Shah, *Contagious Divides: Epidemics and Race in San Francisco's Chinatown* (Berkeley: University of California Press, 2001); Amy Greenburg, *Manifest Manhood and the Antebellum American Empire* (New York: Cambridge University Press, 2006); Laura Wexler, *Tender Violence: Domestic Visions in an Age of U.S. Imperialism* (Chapel Hill: University of North Carolina Press, 2000); Laura Briggs, *Race, Sex, Science and U.S. Imperialism in Puerto Rico* (Berkeley: University of California Press, 2002); Ann Laura Stoler, ed., *Haunted by Empire: Geographies of Intimacy in North American History.*

16. George Potter, *To the Golden Door: The Story of the Irish in Ireland and America* (Boston: Little, Brown, 1960), 252–253; Jenny Franchot, *Roads to Rome: The Antebellum Protestant Encounter with Catholicism* (Berkeley: University of California Press, 1994), 137, 144–145, 154–155; Susan M. Griffin, "Awful Disclosures: The Escaped Nun's Tale," in *Anti-Catholicism and Nineteenth-Century Fiction* (Cambridge: Cambridge University Press, 2004), 27–61.

17. John Higham, *Strangers in the Land: Patterns of American Nativism, 1860–1925* (New York: Atheneum, 1963); Tyler Anbinder, *Nativism and Slavery: The Northern Know Nothings and the Politics of the 1850s* (New York: Oxford University

Press, 1992); Dale T. Knobel, *America for the Americans: The Nativist Movement in the United States* (New York: Twayne, 1996), Faye Dudden, *Serving Women: Household Service in Nineteenth-Century America* (Middletown, CT: Wesleyan University Press, 1983), 69.

18. Jay P. Dolan, *The Immigrant Church: New York's Irish and German Catholics, 1815–1865* (Notre Dame, IN: University of Notre Dame Press, 1983), 56–57.

19. Kenny, *American Irish*, 289–290; Kerby Miller, "Class, Culture and Ethnicity: The Construction of Irish America in the Nineteenth Century," in *Ireland and Irish America: Culture, Class and Transnational Migration* (Dublin: Field Day Press, 2008), 268.

20. Steven P. Erie, *Rainbow's End: Irish Americans and the Dilemmas of Urban Machine Politics, 1840–1985* (Berkeley: University of California Press, 1988).

21. Kenny, *American Irish*, 129; Potter, *To the Golden Door*, 54–61, 317–318, 337; Kevin Kenny, *Making Sense of the Molly Maguires* (New York: Oxford University Press, 1998).

22. Roy Rosenzweig, *Eight Hours for What We Will: Workers and Leisure in an Industrial City, 1870–1920* (Cambridge: Cambridge University Press, 1983), 36–40; Richard B. Stott, *Workers in the Metropolis: Class, Ethnicity and Youth in Antebellum New York City* (Ithaca: Cornell University Press, 1990), 143, 217–222, 231, 241–251; Michael Kaplan, "City Tavern Violence and the Creation of a Working-Class Male Identity," *Journal of the Early Republic* 15 no. 4 (Winter 1995): 591–617; Patricia Kelleher, "Class and Catholic Irish Masculinity in Antebellum America: Young Men on the Make in Chicago," *Journal of American Ethnic History* 28, no. 4 (Summer 2009), 12.

23. Diner, *Erin's Daughters*, 55–62.

24. Franchot, *Roads to Rome*, 144.

25. Roger Daniels, "Minorities from Other Regions: Chinese, Japanese, and French Canadians," in *Coming to America: A History of Immigration and Ethnicity in American Life*, 2nd ed. (New York: Perennial, 2002), 238–264.

26. Edmund S. Morgan, "Slavery and Freedom: The Great Paradox in American History," *Journal of American History* 59, no. 1 (June 1972): 5–29; Aihwa Ong, *Buddha Is Hiding: Refugees, Citizenship and the New America* (Berkeley: University of California Press, 2003), 11.

27. Amy Louise Wood, *Lynching and Spectacle: Witnessing Racial Violence in America, 1890–1940* (Chapel Hill: University of North Carolina Press, 2011); Heather Cox Richardson, *The Death of Reconstruction: Race Labor and Politics in the Post–Civil War North, 1861–1901* (Cambridge: Harvard University Press, 2004); Thomas J. Sugrue, *Sweet Land of Liberty: The Forgotten Struggle for Civil Rights in the North* (New York: Random House, 2009);

28. Tyler Anbinder, *Five Points: The 19th Century New York City Neighborhood That Invented Tap Dance, Stole Elections and Became the World's Most Notorious Slum* (New York: Free Press, 2001); David Roediger, *The Wages of Whiteness: Race and the Making of the Working Class*, 2nd ed. (New York: Verso, 1999); Eric Lott,

Love and Theft: Blackface Minstrelsy and the American Working Class (New York: Oxford University Press, 1993), 6.

29. Graham Hodges, "Desirable Companions and Lovers: The Irish and African Americans in the Sixth Wards, 1830–1870," in Bayor and Meagher, *The New York Irish*, 107–124; Noel Ignatiev, *How the Irish Became White* (New York: Routledge, 1995), 40–42. The Irish were not the first to prompt cultural anxieties about interracial intimacies between Blacks and whites. See Kathleen Brown, *Good Wives, Nasty Wenches and Anxious Patriarchs: Gender, Race and Power in Colonial Virginia* (Chapel Hill: University of North Carolina Press, 1996); Martha Hodes, *White Women, Black Men: Illicit Sex in the Nineteenth-Century South* (New Haven: Yale University Press, 1997).

30. Roediger, *Wages of Whiteness*; Jane Leslie Helleiner, *Irish Travelers: Racism and the Politics of Culture* (Toronto: University of Toronto Press, 2000); Elizabeth Cullingford, *Ireland's Others: Ethnicity and Gender in Irish Literature and Popular Culture* (Notre Dame: University of Notre Dame Press, 2001); Nini Rogers, *Ireland, Slavery and Anti-Slavery: 1612–1865* (New York: Palgrave Macmillan, 2007); Michael Holmes, "The Irish and India: Imperialism, Nationalism and Internationalism," in *The Irish Diaspora*, ed. Andy Bielenberg (New York; Longman, 2000), 235–250; Timothy J. Meagher, "The Fireman on the Stairs: Communal Loyalties in the Making of Irish America," in *Making the Irish American: History and Heritage of the Irish in the United States*, ed. Joseph Lee and Marion R. Casey (New York: NYU Press, 2006), 654.

31. John T. McGreevy, *Catholicism and American Freedom: A History* (New York: Norton, 2003), 52–58; Angela F. Murphy, *American Slavery Irish Freedom: Abolition, Immigrant Citizenship and the Transatlantic Movement for Irish Repeal* (Baton Rouge: Louisiana State University Press, 2010); Dudden, *Serving Women*, 64; Roediger, *Wages of Whiteness*; Alexander Saxton, *The Rise and Fall of the White Republic: Class Politics and Mass Culture in Nineteenth-Century America* (New York: Verso, 1990); Kaplan, "City Tavern Violence."

32. Iver Bernstein, *The New York City Draft Riots: The Significance for American Society and Politics in the Age of the Civil War* (New York: Oxford University Press, 1990).

33. Lauren Onkey, *Blackness and Transatlantic Irish Identity: Celtic Soul Brothers* (New York: Routledge, 2010), 64; Mike Cronin and Daryl Adair, *The Wearing of the Green: A History of St. Patrick's Day* (New York: Routledge, 2002); Marilyn Halter, *Shopping for Identity: The Marketing of Ethnicity* (New York: Schocken Books, 2000), 168; "How Irish Was My Surname: Via Ireland, a Chapter in the Story of Black America," *New York Times*, March 17, 2003, B1; "A Black Grand Marshall," *Irish Voice*, March 19, 2003, 20; Maureen O'Dowd, "Don't Be a Stranger," *New York Times*, May 25, 2011, A27. The St. Patrick's Day parade in Queens, New York, however, is an exception. Adrian Mulligan, "Countering Exclusion: The 'St. Pat's for All' Parade," *Gender, Place and Culture: A Journal of Feminist Geography* 15, no. 2 (April 2008): 153–167.

34. Timothy J. Meagher, "Introduction," in *From Paddy to Studs: Irish-American Communities in the Turn of the Century Era, 1880–1920*, ed. Timothy J. Meagher (New York: Greenwood Press, 1986), 9.
35. Joseph Lee, "Irish Responses to Stereotype," *Radharc* 1 (November 2000): 23–31.
36. Thomas J. Rowland, "Irish American Catholics and the Quest for Respectability in the Coming of the Great War, 1900–1917," *Journal of American Ethnic History* 15, no. 2 (Winter 1996): 3–42; Deirdre M. Moloney, *American Catholic Lay Groups and Transatlantic Social Reform in the Progressive Era* (Chapel Hill: University of North Carolina Press, 2002), 132; David Noel Doyle, *Irish Americans, Native Rights and National Empires* (New York: Arno Press, 1976), 55; Kelleher, "Class and Catholic Irish Masculinity," 23.
37. Jay P. Dolan, *The American Catholic Experience: A History from Colonial Times to the Present* (South Bend: University of Notre Dame Press, 1992), 219, 252–253.
38. Miller, "Class, Culture and Ethnicity," 265.
39. Kenny, *American Irish*, 185–186, 200.
40. Diner, *Erin's Daughters*, 70–94; Dudden, *Serving Women*, 64; Margaret Lynch-Brennan, "Ubiquitous Bridget: Irish Immigrant Women in Domestic Service in America, 1840–1930," in Lee and Casey, *Making the Irish American*, 332–353; Colleen McDannell, "Going to the Ladies Fair: Irish Catholics in New York City," in Bayor and Meagher, *The New York Irish*, 234–251. Protestant reformers also saw the "redemptive potential" of Irish women; see Gunja SenGupta, "Celtic Sisters, Saxon Keepers," in *From Slavery to Poverty: The Racial Origins of Welfare in New York, 1840–1918* (New York: NYU Press, 2009), 170–206.
41. Francis Walsh, "Lace Curtain Literature: Changing Perceptions of Irish American Success," *Journal of American Culture* 2, no. 1 (1979): 139–146; Roediger, *Working towards Whiteness*, 190–191; Margaret M. Mulrooney, *Black Powder, White Lace: The du Pont Irish and Cultural Identity in Nineteenth-Century America* (Hanover: University of New Hampshire Press, 2002), 186–187.
42. Moloney, *American Catholic Lay Groups*, 170; William H. A. Williams, "Green Again: Irish-American Lace-Curtain Satire," *New Hibernia Review* 6, no. 2 (Summer, 2002): 9–24
43. M. Alison Kibler, "The Stage Irishwoman," *Journal of American Ethnic History* 24, no. 3 (Spring 2005): 5–30; Potter, *To the Golden Door*, 82; Diner, *Erin's Daughters*, 116–118; Kenny, *American Irish*, 230.
44. Matthew Frye Jacobson, *Barbarian Virtues: The United States Encounters Foreign Peoples at Home and Abroad, 1876–1917* (New York: Hill and Wang, 2000), 213–216; Miller, "Class, Culture and Ethnicity," 268.
45. Susannah Ural Bruce, *The Harp and the Eagle: Irish American Volunteers and the Union Army, 1861–1865* (New York: NYU Press, 2006), 184, 189, 218, 258; Christian G. Samito, *Becoming American under Fire: Irish Americans, African Americans and the Politics of Citizenship during the Civil War Era* (Ithaca: Cornell University Press, 2009), 118, 120–121.

46. *Booklet of Information Regarding the American Irish Historical Society* (New York: American Irish Historical Society, 1905); General Edward Moseley, "Annual Address" (paper presented at the annual meeting of the American Irish Historical Society, New York, February 1898); Thomas Lonergan, "The Irish Chapter in American History" (paper presented at the annual meeting of the American Irish Historical Society, New York, January 1912).

47. Michael O'Brien, "Irish Firsts in American History" (paper presented at the annual meeting of the American Irish Historical Society, New York, April 1917); Lonergan, "Irish Chapter in American History."

48. Timothy J. Meagher, *Inventing Irish America: Generation, Class and Ethnic Identity in a New England City, 1880–1928* (Notre Dame, IN: University of Notre Dame Press, 2001), 162; Meagher, *From Paddy to Studs*, 10.

49. Moloney, *American Catholic Lay Groups*, 62; Meagher, *Inventing Irish America*, 253.

50. Kenny, *American Irish*, 200; John Duffy Ibson, *Will the World Break Your Heart? Dimensions and Consequences of Irish American Assimilation* (New York: Garland, 1990), 167, 172; Monica McGoldrick, ed., "Irish Families," in *Ethnicity and Family Therapy*, 3rd ed. (New York: Guildford, 2005), 595–615.

51. Diner, *Erin's Daughters*, 113; Elizabeth Malcolm, *Ireland Sober, Ireland Free: Drink and Temperance in Nineteenth-Century Ireland* (Syracuse, NY: Syracuse University Press, 1986), 332–333; Richard Strivers, *Hair of the Dog: Irish Drinking and Its American Stereotype*, rev. ed. (New York: Continuum, 2000), 174. Other groups had similar encounters with racial caricatures. Krystyn Moon, *Yellowface: Creating the Chinese in American Popular Music and Performance, 1850s–1920s* (New Brunswick, NJ: Rutgers University Press, 2006); Jonathan Munby, *Under a Bad Sign: Criminal Self-Representation in African American Popular Culture* (Chicago: Chicago University Press, 2011).

52. John T. Ridge, *Erin's Sons in America: The Ancient Order of Hibernians* (New York: Ancient Order of Hibernians 150th Anniversary Committee, 1986).

53. *National Hibernian*, May 1915, 10; June 1915, 11; October 1915, 12.

54. *Booklet of Information Regarding the American Irish Historical Society*.

55. Lonergan, "Irish Chapter in American History."

56. *National Hibernian*, May 1915, 7.

57. Quoted in John T. Ridge, "Irish County Societies in New York," in Bayor and Meagher, *The New York Irish*, 297.

58. *Irish American Advocate*, February 13, 1904.

59. Charles Fanning, "Respectability and Realism: Ambivalent Fictions," in *The Irish Voice in America: 250 Years of Irish American Fiction* (Lexington: University Press of Kentucky, 1990), 153–197; Colleen McDannell, "True as We Need Them: Catholicism and the Irish-American Male," *American Studies* 27, no. 2 (Fall 1986): 19–36.

60. Nell Irving Painter, *The History of White People* (New York: Norton, 2010), 206; Lynn Dumenil, "The Tribal Twenties: 'Assimilated' Catholics' Response to

Anti-Catholicism in the 1920s," *Journal of American Ethnic History* 11, no. 1 (Fall 1991): 21–50.

61. Higham, *Strangers in the Land*, 77–87; Dolan, *American Catholic Experience*, 255; Daniel J. Tichenor, *Dividing Lines: The Politics of Immigration Control in America* (Princeton: Princeton University Press, 2002), 71–72.

62. Justin Nordstrom, *Danger on the Doorstep: Anti-Catholicism and American Print Culture in the Progressive Era* (Notre Dame, IN: Notre Dame University Press, 2006), 120–124, 129–138.

63. Thomas J. Rowland, "Irish American Catholics and the Quest for Respectability in the Coming of the Great War," *Journal of American Ethnic History* 15, no. 2 (Winter 1996): 3–32.

64. Jeanne Petit, "Our Immigrant Coreligionists: The National Catholic Welfare Conference as an Advocate for Immigrants in the 1920s," in *Immigrant Rights in the Shadows of Citizenship*, ed. Rachel Ida Buff (New York: NYU Press, 2008), 315–328; Meagher, *Inventing Irish America*, 327, 355.

65. Roediger, *Wages of Whiteness*; Ignatiev, *How the Irish Became White*; John J. Appel, "From Shanties to Lace Curtains: The Irish Image in Puck, 1876–1910," *Comparative Studies in Society and History* 13, no. 4 (October 1971), 371; Kathleen Donovan, "Good Old Pat: An Irish-American Stereotype in Decline," *Eire-Ireland* 15, no. 3 (Fall 1980): 6–14; Margaret Connors, "Historical and Fictional Stereotypes of the Irish," in *Irish American Fiction: Essays in Criticism*, ed. Daniel J. Casey and Robert E. Rhodes (New York: AMS, 1979), 1–12; Kerry Soper, "From Swarthy Ape to Sympathetic Everyman and Subversive Trickster: The Development of Irish Caricature in American Comic Strips between 1890 and 1920," *Journal of American Studies* 39 (2005): 257–296.

66. Francis R. Walsh, "The Callaghans and the Murphys: A Case Study," *Historical Journal of Film and Radio* 10, no. 1 (March 1990): 33–46; Ruth Barton, "Introduction," in *Screening Irish America: Representing Irish America in Film and Television*, ed. Ruth Barton (Dublin: Irish Academic Press, 2009) 1–14; Kevin Rockett, "The Irish Migrant and Film," in Barton, *Screening Irish America*, 17–44; Christopher Shannon, *Bowery to Broadway: The American Irish in Classic Hollywood Cinema* (Scranton, PA: University of Scranton Press, 2010), xxxiv.

67. Matthew J. O'Brien, "Hibernians on the March: Irish-American Ethnicity and the Cold War," in *After the Flood: Irish America, 1945–1960*, ed. James Silas Rogers and Matthew J. O'Brien (Dublin: Irish Academic Press, 2009), 57–70; Anthony Burke Smith, *The Look of Catholics: Portrayals in Popular Culture from the Great Depression to the Cold War* (Lawrence: University Press of Kansas, 2010).

68. *Bronx Irish at the Ramparts*, directed by Marcia Rock (New York: Rutt Video, 1995), videocassette (VHS), 28 mins.; Robert W. Snyder, "The Neighborhood That Changed: The Irish of Washington Heights and Inwood since 1945," in Bayor and Meagher, *The New York Irish*, 439–460. The Irish also moved in significant numbers farther north to Rockland County. Morton D. Winsberg, "The

Suburbanization of the Irish in Boston, Chicago and New York," *Eire-Ireland* 21, no. 3 (Fall 1986): 90–104.

69. For a concise overview of Irish history, see Eileen Reilly, "Modern Ireland: An Introductory Survey," in Lee and Casey, *Making the Irish American*, 63–147. Also see Joseph Lee, *Ireland, 1912–1985: Politics and Society* (Cambridge: Cambridge University Press, 1989); Mary E. Daly, *The Slow Failure: Population Decline and Independent Ireland, 1922–1973* (Madison: University of Wisconsin Press, 2006); Clair Wills, "Women, Domesticity and the Family: Recent Feminist Work in Irish Cultural Studies," *Cultural Studies* 15, no. 1 (2001): 33–57.

70. James M. Smith, *Ireland's Magdalen Laundries and the Nation's Architecture of Containment* (Notre Dame, IN: University of Notre Dame Press, 2007); Moira Maguire, *Precarious Childhood in Post-independence Ireland* (Manchester: Manchester University Press, 2009), 49–52, 129; Paul Michael Garrett, "The Abnormal Flight: The Migration and Repatriation of Irish Unmarried Mothers," *Social History* 25, no. 3 (2000): 330–343.

71. Daly, *Slow Failure*.

72. Ibid.; John Corbally, "The Jarring Irish: Postwar Immigration to the Heart of Empire," *Radical History Review* 2009, no. 104 (Spring 2009): 103–125.

73. Linda Dowling Almeida, *Irish Immigrants in New York City, 1945–1995* (Indianapolis: Indiana University Press, 2001), 23.

74. The *Irish Echo* was founded in 1928 during the migration of approximately 20,000 Irish immigrants who arrived in New York City during Ireland's civil unrest of the 1920s. The GAA was established in 1884 to promote Irish sports as part of a larger nationalist movement in Ireland. U.S. branches consequentially opened in cities where Irish immigrants had continued to settle during that era. For a discussion of the GAA in New York City, see Sara Brady, "Irish Sport and Culture at New York's Gaelic Park" (PhD diss., New York University, 2005); Miriam Nyhan, "County Associations in Irish New York, 1945–1965," *New York Irish History* 22 (2008): 27–36.

75. Diarmaid Ferriter, *A Nation of Extremes: The Pioneers in Twentieth-Century Ireland* (Dublin: Irish Academic Press, 1999).

76. Rebecca S. Miller, "Irish Traditional and Popular Music in New York City: Identity and Social Change, 1930–1975," in Bayor and Meagher, *The New York Irish*, 481–506; "Dude, Where's the Bar? Partying with the Irish Pioneers," *Irish Voice*, November 4, 2003, 10; Frances Browner, ed., *When Mem'ry Brings Us Back Again* (Yonkers: Aisling Irish Community Center, 2006).

77. George Lipsitz, *The Possessive Investment in Whiteness: How White People Profit from Identity Politics* (Philadelphia: Temple University Press, 1998); Lisabeth Cohen, *A Consumer's Republic: The Politics of Mass Consumption in Postwar America* (New York: Knopf, 2003); Kenneth T. Jackson, *Crabgrass Frontier: The Suburbanization of the United States* (New York: Oxford University Press, 1985).

78. Eileen Anderson, "Irish New Yorkers and the Puerto Rican Migration," in Rogers and O'Brien, *After the Flood,* 87–99.

79. Browner, *When Mem'ry Brings Us Back Again.*

80. Nathan Glazer and Daniel Patrick Moynihan, *Beyond the Melting Pot: The Negroes, Puerto Ricans, Jews Italians and Irish of New York City* (Cambridge: MIT Press, 1963), 12, 314. For the Chicago school model of assimilation, see Robert Park and Ernest Burgess, *Introduction to the Science of Sociology,* 2nd ed. (Chicago: University of Chicago Press, 1924).

81. Douglas S. Massey and Robert J. Sampson, "Moynihan Redux: Legacies and Lessons," *Annals of the American Academy of Political and Social Science* 621, no. 1 (January 2009): 6–27; Philip Kasinitz, "Beyond the Melting Pot: The Contemporary Relevance of a Classic," *International Migration Review* 34, no. 1 (Spring 2000): 248–255.

82. Matthew Frye Jacobson, *Roots Too: White Ethnic Revival in Post–Civil Rights America* (Cambridge: Harvard University Press, 2006), 7–9.

83. Halter, *Shopping for Identity.* Halter, however, does not address how ethnic marketing appeals to agendas of race. See Arlene Davila, *Latinos Inc.: The Marketing and Making of a People* (Berkeley: University of California Press, 2001).

84. Richard Jensen, "No Irish Need Apply: A Myth of Victimization," *Journal of Social History* 36, no. 2 (Winter 2002): 405–427. Kevin Kenny addresses this critique in "Race, Violence and Anti-Irish Sentiment in the Nineteenth Century," in Lee and Casey, *Making the Irish American,* 364–378.

85. Ed O'Donnell, "New York Sun Asks That Irish Not Apply," *Irish Echo,* May 9, 2007, 22; Potter, *To the Golden Door,* 168.

86. Diane Negra, "The Irish in Us: Irishness, Performativity and Popular Culture," in *The Irish in Us: Irishness, Performativity and Popular Culture,* ed. Diane Negra (Durham, NC: Duke University Press, 2006), 1. Hamilton Carroll explains that once race privilege becomes visible, it has the capacity to locate itself elsewhere, in ethnicity or Irishness. Carroll, *Affirmative Reaction: New Formations of White Masculinity* (Durham, NC: Duke University Press, 2011).

87. Roediger, *Wages of Whiteness*; Ignatiev, *How the Irish Became White*; Cheryl I. Harris, "Whiteness as Property," *Harvard Law Review* 106, no. 8 (June 1993): 1707–1791. George Lipsitz addresses whiteness in the post–World War II Fordist era; see Lipsitz, *Possessive Investment in Whiteness.*

88. Catherine Eagan, "Still Black and Proud: Irish America and Racial Politics of Hibernophilia," in Negra, *The Irish in Us,* 84–109.

89. Brian Dooley, *Black and Green: The Fight for Civil Rights in Northern Ireland and Black America* (Chicago: Pluto Press, 1998), 86–91; Andrew J. Wilson, *Irish America and the Ulster Conflict, 1968–1995* (Washington, DC: Catholic University Press, 1995).

90. Natasha Casey, "The Best Kept Secret in Retail: Selling Irishness in Contemporary America," in Negra, *The Irish in Us,* 88.

91. Stephanie Rains, *The Irish American in Popular Culture, 1945–2000* (Dublin: Irish Academic Press, 2007).

92. Catherine Nash, *Of Irish Descent: Origins Stories, Genealogy and the Politics of Belonging* (Syracuse, NY: Syracuse University Press, 2008).

93. Kerby Miller, "'Scotch-Irish,' 'Black Irish' and 'Real Irish': Emigrants and Identities in the Old South," in Bielenberg, *Irish Diaspora*, 141.

94. Natasha Casey calls this trend a "deviant" consumption of Irishness; Casey, "The Best Kept Secret in Retail," 94.

95. Almeida, *Irish Immigrants in New York City*, 60–62.

96. Ibid., 61–62.

97. Mary P. Corcoran, *Irish Illegals: Transients between Two Societies* (Westport, CT: Greenwood Press, 1993).

98. Almeida, *Irish Immigrants in New York City*, 81.

99. Anne Maguire, *Rock the Sham: The Irish Lesbian and Gay Organization's Battle to March in New York's St. Patrick's Day Parade* (New York: Street Level Press, 2006), 38.

100. Ibid., 17. Sallie A. Marston, "Making Difference: Conflict over Irish Identity in the New York City St. Patrick's Day Parade," *Political Geography* 21 (2002): 373–392; Mulligan, "Countering Exclusion."

101. Almeida, *Irish Immigrants in New York City*, 74, 78.

102. Corcoran, *Irish Illegals*, 131.

103. Lisa Duggan, *The Twighlight of Equality: Neoliberalism, Cultural Politics and the Attack on Democracy* (Boston: Beacon Press, 2003); Patricia Hill Collins, "Like One of the Family: Race, Ethnicity and the Paradox of U.S. National Identity," *Ethnic and Racial Studies* 24, no. 1 (January 2001): 3–28; Wahneema Lubiano, "Black Ladies, Welfare Queens, and State Minstrels: Ideological War by Narrative Means," in *Race-ing Justice, En-gendering Power: Essays on Anita Hill, Clarence Thomas and the Construction of Social Reality*, ed. Toni Morrison (New York: Pantheon, 1992), 323–363; Leo Chavez, *Covering Immigration: Popular Images and the Politics of the Nation* (Berkeley: University of California Press, 2001); Joseph Nevins, *Operation Gatekeeper: The Rise of the "Illegal Alien" and the Making of the U.S.-Mexican Boundary* (New York: Routledge, 2002); Justin Akers Chacon and Mike Davis, *No One Is Illegal: Fighting Racism and State Violence on the U.S.-Mexico Border* (Chicago: Haymarket Books, 2006).

104. According to Mary P. Corcoran, "Irish construction workers occupy a privileged position in the informal economy," made possible by their use of ethnic connections in construction unions. In addition, "Irish workers in the bar trade occupy the highest paid positions as waiters/waitresses and bartenders," while the "kitchen and janitorial jobs are almost exclusively reserved for Central and South Americans. Even in domestic work, Irish immigrant women report that an American family enhances their prestige by having a white nanny rather than a black nanny in their service." Corcoran, *Irish Illegals*, 185.

105. "Lost in Yonkers (and the North Bronx Too!): Influx of New Residents and Businesses Creates Booming Irish Mecca," *Irish Voice*, September 24, 1996, 22. Granuaile is a bar named after a female Irish sea pirate in Irish mythology, the An Bodhran is a bar named after an Irish musical instrument most similar to a drum, and An Sioppa Beag is a deli whose name literally translates as "the small shop." Incidentally, two of these establishments have either been sold and reopened under a new name or have closed.

NOTES TO CHAPTER 3

1. Lisa Duggan, *TheTwilight of Equality? Neoliberalism, Cultural Politics and the Attack on Democracy* (Boston: Beacon Press, 2003), x–xiii; David Harvey, *A Brief History of Neoliberalism* (New York: Oxford University Press, 2005); Neil Smith, *The Endgame of Globalization* (New York: Routledge, 2005); Andrea McArdle and Tanya Erzen, eds., *Zero Tolerance: Quality of Life and the New Police Brutality in New York City* (New York: NYU Press, 2001).

2. Peter Marcuse, "Abandonment, Gentrification and Displacement: The Linkages in New York City," in *Gentrification of the City*, ed. Neil Smith and Peter Williams (Boston: Allen and Unwin, 1986), 153–177; Mike Davis, *City of Quartz: Excavating the Future of Los Angeles* (New York: Verso, 1990); Janet Abu-Lughod, *From East Village to Urban Village: The Battle for New York's Lower East Side* (Cambridge: Blackwell Press, 1994).

3. Neil Smith, *The New Urban Frontier: Gentrification and the Revanchist City* (New York: Routledge, 1996).

4. "The Battle for Ridge Hill," Channel 12 News Westchester, March 8, 2006.

5. Michael Omi and Howard Winant, *Racial Formation in the United States, from the 1960s to the 1990s*, 2nd ed. (New York: Routledge, 1994); Duggan, *Twilight of Equality*.

6. Jan Lin, however, demonstrates how communities of color use ethnic heritage to create more equitable urban environments. Lin, *The Power of Urban Ethnic Spaces* (New York: Routledge, 2010).

7. Arlene Davila, *Barrio Dreams: Puerto Ricans, Latinos and the Neoliberal City* (Berkeley: University of California Press, 2004); Derek Hyra, *The New Urban Renewal: The Economic Transformation of Harlem and Bronzeville* (Chicago: University of Chicago Press, 2008). Lance Freeman, however, treats urban redevelopment as a very complex process. In his study of New York City, gentrification can be emancipatory for middle-class Blacks but revanchist for working-class communities of color. Freeman, *There Goes the Hood: Views of Gentrification from the Ground Up* (Philadelphia: Temple University Press, 2006).

8. Peadar Kirby, *The Celtic Tiger in Collapse: Explaining the Weaknesses of the Irish Model*, 2nd ed. (London: Palgrave Macmillan, 2010), 5, 31–33.

9. Ibid., 2; Kieran Allen, *Ireland's Economic Crash: A Radical Agenda for Change* (Dublin: Liffey Press, 2009), 44–51; "After Months of Resisting, Ireland Applies for a Bailout," *New York Times*, November 22, 2010, A1; Patrick J. Drudy and

Micheal L. Collins, "Ireland: From Boom to Austerity," *Cambridge Journal of Regions, Economy and Society* 4 (2011): 339–354.

10. Kieran Allen, ed., *The Celtic Tiger: The Myth of Social Partnership in Ireland* (Manchester: Manchester University Press, 2000); Denis O'Hearn, "Macroeconomic Policy in the Celtic Tiger: A Critical Reassessment," in *The End of Irish History: Critical Reflections on the Celtic Tiger*, ed. Colin Coulter and Steve Coleman (Manchester: Manchester University Press, 2003), 34–55.

11. Sinead Kennedy, "Irish Women and the Celtic Tiger," in Coulter and Coleman, *End of Irish History*, 95–109; Steve Loyal, "Welcome to the Celtic Tiger: Racism, Immigration and the State," in Coulter and Coleman, *End of Irish History*, 74–94; "Heading Home? Expo Pulls in Crowds While Some U.S. Citizens Think of Taking the Plunge," *Irish Echo*, October 25, 2006, 3.

12. O'Hearn, "Macroeconomic Policy in the Celtic Tiger," 47–49.

13. Kieran Allen, "Neither Boston nor Berlin: Class Polarisation and Neoliberalism in the Irish Republic," in Coulter and Coleman, *End of Irish History*, 68.

14. Ibid., 68; Colin Coulter, "The End of Irish History? An Introduction to the Book," in Coulter and Coleman, *End of Irish History*, 22.

15. "Irish Shoppers Blitz New York," *Irish Voice*, November 17, 2004, 8; "Irish Visit U.S. in Record Numbers," *Irish Voice*, February 8, 2006, 4; "Irish Miracle on 34th Street," *Irish Voice*, November 29, 2006, 10; "An Irish Taste for Real Estate," *New York Times*, May 8, 2007, A1; "New Air Route to Open," *New York Times*, January 30, 2007, B7; "Mayor Promotes Tourism during Visit to Ireland," *New York Times*, February 5, 2007, B4; Brendan Bartley and Rob Kitchin, "Ireland in the Twenty-First Century," in *Understanding Contemporary Ireland*, ed. Brendan Bartley and Rob Kitchin (Dublin: Pluto Press, 2007), 1–26. According to Bartley and Kitchin, on average, 31,000 people per year left Ireland between 1990 and 2003. Piaras Mac Einri notes that approximately 44,600 left Ireland for the United States between 1995 and 2004; see Mac Einri, "Immigration: Labour Migrants, Asylum Seekers and Refugees," in Bartley and Kitchin, *Understanding Contemporary Ireland*, 236–248.

16. Ian O'Donnell and Eoin O'Sullivan, *Crime Control in Ireland: The Politics of Intolerance* (Cork: Cork University Press, 2001); quoted in Peadar Kirby, Luke Gibbons, and Michael Cronin, eds., *Reinventing Ireland: Culture, Society and the Global Economy* (London: Pluto Press, 2002), 9.

17. "Voters Reject Automatic Citizenship for Babies Born in Ireland," *New York Times*, June 13, 2004, A7.

18. Ireland's first Gaelic television station made its debut in 1996 only to be followed by a Gaelic-language newspaper in 2003. Groups like Altan and Clannad have enjoyed commercial success in Ireland, and before becoming a global phenomenon, the sound track for Riverdance spent eighteen weeks as number one on the Irish music charts in 1994. For an examination of Irish tourism, see Michael Cronin and Barbara O'Connor, eds., *Tourism and Cultural Change: Irish Tourism: Image, Culture and Identity* (Buffalo, NY: Channel View Publications, 2003).

19. Elizabeth Malcolm, "The Rise of the Pub in Irish Popular Culture," in *Irish Popular Culture, 1650–1850*, ed. James S. Donnelly and Kerby Miller (Dublin: Irish Academic Press, 1998), 50–72.

20. James Roberts, Drink, *Temperance and the Working-Class in Nineteenth-Century Germany* (Boston: Allen and Unwin, 1984).

21. Elizabeth Malcolm, *Ireland Sober, Ireland Free: Drink and Temperance in Nineteenth-Century Ireland* (Syracuse, NY: Syracuse University Press, 1986), 299–303; Hasia Diner, Hungering for America: Italian, Irish and Jewish Foodways in the Age of Migration (Cambridge: Harvard University Press, 2001), 85.

22. Hasia Diner, *Erin's Daughters in America: Irish Immigrant Women in the Nineteenth Century* (Baltimore: Johns Hopkins University Press, 1983).

23. Cian Molloy, *The Story of the Irish Pub: An Intoxicating History of the Licensed Trade in Ireland* (Dublin: Liffey Press, 2003), 80.

24. Mary P. Corcoran, Karen Keaveney, and Patrick J. Duffy, "Transformations in Housing," in Bartley and Kitchin, *Understanding Contemporary Ireland*, 249–263; Denis Linehan, "'For the Way We Live Today': Consumption, Lifestyle and Place," in Bartley and Kitchin, *Understanding Contemporary Ireland*, 289–300; "Barely a Whimper as Ireland's Pubs Comply with Ban," *Financial Times* (London), September 10, 2004, 4; "Overcharging by Publicans," *Irish Times*, January 8, 2004, 15; "Smoking Ban and Pub Prices Linked to Home Drinking," *Irish Times*, September 3, 2004, 2; "Pub Arithmetic," *Irish Times*, July 31, 2004, 12; "Irish Retail Show Bar Sales Falling," *Irish Times*, August 20, 2004, http://www.irishtimes.com/newspaper/breaking/2004/0820/breaking26.html; "Is Alcohol Too Cheap?," *Irish Times*, October 1, 2010, 17.

25. Denis Conniffe and Daniel McCoy, *Alcohol Use in Ireland: Some Social and Economic Implications* (Denver, CO: Academic Books, 1993), 33; Malcolm MacLachlan and Caroline Smyth, eds., *Binge Drinking and Youth Culture: Alternative Perspectives* (Dublin: Liffey Press, 2004); Carmen Kuhling and Kieran Keohane, "Binge Drinking and Overeating: Globalisation and Insatiability," in *Cosmopolitan Ireland: Globalisation and Quality of Life*, ed. Kieran Keohane and Carmen Kuhling (Dublin: Pluto Press, 2007), 129–152; "Stricter Road Rules May Empty Ireland's Pubs," *New York Times*, February 12, 2007, http://www.nytimes.com/2007/02/12/world/europe/12ireland.html.

26. Molloy, *Story of the Irish Pub*, 87–88; Guinness, http://www.guinness.com/en-us/thestory.html; "The Guinness Irish Pub Concept," http://irishpubconcept.com/why/designs.asp; http://irishpubconcept.com/planning/; "The Pub Diaspora," *Europe*, February 1997, 44–45.

27. Nine Fine Irishmen, http://www.ninefineirishmen.com/.

28. The Irish Pub Company, http://www.irishpubcompany.com/index.htm; http://www.irishpubcompany.com/services.htm.For a discussion of the Irish pub within Irish tourism, see Mark McGovern, "The Cracked Pint Glass of the Servant: The Irish Pub, Irish Identity and the Tourist Eye," in Cronin and Connor, *Irish Tourism*, 83–103.

29. Matthew Ruben, "Suburbanization and Urban Poverty under Neoliberalism," in *The New Poverty Studies: The Ethnography of Power, Politics and Impoverished People in the United States*, ed. Judith Goode and Jeff Maskovsky (New York: NYU Press, 2001), 438.

30. "Usual Civic Fights Subside as Yonkers Hopes for $3.1 Billion Project," *New York Times*, February 27, 2006, B1; "A Monarch Rises at Ridge Hill in Yonkers," *Journal News*, December 13, 2010, 1A; "A Go in Yonkers: Developers Given Six Months to Prepare Master Renewal Plan," *Journal News*, April 6, 2006, 4B; "Trump Voices Interest in Yonkers Development," *Journal News*, May 4, 2006, 11A; Struever, Fidelco, and Cappelli, "A Bold New Future for Yonkers," http://www.sfcyonkers.com/.

31. The City of Yonkers, "Ashburton Avenue Master Plan," http://www.yonkersny.gov/Index.aspx?page=676; "New Take on Public Housing: Destroying It to Save It," *New York Times*, August 7, 2006, http://www.nytimes.com/2006/08/07/nyregion/07yonkers.html.

32. Forest City Ratner Companies, "Ridge Hill, Yonkers," http://www.ridgehill.com/index.html; "Yonkers Raceway Casino Rises to Top Earner," *New York Times*, December 17, 2006, WC2; "A Dowdy Mall Warily Awaits Its Makeover," *New York Times*, January 16, 2005, B3; Dennis R. Judd and Susan S. Fainstein, eds., *The Tourist City* (New Haven: Yale University Press, 1999).

33. John Logan and Harvey Molotch, "The City as Growth Machine," in *Urban Fortunes: The Political Economy of Place* (Berkeley: University of California Press, 1987), 50–98. Yonkers residents have raised objections to components of the city's plans for redevelopment. Some have voiced concern over the traffic and noise related to these projects, while others point to the city's troubled, underfunded public schools. Charges of corruption and mismanagement by city politicians and officials also have been raised. Nevertheless, most believe "growth" is good for Yonkers. For a fuller account of these critiques, see "Approval of Ridge Hill Nullified," *Journal News*, May 3, 2006, 1A; "Town, Two Villages Sue to Block Ridge Hill," *Journal News*, April 8, 2006, 3A; "FBI Subpoenas Records from Yonkers," *Journal News*, March 8, 2007, 1A; "Some Yonkers Residents Support Federal Probe into City Hall," *Journal News*, March 25, 2007, 5A; "State Audit Accuses Yonkers of Underfinancing Public Schools," *New York Times*, July 20, 2005, B1; "Audit Calls Yonkers Schools Archaic," *New York Times*, April 7, 2006, B3, "Audit Calls for Overhaul of Yonkers Schools' Financial System," *Journal News*, April 7, 2006, 1A.

34. Dennis R. Rudd, "Constructing the Tourist Bubble," in Judd and Fainstein, *Tourist City*, 35–53; "Anti-crime Nets 280," *Journal News*, July 15, 2005, 1B; "Neighborhoods Living in Fear," *Journal News*, September 28, 2005, 1A; "Yonkers Gets $375G to Boost Crime Fighting," *Journal News*, February 22, 2006, 8A; "Downtown Visitors Need to Feel Safe," *Journal News*, April 18, 2006, 6B; "Security Measures in Downtown Yonkers," i, May 2, 2006, 6B; "Another Crime Summer," *Journal News*, June 20, 2006, 6B; "Spittin' on the Street? Ticket!,"

Journal News, June 26, 2006, 1A; "Yonkers Mulls Teen Curfew," *Journal News*, December 21, 2006, 1A; "Yonkers Anti-gang Coalition Ponders Ban on Saggy Pants," *Journal News*, September 20, 2007, 3A; "Yonkers Police Ask Day Laborers to Move, Prompting Harassment Complaints," *Journal News*, December 28, 2006,8A; "Some Yonkers Day Laborers Support City Search for Hiring Site, Others Frustrated," *Journal News*, January 3, 2007, 3A; "Yonkers Day Laborers Arrested, Charged with Trespassing," *Journal News*, March 16, 2007, 16A. In response to this controversy, Catholic Charities established an outreach office for day laborers; see "Yonkers Day Laborers to Get Outreach Office," *Journal News*, August 8, 2009, 1A.

35. "Yonkers OK's $929 Million City-School Budget," *Journal News*, June 24, 2011,5A; "Comptroller Pans Yonkers on Debt Burden, Budget Estimates," *Journal News*, August 21, 2010, 7A; "Yonkers Council Adopts $894.1M Budget," *Journal News*, July 15, 2010, 4A; "Yonkers Bracing for an Expected 151 Layoffs," *New York Times*, December 21, 2008, WE2; "Monarch Rises at Ridge Hill in Yonkers"; "Ex-official in Yonkers Faces Charges of Corruption," *New York Times*, January 7, 2010, A26; "Three Indicted in Yonkers Vote-Selling Scam," *Journal News*, January 7, 2010, 1A; "County Raises Financial Doubts about Yonkers Redevelopment," *Journal News*, September 17, 2008, 5A; "County Again Criticizes Financing Plan forYonkers Redevelopment," *Journal News*, December 14, 2008, 5A; "Yonkers City Council Approves $1.5 Billion Downtown Redevelopment Deal," *Journal News*, October 15, 2009, 3A; "Yonkers Raceway to Pay $3.9M to City Each Year," *Journal News*, August 10, 2011, 5A; "Kimber Seeks Tax Breaks for Yonkers Site," *Journal News*, June 9, 2011, 5A; "Weapons Manufacturer to Get $700,000 Grant for Yonkers and Greenburgh Expansion," *Journal News*, December 11, 2009, 7A; "Anabi, Jereis, Convicted on All Bribe, Corruption Counts," *Journal News*, March 30, 2012, http://www.lohud.com/apps/pbcs.dll/article?AID=2012303300049.

36. "Lofts Provide a SoHo Feel in Yonkers," *New York Times*, October 9, 2005, WC10; "When Commercial Sites Get Morphed into Mini-Sohos," *New York Times*, October 9, 2005, WC5; "Making the Yonkers-Manhattan Commute by Water," *New York Times*, May 6, 2007, WC2; "Arriving on Track 1, a Reborn Yonkers Station," *New York Times*, March 28, 2004, WC3. Also see the special advertising supplement, "The Rebirth of Yonkers," *New York Times*, October 16, 2006.

37. Quoted in Kenneth T. Jackson, *Crabgrass Frontier: The Suburbanization of the United States* (New York: Oxford University Press, 1985), 244.

38. George Lipsitz, *The Possessive Investment in Whiteness: How White People Profit from Identity Politics* (Philadelphia: Temple University Press, 1998); Eric Avila, *Popular Culture in the Age of White Flight: Fear and Fantasy in Suburban Los Angeles* (Berkeley: University of California Press, 2004).

39. Dolores Hayden, "What Would a Non-sexist City Look Like? Speculations on Housing, Urban Design and Human Work," *Signs* 5, no. 3 (Spring 1980): 170–187; Lizabeth Cohen, *A Consumer's Republic: The Politics of Mass Consumption*

in Postwar America (New York: Knopf, 2003); Ray Oldenburg, *The Great Good Place: Cafes, Coffee Shops, Community Centers, Beauty Parlors, General Stores, Bars, Hangouts and How They Get You through the Day* (New York: Paragon House, 1989).

40. Congress for New Urbanism, http://www.cnu.org/; Sharon Zukin, *The Culture of Cities* (New York: Blackwell, 1995); John Hannigan, *Fantasy City: Pleasure and Profit in the Postmodern Metropolis* (New York: Routledge, 1998).

41. Jean Comaroff and John L. Comaroff, "Millennial Capitalism: First Thoughts on a Second Coming," *Public Culture* 12 no. 2 (Spring 2000): 291–343; Marilyn Halter, *Shopping for Identity: The Marketing of Ethnicity* (New York: Schocken Books, 2000); Arlene Davila, *Latinos Inc.: The Marketing and Making of a People* (Berkeley: University of California Press, 2001).

42. "Fado Irish Pubs Plan Store, Menu Updates in Expansion Push," *Nation's Restaurant News*, May 22, 2006, 182.

43. "Top 50 Growth Chains," *Restaurant Business*, July 15, 2005, 38–39; *Restaurant and Foodservice Market Research Handbook* (Loganville, GA: Richard K. Miller and Associates, 2007), 130–133. Other Irish pub chains include Ri-Ra Irish Pub and Restaurants, operating along the East Coast, and Pennsylvania-based Molly Brannigan's and Philadelphia-based McFadden's, which also operate in Baltimore and New York. Other Irish pub designers include Angela Murphy Design Associates; Irish Pub Design & Development Co.; Gemmel, Griffin, Dunbar Virtual Pub; John Duffy Design Group; Irish First; and Sonas Design. Irish pubs have received considerable attention in U.S. restaurant and travel magazines. See "Hennessy's Taverns Charm California Crowds," *Night Club & Bar Magazine*, March 1993, 16; "Trendsetters: McGuire's Pensacola," *Night Club & Bar Magazine*, January 1997, 96; "Irish Invasion," *Restaurant Hospitality*, January 1999, 56; "Coming to Your Neighborhood," *Restaurants and Institutions*, August 2000, 48; "Been There, Done That?," *Restaurants and Institutions*, November 2000, 71; "A Bit of the Emerald Isle in a Florida Backyard," *New York Times*, October 9, 2003, F10.

44. Michael Holt and Joshua Goldstein, "How 4.5 Million Irish Immigrants Became 40 Million Irish Americans: Demographic and Subjective Aspects of the Ethnic Composition of White Americans," *American Sociological Review* 59, no. 1 (February 1994): 64–82.

45. Bennigan's Grill and Tavern, http://www.bennigan's.com/; "Guinness on the Piazza: Irish Theme Pubs," *Financial Times* (London), September 29, 1997, 15.

46. Nine Fine Irishmen, http://irishpubconcept.com/why/press.asp. The company's emphasis on hiring an Irish staff is not without controversy. In 1999, three waitresses filed a claim against the Hilton Hotel Corporation for being edged out of their jobs by management's decision to recruit an Irish staff for its Irish-themed bar. "Hotels Demand for Irish Only Staff Leads to Suit by 3 Boston Waitresses," *Houston Chronicle*, June 18, 1999, 6; "Irish Theme Bar Hit with Bias Complaint," *Chicago Tribune*, June 18, 1999, 24.

47. Scholars have understood the quest for authenticity as a cultural construct of the Western modern world.See Dean MacCannell, *The Tourist: A New Theory of the Leisure Class* (New York: Schocken Books, 1976); Richard Handler, "Authenticity," *Anthropology Today* 1, no. 2 (February 1986): 2–4; Vincent J. Cheng, *Inauthentic: The Anxiety over Culture and Identity* (New Brunswick, NJ: Rutgers University Press, 2004); David Harvey, *Spaces of Capital: Towards a Critical Geography* (New York: Blackwell, 2001); "Fado's Irish Stew: A Huge Serving of Décor," *Washington Post*, June 12, 1998, N8; "Drinking Problems: Soft Focus History in the Irish Theme Pub," *Left Curve*, December 31, 2000, 50; "Ireland's Crack Habit: Explaining the Faux Irish Pub Revolution," *Slate*, March 16, 2006, http://www.slate.com/default.aspx?id=3944&qt=faux+irish+pub; Kymberly Helbig Porter, "Being Irish: The Market, Transnationalism and the Experience of Ethnicity" (PhD diss., University of Pennsylvania, 2002); Caroline K. Lego, Natalie T. Wodo, Stephanie L. McFee, and Michael R. Solomon, "A Thirst for the Real Thing in Themed Retail Environments: Consuming Authenticity in Irish Pubs," *Journal of Foodservice Business* 5, no. 2 (2002): 61–74.

48. Louis Wirth, "Urbanism as a Way of Life," *American Journal of Sociology* 44 (1938): 1–24; Fado Irish Pubs, http://www.fadoirishpub.com/austin/irish-pub-experience; Raglan Road Irish Pub, http://www.raglanroadirishpub.com/; B. Joseph Pine and James H. Gilmore, *The Experience Economy: Work Is Theatre and Every Business a Stage* (Cambridge: Harvard Business School Press, 1999).

49. Hamilton Carroll, *Affirmative Reaction: New Formations of White Masculinity* (Durham, NC: Duke University Press, 2011).

50. Sharon Salinger, *Taverns and Drinking in Early America* (Baltimore: Johns Hopkins University Press, 2002); Eric Burns, *The Spirits of America: A Social History of Alcohol* (Philadelphia: Temple University Press, 2003); Jack Blocker, "Kaleidoscope in Motion: Drinking in the United States, 1400–2000," in *Alcohol: A Social and Cultural History*, ed. Mack P. Holt (New York: Berg, 2006), 227; Mark Edward Lender and James Kirby Martin, *Drinking in America: A History* (New York: Free Press, 1987), 46; Roy Rosenzweig, *Eight Hours for What We Will: Workers and Leisure in an Industrial City, 1870–1920* (Cambridge: Cambridge University Press, 1983), 40–44; Diner, *Hungering for America*, 133–134.

51. Madelon Powers, *Faces along the Bar: Lore and Order in the Workingman's Saloon, 1870–1920* (Chicago: University of Chicago Press, 1998), 8.

52. Perry Duis, *The Saloon: Public Drinking in Chicago and Boston, 1880–1920* (Urbana: University of Chicago Press, 1983), 127–140, 176–181.

53. Diner, *Hungering for America*, 134, 140–141; Duis, *Saloon*, 153.

54. John Rumbarger, *Profits, Power and Prohibition: Alcohol Reform and the Industrializing of America, 1800–1930* (Albany: State University of New York Press, 1989); Jack S. Blocker Jr., *American Temperance Movements: Cycles of Reform* (Boston: Twayne, 1989); Edward Behr, *Prohibition: Thirteen Years That Changed America* (New York: Arcade, 1996); Catherine Murdock, *Domesticating Drink: Women, Men and Alcohol in America, 1870–1940* (Baltimore: Johns Hopkins University

Press, 1998); Thomas Pegram, *Battling Demon Rum: The Struggle for a Dry America, 1800–1933* (Chicago: Ivan R. Dee, 1998), Elaine Franz Parsons, *Manhood Lost: Fallen Drunkards and Redeeming Women in the Nineteenth-Century United States* (Baltimore: Johns Hopkins University Press, 2003).

55. Lori Rotskoff, *Love on the Rocks: Men, Women and Alcohol in Post–World War II America* (Chapel Hill: University of North Carolina Press, 2002).

56. Madelon Powers, "Doom from Within: The Inevitable Doom of the American Saloon," in *Drinking: Behavior and Belief in Modern History*, ed. Susanna Barrows and Robin Room (Berkeley: University of California Press, 1991), 112–131.

57. "Too, Too, Too Many Empty Bar Stools," *New York Times*, August 1, 2004, CY 9; "Last Call for the Home of the Dollar Drink," *New York Times*, July 11, 2004, CY 5; "Kiss them 'Bye: Storied Blarney Stones Are Drying Up," *New York Post*, March 15, 2006, 43; Dick Moore, "A Tavern Trip," *Yonkers Historical Society Newsletter*, Summer 1993, 5.

58. Mary P. Corcoran, *Irish Illegals: Transients between Two Societies* (Westport, CT: Greenwood University Press, 1993), 91; "There's the Irish Bar and Then There's the Irish Bar," *New York Times*, March 17, 2002, B8.

59. Linda Dowling Almeida, *Irish Immigrants in New York City* (Indianapolis: Indiana University Press, 2001), 81.

60. Corcoran, *Irish Illegals*, 92.

61. "Seven Arrested in Parking Lot Melee," *Journal News*, December 3, 1991, 6A; "Irish Immigrants Accuse Police of Savage Attack," *Journal News*, December 7, 1991, 5A; "Seven Accuse Police of Bias in Assault," *New York Times*, December 8, 1991, B1; "Bloodied and Beaten: A Nightmare in Yonkers," *Irish Voice*, December 17, 1991, 1; "Police Brutality," *Irish Echo*, December 17, 1991, 5–6; "Irish Immigrants Cleared of Assault Charges," *Journal News*, September 2, 1992, 5A; "2 Officers Indicted in 1991 Beating," *Journal News*, May 7, 1993, 5A; "2 Yonkers Officers Accused of Beating a Woman and 2 Men," *New York Times*, May 7, 1993, B5; "Irish Family Describes Anger over Beating," *New York Times*, May 8, 1993, B26; "2 Men Tell of Injuries in Police Assault Case," *New York Times*, December 21, 1993, B5; "Yonkers Cop: I Was Fighting for My Life," *Herald Statesman*, December 28, 1993, 13A; "Jury Still Weighing Beating Claims," *Herald Statesman*, December 29, 1993, 14A; "Yonkers Officer Denies a Side Trip for Beating," *New York Times*, December 28, 1993, B5.

62. "After Fistfight, Yonkers Officers Invented Tale of Black Assailant," *New York Times*, April 24, 1993, B1; "Police Review Panel for Yonkers," *New York Times*, October 3, 1990, B4; "Yonkers Police Commissioner Is Injured in Car Bombing," *New York Times*, November 4, 1992, B17; "Police Chief Returns to Work after Being Hurt in Car Bombing," *New York Times*, November 7, 1992, B1; *United States v. Nickels et al.*, 18 F. 242 (S.D.N.Y., 1993).

63. Ronald Weitzer, *Policing under Fire: Ethnic Conflict and Police-Community Relations in Northern Ireland* (Albany: State University of New York Press, 1995); Joanne Wright, *Policing and Conflict in Northern Ireland* (Hampshire:

Macmillan, 2000); Graham Ellison, *The Crowned Harp: Policing Northern Ireland* (London: Pluto Press, 2000). Police reform in Northern Ireland, however, has been one of the provisions of the 1998 Good Friday Peace Agreement.

64. "2 Yonkers Cops Cleared of Charges," *Journal News*, December 30, 1993, 4A; "Bitter Tale Nears End," *Daily News*, September 7, 1991, 29; "Yonkers Spends $700,000 to Settle Police Assault Suit," *New York Times*, May 15, 1998, B9.

65. "A Lively Public House in Yonkers," *New York Times*, May 11, 1997, WC13.

66. "Braveheart of Yonkers," *New York Times*, July 30, 2000, WC1.

67. "Neighbors Toast Board for Bar Moratorium," *Herald Statesman*, March 30, 1996, 3A.

68. "Irish Charged in Yonkers Fracas," *Irish Echo*, January 17, 1996, 1; "Irish Trio Charged in Brawl with Yonkers Police, Brutality Allegations Rise Again," *Irish Voice*, January 17, 1996, 3; "Irish Men Face Assault Charges in New York," *Irish Times*, July 30, 1997, 4; "Irishmen Accept US Plea Bargain," *Irish Times*, August 6, 1997, 4.

69. "Yonkers Refuses to Give Details on Police Misconduct," *Journal News*, July 17, 2006, 6A; "Silence in Yonkers," *Journal News*, July 18, 2006, 6B; "Yonkers Police Tactics on Radar," *Journal News*, August 22, 2006, A5; "Department of Justice to Investigate Yonkers Police," *Journal News*, August 30, 2007, 1A; "As Feds Begin Probe, Yonkers Police Face Spate of Brutality Suits," *Journal News*, August 31, 2007, 1A; "Federal Investigation Clears Yonkers Police," *Journal News*, June 20, 2009, 1A.

70. "Many Bars Not Smoke Free," *Irish Voice*, April 8, 2003, 8; "Smoke Ban Defied in the Bronx," *Irish Voice*, April 29, 2003, 6.

71. Linda Dowling Almeida has referred to the 1980s Irish as the "new" Irish; see Almeida, *Irish Immigrants in New York City*; "Dublin on the Thruway," *New York Times*, August 25, 2002, WC1. Also see "Irish on the Move: Migration to Suburbs an Established Pattern," *Irish Echo*, July 7, 2004, 3.

72. Mary P. Corcoran, "The Process of Migration and the Reinvention of Self: The Experience of Returning Irish Emigrants," *Eire-Ireland* 37, nos. 1–2 (Spring–Summer 2002): 175–191. Between 1995 and 2004, approximately 26,700 people left the United States for Ireland. Mac Einri, "Immigration," 238; Deirdre Conlon, "'Germs' in the Heart of the Other: Emigrant Scripts, the Celtic Tiger and the Lived Realities of Return," in *The Legacy of Ireland's Economic Expansion: Geographies of the Celtic Tiger*, ed. Peadar Kirby and Padraig Carmody (London: Routledge, 2010), 98–114.

73. "Yonkers Tavern Avoids Shutdown," *Irish Echo*, December 1, 2004, 5; "Community Rallies for Rory Dolan's," *Irish Echo*, January 26, 2005, 8.

74. Sara Brady has referred to more recent Irish arrivals as the "newer" Irish, in "Newer Irish in New York: Technology and the Experience of Immigration," *Foilsiu* 1, no. 1 (Spring 2001): 95–106; Bartley and Kitchin, "Ireland in the Twenty-First Century," 1–26; Mac Einri, "Immigration," 236–248; Feargal Cochrane, *The End of Irish America? Globalisation and the Irish Diaspora*

(Dublin: Irish Academic Press, 2010); "Immigrants Prone to Alcoholism, Suicide, Depression," *Journal News*, July 17, 2005, 1B; "Driver's Licenses State by State," *Irish Voice*, December 1, 2004, 8; "Checkmate," *Irish Voice*, August 24, 2004, 1; "Back Home in Ireland, Greener Pastures: Immigrants Reverse Their Trek as American Dreams Fade," *New York Times*, November 10, 2004, B1; "Giving Up on America," *Irish Voice*, May 19, 2004, 6; "Are the Irish Leaving NYC for Good?," *Irish Voice*, December 15, 2004, 12.

75. "Man Stabs Officer and Is Killed by Another in Yonkers," *New York Times*, January 5, 2006, B1; "Off-Duty Officer Cleared," *New York Times*, April 27, 2006, B4.

NOTES TO CHAPTER 4

1. Although I have lived in southeast Yonkers for much of my life, I participated in its St. Patrick's Day parade and postparade festivities for the first time in 2007. In addition to extended taped interviews with my informants, I compiled the account that follows from my field notes for 2007 and return visits during the 2008 and 2010 St. Patrick's Day season.

2. An Irish coffee usually contains coffee, Irish whiskey and whipped cream.

3. It is believed that St. Patrick explained the mystery of the Holy Trinity to the pagan Irish with the three leaves of the shamrock. The shamrock became a political symbol in Ireland by the end of the eighteenth century. See Ewan Morris, *Our Own Devices: National Symbols and Political Conflict in Twentieth Century Ireland* (Dublin: Irish Academic Press, 2005).

4. The ILIR was established in 2005 to lobby for comprehensive immigration reform and change the legal status of the 50,000 undocumented Irish immigrants thought to be living in the United States. The organization is discussed at greater length in chapter 6.

5. This song is quite popular around St. Patrick's Day. However, one bar owner in New York City, frustrated by drunken renditions of the tune, has decided to ban it. "Oh Danny Boy—Shut Up!," *Irish Voice*, March 12, 2008, http://www.irishcentral.com/news/Oh-Danny-Boy—-Shut-Up_-1256.html.

6. Mary P. Ryan, *Civic Wars: Democracy and Public Life in the American City during the Nineteenth Century* (Berkeley: University of California Press, 1997), 55, 72–73; Mike Cronin and Daryl Adair, *Wearing of the Green: A History of St. Patrick's Day* (New York: Routledge, 2002), 10, 17, 37, 72.

7. Kenneth Moss, "St. Patrick's Day Celebrations and the Formation of Irish-American Identity, 1845–1875," *Journal of Social History* 29, no. 1 (Fall 1995): 125–148; Sallie A. Marston, "Public Rituals and Community Power: St. Patrick's Day Parades in Lowell, Massachusetts, 1841–1874," *Political Geography Quarterly* 8, no. 3 (July 1989): 255–269; Jane Gladden Kelton, "New York City's St. Patrick's Day Parade: Invention of Contention and Consensus," *TDR: The Drama Review* 29, no. 3 (Autumn 1995): 93–105; Ryan, *Civic Wars*, 72, 79–81, 83; Cronin and Adair, *Wearing of the Green*, 34–37.

8. Timothy J. Meagher, "Why Should We Care for a Little Trouble or a Walk through the Mud: St. Patrick's and Columbus Day Parades in Worcester, Massachusetts, 1845–1915," *New England Quarterly* 58, no. 1 (March 1985): 5–26; Cronin and Adair, *Wearing of the Green*, 26.

9. Ryan, *Civic Wars*, 202, 229–234; Cronin and Adair, *Wearing of the Green*, 72–73, 156, 164–167, 170, 232.

10. Program for St. Patrick's Day parade, 2007, prepared by the Yonkers St. Patrick's Day parade committee.

11. Morris, *Our Own Devices*.

12. "Seeing Green Despite the Cold," *Journal News*, March 5, 2007, 1B; "Kicking Off the Irish Season," *Journal News*, March 3, 2008, 1B; "Irish Tradition Alive in Yonkers," *Journal News*, March 7, 2010, 3A.

13. Adam Nossiter, "Jamaican Way Station in the Bronx: Community of Striving Immigrants Fosters Middle-Class Values," *New York Times*, October 25, 1995, http://www.nytimes.com/1995/10/25/nyregion/jamaican-way-station-bronx-community-striving-immigrants-fosters-middle-class.html.

14. Wahneema Lubiano, "Black Ladies, Welfare Queens, and State Minstrels: Ideological War by Narrative Means," in *Race-ing Justice, En-gendering Power: Essays on Anita Hill, Clarence Thomas and the Construction of Social Reality*, ed. Toni Morrison (New York: Pantheon, 1992), 323–363.

15. Jay P. Dolan, "A New Catholicism," in *The American Catholic Experience: A History from Colonial Times to the Present* (South Bend, IN: University of Notre Dame Press, 1992), 421–454.

16. Eduardo Bonilla-Silva, *Racism without Racists: Color-Blind Racism and the Persistence of Racial Inequality in America*, 3rd ed. (New York: Rowman and Littlefield, 2009).

17. This is not unique to contemporary Irish American culture. See, for example, Yen Le Espiritu, *Home Bound: Filipino American Lives across Cultures, Communities and Countries* (Berkeley: University of California Press, 2003).

18. In 2006, the Yonkers Puerto Rican Day parade added Hispanic to its title. It is now called the Yonkers Puerto Rican/Hispanic Day parade.

19. The Wolfe Tones emerged as part of the rise of modern folk music during the 1960s. Their contemporaries in Ireland include the Clancy Brothers and Tommy Maken, who became popular during the 1960s and 1970s. Their name comes from Wolfe Tone, an early eighteenth-century Irish rebel.

20. Jane H. Hill, *The Everyday Language of White Racism* (Malden, MA: Wiley-Blackwell, 2008).

21. Finola Kennedy, *Cottage to Crèche: Family Change in Ireland* (Dublin: Institute of Public Administration, 2001); James M. Smith, *Ireland's Magdalen Laundries and the Nation's Architecture of Containment* (Notre Dame, IN: University of Notre Dame Press, 2007); Moira Maguire, *Precarious Childhood in Post-independence Ireland* (Manchester: Manchester University Press, 2009).

22. Tom Inglis, *Moral Monopoly: The Rise and Fall of the Catholic Church in Modern Ireland*, 2nd ed. (Dublin: University College Dublin Press, 1998); Louise Fuller, *Irish Catholicism since 1950: The Undoing of a Culture* (Dublin: Gill and Macmillan, 2002).

NOTES TO CHAPTER 5

1. Mary P. Corcoran, *Irish Illegals: Transients between Societies* (Westport, CT: Greenwood Press, 1993); Linda Dowling Almeida, *Irish Immigrants in New York City* (Indianapolis: Indiana University Press, 2001).
2. Sara Brady, "Newer Irish in New York: Technology and the Experience of Immigration," *Foilsiu* 1, no. 1 (Spring 2001): 95–106; Brendan Bartley and Rob Kitchin, "Ireland in the Twenty-First Century," in *Understanding Contemporary Ireland*, ed. Brendan Bartley and Rob Kitchin (Dublin: Pluto Press, 2007), 1–26; Piaras Mac Einri, "Immigration: Labour Migrants, Asylum Seekers and Refugees," in Bartley and Kitchin, *Understanding Contemporary Ireland*, 236–248.
3. Michael Dahan and Gabriel Sheffer, "Ethnic Groups and Distance Shrinking Technologies," *Nationalism and Ethnic Politics* 7, no. 1 (Spring 2001): 85–107.
4. Lisa Lowe, *Immigrant Acts: On Asian American Cultural Politics* (Durham, NC: Duke University Press, 1996)
5. Wahneema Lubiano, "Black Ladies, Welfare Queens, and State Minstrels: Ideological War by Narrative Means," in *Race-ing Justice, En-gendering Power: Essays on Anita Hill, Clarence Thomas and the Construction of Social Reality*, ed. Toni Morrison (New York: Pantheon, 1992), 323–363; Eduardo Bonilla-Silva, *Racism without Racists: Color-Blind Racism and the Persistence of Racial Inequality in America*, 3rd ed. (New York: Rowman and Littlefield, 2009).
6. "Immigrants Prone to Alcoholism, Suicide, Depression," *Journal News*, July 7, 2005, 1B; "Suicide and Depression Major Problems for Young Irish in New York," *Irish Voice*, October 17, 2012, http://www.irishcentral.com/news/Suicide-and-depression-major-problems-for-young-Irish-in-New-York-174548571.html; Lisa Newton, *Illegal, Alien or Immigrant: The Politics of Immigration Reform* (New York: NYU Press, 2008), 152.
7. Jacob Riis, *Children of the Poor* (1892; reprint, New York: Arno Press, 1971); "In Alabama a Harsh Bill for Residents Here Illegally," *New York Times*, June 3, 2001, A10; "Birthright Citizenship Looms as Next Immigration Battle," *New York Times*, January 5, 2011, A1.
8. Pierrette Hondagneu-Soleto, *Domestica: Immigrant Workers Cleaning and Caring in the Shadows of Affluence* (Berkeley: University of California Press, 2001).
9. Carola Suárez-Orozco, Hirokazu Yoshikawa, Robert T. Teranishi, and Marcelo M. Suárez-Orozco, "Growing Up in the Shadows: The Developmental Implications of Unauthorized States," *Harvard Educational Review* 81, no. 3 (September 2011): 438–473.

10. Louise Cainkar, "Thinking Outside the Box: Arabs and Race in the United States," in *Race and Arab Americans before and after 9/11: From Invisible Citizens to Visible Subjects*, ed. Amaney Jamal and Nadine Naber (Syracuse, NY: Syracuse University Press, 2008), 46–80.

11. "Report Details Abuse in Irish Reformatories," *New York Times*, May 21, 2009, A1; "Report Says Irish Bishops and Police Hid Abuse," *New York Times*, November 27, 2009, A10; "Irish Rupture with the Vatican Sets Off a Transformation," *New York Times*, September 18, 2011, A8.

12. David Roediger, *The Wages of Whiteness: Race and the Making of the Working Class*, 2nd ed. (New York: Verso, 1999).

13. Philip Kretsedemas, "Concerned Citizens, Local Exclusions: Local Immigration Laws and the Legacy of Jim Crow," in *The Immigration Crucible: Transforming Race, Nation and the Limits of the Law* (New York: Columbia University Press, 2012), 73–103; Arlene Davila, *Latino Spin: Public Image and the Whitewashing of Race* (New York: NYU Press, 2008).

14. Shellee Colen, "Like a Mother to Them: Stratified Reproduction and West Indian Childcare Workers and Employers in New York," in *Conceiving the New World Order: The Global Politics of Reproduction*, ed. Faye Ginsburg and Rayna Rapp (Berkeley: University of California Press, 1995), 78–102.

15. While undocumented Irish immigrants may eschew more conventional heterosexual conventions like marriage, they do not disregard heterosexuality. Anne Maguire addressed the difficulty of being both Irish and gay in New York City. See Maguire, *Rock the Sham: The Irish Lesbian and Gay Organization's Battle to March in New York's St. Patrick's Day Parade* (New York: Street Level Press, 2006).

16. James R. Barrett and David Roediger, "Inbetween Peoples: Race, Nationality and the 'New Immigrant' Working Class," *Journal of American Ethnic History* 16, no. 3 (Spring 1997): 3–44.

NOTES TO CHAPTER 6

1. "States Resisting Program Central to Obama's Immigration Strategy," *New York Times*, May 6, 2011, A18; "Immigration Program Is Rejected by Third State," *New York Times*, June 7, 2011, A13.

2. Philip Kretsedemas, "Immigration Enforcement and the Complication of National Sovereignty: Understanding Local Enforcement as an Exercise in Neoliberal Governance," *American Quarterly* 60, no. 3 (September 2008): 553–573; Kretsedemas, *The Immigration Crucible: Transforming Race, Nation and the Limits of the Law* (New York: Columbia University Press, 2012), 23–24; "Birthright Citizenship Looms as Next Immigration Battle," *New York Times*, January 5, 2011, A1; "Arizona Lawmakers Push New Round of Immigration Restrictions," *New York Times*, February 24, 2010, A16; "In Alabama, a Harsh Bill for Residents Here Illegally," *New York Times*, June 4, 2011, A10; "Latinos and Democrats Press

Obama to Curb Deportations," *New York Times*, April 20, 2011, A18; "Obama to Permit Young Migrants to Remain in the U.S.," *New York Times*, June 16, 2012, A1; "Court Splits Immigration Law Verdicts; Upholds Hotly Debated Centerpiece, 8–0," *New York Times*, June 26, 2012, A1; "Appeals Court Draws Boundaries on Alabama's Immigration Law," *New York Times*, August 22, 2012, A19.

3. Bill Ong Hing, *Defining America through Immigration Policy* (Philadelphia: Temple University Press, 2004), 43–48; Daniel Kanstroom, *Deportation Nation: Outsiders in American History* (Cambridge: Cambridge University Press, 2007), 104–118; Eithne Luibhéid, *Entry Denied: Controlling Sexuality at the Border* (Minneapolis: University of Minnesota Press, 2002), 3–5; Kevin R. Johnson, *The Huddled Masses Myth: Immigration and Civil Rights* (Philadelphia: Temple University Press, 2004), 134; Patrick Ettinger, *Imaginary Lines: Border Enforcement and the Origins of Undocumented Immigration, 1882–1930* (Austin: University of Texas Press, 2009), 69–71.

4. Elazar Barkan, *The Retreat of Scientific Racism: Changing Concepts of Race in Britain and the United States between the World Wars* (New York: Cambridge University Press, 1992), 199–200; Peter Schrag, *Not Fit for Our Society: Immigration and Nativism in America* (Berkeley: University of California Press, 2010), 96–98; Michael O'Brien, "A Hidden Phase of American History," in *Repeal the National Origins Act of 1924* (New York: American Irish Historical Society, 1928).

5. Edward F. McSweeney, "The National Origins Myth," in *Repeal the National Origins Act of 1924*; Lynn Dumeneil, "The Tribal Twenties: Assimilated Catholics Response to Anti-Catholicism in the 1920s," *Journal of American Ethnic History* 11, no. 1 (Fall 1991): 21–49; Jeanne Petit, "Our Immigrant Coreligionists: The National Catholic Welfare Conference as an Advocate for Immigrants in the 1920s," in *Immigrant Rights in the Shadows of Citizenship*, ed. Rachel Ida Buff (New York: NYU Press, 2008), 315–328.

6. *National Origins Provision, Immigration Act of 1924: Hearings before the House Committee on Immigration and Naturalization*, 69th Cong., 2nd sess. (1927) (statement of Joseph Carey, president of the American Irish Republican League); Petit, "Immigrant Coreligionists"; Roger Daniels, *Coming to America: A History of Immigration and Ethnicity in American Life*, 2nd ed. (New York: Perennial, 2002), 51–59; Mae Ngai, *Impossible Subjects: Illegal Aliens and the Making of Modern America* (Princeton: Princeton University Press, 2005).

7. Daniels, *Coming to America*, 61–64; Matthew J. O'Brien, "Transatlantic Connections and the Sharp Edge of the Great Depression," in *New Directions in Irish American History*, ed. Kevin Kenny (Madison: University of Wisconsin Press, 2003), 78–98; Francisco E. Balderrama and Raymond Rodriguez, *Decade of Betrayal: Mexican Repatriation in the 1930s* (Albuquerque: University of New Mexico Press, 2006).

8. Rachel Ida Buff, *Immigration and the Political Economy of Home: West Indian Brooklyn and Indian Minneapolis, 1945–1992* (Berkeley: University of California

Press, 2001), 48–59; Ngai, *Impossible Subjects,* 238; Hing, *Defining America through Immigration Policy,* 76, 82–83.

9. Daniel J. Tichenor, *Dividing Lines: The Politics of Immigration Control in America* (Princeton: Princeton University Press, 2002), 214–216; quoted in Hing, *Defining America through Immigration Policy,* 94–96; Daniels, *Coming to America,* 343.

10. Andrew Wilson, *Irish-America and the Ulster Conflict, 1968–1995* (Washington, DC: Catholic University of America Press, 1995); Patrick Hennesey, "American Irish Immigration Committee," in *Irish American Voluntary Organizations,* ed. Michael Funchion (Westport, CT: Greenwood Press, 1983), 43–46.

11. *Hearings before Subcommittee No. 1 of the Committee on the Judiciary House of Representatives,* 1968, Archives of Irish America Vertical File Collection, AIA.013, Box 2, American Irish Immigration Center Folder, Archives of Irish America, Tamiment Library, New York University.

12. Ibid.; Tichenor, *Dividing Lines,* 235; Mary E. Daly, *The Slow Failure: Population Decline and Independent Ireland 1920–1973* (Madison: University of Wisconsin Press, 2006), 33–39, 159–160.

13. Ngai, *Impossible Subjects*; Ettinger, *Imaginary Lines.*

14. Lisa Newton, *Illegal, Alien or Immigrant: The Politics of Immigration Reform* (New York: NYU Press, 2008), 148.

15. Schrag, *Not Fit for Our Society,* 166; Newton, *Illegal, Alien or Immigrant,* 4–5.

16. Linda Dowling Almeida, *Irish Immigrants in New York City* (Indianapolis: Indiana University Press, 2001).

17. Ray O'Hanlon, *The New Irish Americans* (Niwot, CO: Roberts Rinehart, 1998), 62–63.

18. A. P. Lobo and J. J. Salvo, "Resurgent Irish Immigration to the US in the 1980's and 1990's: A Socio-demographic Profile," *International Migration* 36, no. 2 (1998): 262; Roger Daniels, *Guarding the Golden Door: American Immigration Policy and Immigrants since 1882* (New York: Hill and Wang, 2004), 230–231, 238.

19. "No More Tourist Visas for the Irish," *Irish Voice,* October 18, 2004, 3, http://irishvoice.com/; U.S. Department of State, "Visa Waiver Program," http://travel.state.gov/visa/temp/without/without_1990.html#countries.

20. O'Hanlon, *New Irish Americans,* 108.

21. Ibid., 36.

22. Almeida, *Irish Immigrants in New York City,* 76.

23. O'Hanlon, *New Irish Americans,* 110.

24. Almeida, *Irish Immigrants in New York City,* 73.

25. O'Hanlon, *New Irish Americans,* 99.

26. Informational pamphlet, date unknown, Irish Immigration Reform Movement Records (IIRMR), AIA 016, Box 1, Folder 3, Archives of Irish America, Tamiment Library, New York University; Statement of the IIRM, *Hearings before the Subcommittee on Immigration and Refugee Affairs,* U.S. Senate, October 23, 1987, IIRMR; AIA 016, Box 8, Folder 6.

27. Hing, *Defining America through Immigration Policy*, 253–255, 184–190; Daniels, *Guarding the Golden Door*, 246; Newton, *Illegal, Alien or Immigrant*, 144–160.

28. The Republic of Ireland received 213 of these visas in 2012. U.S. Department of State, "Diversity Visa Lottery 2012 (DV-2012) Results," http://travel.state.gov/visa/immigrants/types/types_5561.html.

29. "Giving Up on America," *Irish Voice*, May 19, 2004, 6; "Are the Irish Leaving NYC for Good?," *Irish Voice*, December 15, 2004, 12; "In New York, the Irish Pack It In," *New York Times*, March 8, 2006, A6.

30. "A Mother's Wish for Her Children," *Irish Voice*, February 1, 2006, 11; "Some Mother's Daughter Waits," *Irish Voice*, March 15, 2006, 12; "A Snapshot of Lost Lives," *Irish Voice*, February 8, 2006, 10; "A Life Undocumented: Part One," *Irish Voice*, June 8, 2005, 10; "A Life Undocumented: Part Two," *Irish Voice*, June 22, 2005, 11; "A Life Undocumented: Part Three," *Irish Voice*, July 6, 2005, 8; Pat Sullivan, letter, "Don't Favor Illegals," *Irish Voice*, June 4, 2003, 13; E. Maloney, letter, "Undocumented Must Face the Music," *Irish Echo*, January 28, 2004, 15; Helen McClafferty, letter, "Keep America American," *Irish Voice*, April 21, 2004, 15; Jerry Hoosier, letter, "Keep Illegals Out," *Irish Voice*, December 1, 2004, 15; Catroina Lynch, letter, "Illegals Are Law Breakers," *Irish Voice*, December 15, 2004, 15; "Green Card Scammer Hits Irish," *Irish Voice*, October 12, 2005, 6; "Owad Faces Scam Charges," *Irish Voice*, November 16, 2006, 6; "Scam Queen Duped Hundreds of Irish," *Irish Voice*, January 25, 2006, 3.

31. "Major Immigration Surgery," *New York Times*, May 20, 2005, http://www.nytimes.com/2005/05/20/opinion/20fri2.html; "Bill on Illegal-Immigrant Aid Draws Fire," *New York Times*, December 30, 2005, http://www.nytimes.com/2005/12/30/politics/30immig.html.

32. "New Immigration Scam Dupes Irish," *Irish Voice*, May 9, 2007, 13; "Immigration Busts Irish Smuggling Ring," *Irish Voice*, May 10, 2006, 3; "Rumors Worry Yonkers Irish," *Journal News*, May 9, 2006, A1; "Canadian Borders Offer Irish Access," *Journal News*, June 14, 2006, A1.

33. "An Irish Face on the Cause of Citizenship," *New York Times*, March 16, 2006, http://www.nytimes.com/2006/03/16/nyregion/16irish.html.

34. "Niall O'Dowd Responds," *Irish Voice*, January 3, 2007, 13.

35. Anonymous, "Untitled," *Voices from the Irish Lobby for Immigration Reform*, November 16, 2006, https://www.blogger.com/comment.g?blogID=19954943&postID=116365684675175076; Anonymous, "Excerpt from the Hypocritical Anti-immigrant Argument by Robert Nix," *Voices from the Irish Lobby for Immigration Reform*, December 7, 2006, https://www.blogger.com/comment.g?blogID=19954943&postID=116360304921542735.

36. These are the four provinces of Ireland.

37. The Cray and Dempsey Experience, "We're Irish and We're Rockin'," http://www.crayanddempsey.com/irishandrockin.htm.

38. At the time, there was an increasing emphasis on military service as a viable path to citizenship. The Dream Act, for example, proposed a path to citizenship

for young undocumented immigrants based on military service, but it failed to pass by December 2010." Uncle Sam Wants You. But He Needs to Adapt," *New York Times*, September 20, 2007, A2; "How Not to Recruit a Military," *Washington Post*, November 7, 2006, A20; "In Increments, Senate Revisits Immigration Bill," *New York Times*, August 3, 2007, A1; "Pass the Dream Act," *New York Times*, September 20, 2007, A22; "Senate Blocks Bill for Young Illegal Immigrants," *New York Times*, December 18, 2010, http://www.nytimes.com/2010/12/19/us/politics/19immig.html.

39. "A Call to Action," *Irish Voice*, March 14, 2007, 28.

40. "American Dreams, Foreign Flags," *New York Times*, March 30, 2006, A25; "Across the U.S. Protests for Immigrants Draw Thousands," *New York Times*, April 10, 2006, A14; "Immigrant Rallies in Scores of Cities for Legal Status," *New York Times*, April 11, 2006, http://www.nytimes.com/2006/04/11/us/11immig. html; "Eclectic Crowd Joins a Call for the Rights of Immigrants," *New York Times*, April 11, 2006, http://www.nytimes.com/2006/04/11/nyregion/11rally. html.

41. "McCain Calls for Path to Citizenship," *Journal News*, April 1, 2006, A1.

42. Lawrence Downes, "How Green Was My Rally," *New York Times*, December 10, 2006, http://www.nytimes.com/2006/12/10/opinion/10sun3.html; Niall O'Dowd's response, "How Green Is Our Lobby," *Irish Voice*, December 13, 1006, 14.

43. Patrick Hurley, "ILIR Is Blowing the Green Card Game for the Irish," *The Blanket: A Journal of Protest and Dissent*, August 11, 2006, http://indiamond6.ulib. iupui.edu:81/PH1308068g.html; "A Nutcase on Immigration," *Irish Voice*, August 16, 2006, 12.

44. Timothy Taylor, letter, "Stop McCain/Kennedy," *Irish Voice*, March 1, 2006, 19; James Gill, letter, "Come Here Legally," *Irish Voice*, April 26, 2006, 17; Mary O'Connor, letter, "Irish Not Special," *Irish Voice*, May 3, 2006, 15; Robert Morgan, letter, "A Nation of Laws," *Irish Voice*, May 17, 2006, 15; Jerry Hoosier, letter, "They're Illegal Senator," *Irish Voice*, May 17, 2006, 15; Tom Carew, letter, "No Rights for Illegals," *Irish Voice*, May 10, 2006, 19; Frank Stabler, letter, "Keeping It Legal," *Irish Voice*, May 24, 2006, 17; Bryan McMahon, letter, "Sick of Sobbing," *Irish Voice*, June 7, 2006, 17; Tom Mannix, letter, "Illegals Go Home," *Irish Voice*, January 24, 2007, 15.

45. "Irish Make Their Presence Felt in Fight over Illegal Immigration," *San Francisco Chronicle*, February 9, 2007, http://www.sfgate.com/cgi-bin/article. cgi?f=/c/a/2007/02/09/BAG7DO1K5D1.DTL

46. "The ILIR Looks towards Plan B," *Irish Voice*, July 4, 2007, 6; "Ahern Vows Support for Visas," *Irish Voice*, October 3, 2007, 3.

47. "Spitzer Dropping His Driver's License Plan," *New York Times*, November 14, 2007, http://www.nytimes.com/2007/11/14/nyregion/14spitzer.html.

48. Kretsedemas, *Immigration Crucible*, 94; "Nightmare for Jailed Activist," *Irish Voice*, October 10, 2007, 3; Anthony Hillick, letter, "Yep, It's America," *Irish*

Voice, October 17, 2007, 17; Deirdre Sheridan, letter, "He's No Martyr," *Irish Voice*, October 17, 2007, 17; Jim Lang, letter, "Overstaying Is a Crime," *Irish Voice*, October 17, 2007, 17; Daniel J. Murrow, letter, "Immigration Hypocrisy," *Irish Voice*, October 24, 2007, 15; A. P. O'Maille, letter, "The Immigration Debacle," *Irish Voice*, October 24, 2007, 15.

49. "Quid Pro Quo: Shannon Deal Should Lead to Visa Deal," *Irish Echo*, January 2, 2008, 1.

50. Brendan Bartley and Rob Kitchin, "Ireland in the Twenty-First Century," in *Understanding Contemporary Ireland*, ed. Brendan Bartley and Rob Kitchin (Dublin: Pluto Press, 2007), 15; Piaras Mac Einri, "Immigration: Labour Migrants, Asylum Seekers and Refugees," in Bartley and Kitchin, *Understanding Contemporary Ireland*, 236–248.

51. Una Crowley, Mary Gilmartin, and Rob Kitchin, "Vote Yes for Common Sense Citizenship: Immigration and the Paradoxes at the Heart of Ireland's 'Cead Mile Failte,'" *NIRSA Working Papers* 30 (2006): 7–8.

52. Ronit Lentin and Robbie McVeigh, *After Optimism? Ireland, Racism and Globalisation* (Dublin: Metro Eireann Publications, 2006). Also see their earlier work, *Racism and Anti-racism in Ireland* (Belfast: Beyond the Pale, 2002). It is important to note, however, that in the midst of growing racism, a Nigerian immigrant was elected mayor of an Irish town, Ireland's first major Black official. See "African Mayor, Irish Town," *Irish Voice*, August 22, 2007, 6.

53. Crowley, Gilmartin, and Kitchin, "Vote Yes," 7–8.

54. Mac Einri, "Immigration," 238–239.

55. Steve Loyal, "Welcome to the Celtic Tiger: Racism, Immigration and the State," in *The End of Irish History: Critical Reflections on the Celtic Tiger*, ed. Colin Coulter and Steve Coleman (Manchester: Manchester University Press, 2003), 77–78.

56. Crowley, Gilmartin, and Kitchin, "Vote Yes," 15–17; Eithne Lubheid, "Childbearing against the State? Asylum Seeker Women in the Irish Republic," *Women's Studies International Forum* 27 (2004): 339, 343.

57. "Dail Sees Heated Scenes over Citizenship Vote," *Irish Times*, April 7, 2004, www.irishtimes.com/newspaper/breaking/2004/0407/breaking27.html; "Harney Defends Decision to Hold Citizenship Vote," *Irish Times*, April 8, 2004, www.irishtimes.com/newspaper/ireland/2004/0408/1079399171037.html; "Morrison Terms Poll on Citizenship Dangerous," *Irish Times*, April 14, 2004, www.irishtimes.com/newspaper/frontpage/2004/0414/1079399180553.html; "Ireland for Irish Americans," *Irish Voice*, October 10, 2007, 12; Lentin and McVeigh, *After Optimism?*, 37; J. M. Mancini and Graham Finlay, "Citizenship Matters: Lessons from the Irish Citizenship Referendum," *American Quarterly* 60, no. 3 (September 2008): 575–599.

58. Crowley, Gilmartin, and Kitchin, "Vote Yes," 19; Bryan Fanning and Fidele Mutwarasibo, "Nationals/Non-nationals: Immigration, Citizenship and Politics in the Republic of Ireland," *Ethnic and Racial Studies* 30, no. 3 (May 2007): 439–460.

59. "Families Unite at ILIR Dublin Rally," *Irish Voice*, April 18, 2007, 3; "ILIR Goes Home," *Irish Echo*, April 18, 2007, 5; "Families of the Undocumented Rally in Dublin," *Irish Voice*, November 7, 2007, 3.

60. "Irish Illegals Not a Special Case," *Irish Times*, November 16, 2007, 16; Niall O'Dowd's response, "The Irish Are a Long Way from Galas and Golf," *Irish Times*, November 20, 2007, 16; "Uproar over Illegal Irish Comments," *Irish Voice*, November 21, 2007, 3.

61. "No Sympathy for U.S. Illegals," *Irish Voice*, March 8, 2006, 18; "Ahern Talks Visas with Pols," *Irish Voice*, October 10, 2007, 4; "Minister Explores 'Deal' with US over Migrants," *Irish Times*, November 24, 2006, 10; Muzaffar Chishti and Claire Bergeron, "Bipartisan Measures Urge Use of a Temporary Worker Program to Admit Irish Immigrants," *Migration Policy Institute*, March 15, 2012, http://www.migrationinformation.org/usfocus/display.cfm?ID=885; "Some Countries Lobby for More in Race for Visas," *New York Times*, May 12, 2013, A1.

62. "Irish Leader Says Comprehensive Reform Likely Dead," *Irish Voice*, May 6, 2011, http://www.irishcentral.com/news/Irish-leader-says-comprehensive-immigration-reform-likely-dead-121378094.html; "200,000 Will Emigrate from Ireland by 2015," *Irish Voice*, July 22, 2010, http://www.irishcentral.com/news/200000-will-emigrate-from-Ireland-by-2015-99001249.html; "Top Choices for Emigrants: Australia and Canada," *Irish Voice*, December 29, 2009; http://www.irishcentral.com/news/Top-choices-for-Irish-emigrants-Australia-and-Canada-80258512.html; "Irish Immigrants Replenish Irish Ambience of N.Y. Enclave," *New York Times*, March 11, 2011, A21; "Murphy New Chair of ILIR," *Irish Voice*, March 10, 2009, http://www.irishcentral.com/news/Murphy-New-Chair-of-ILIR-4279.html.

NOTES TO CONCLUSION

1. "The Reality of Moving Back," *Irish Voice*, January 23, 2008, 4.

2. "Returning Irish Warned about Welfare," *Irish Voice*, February 13, 2008, 8; "The Habitual Residence Condition," Republic of Ireland, Department of Social and Family Affairs, http://www.welfare.ie/publications/sw108.html/.

3. Black Immigrants Say They Are Now under Siege in Ireland," *Irish Voice*, November 26, 2011, http://www.irishcentral.com/news/Black-immigrants-say-they-are-now-under-siege-in-Ireland—134526888.html; Mary P. Corcoran, "The Process of Migration and the Reinvention of Self: The Experiences of Returning Irish Emigrants," in *New Directions in Irish-American History*, ed. Kevin Kenny (Madison: University of Wisconsin Press, 2003), 302–318. A larger research project is currently under way to document the oral histories of return migrants in Ireland. "Narratives of Migration and Return, "http://migration.ucc.ie/nmr/index.html.

4. Bill Rolston, "Bringing It Back Home: Irish Emigration and Racism," *Race and Class*, 45, no. 2 (October–December 2003): 39–53.

5. "McLean Avenue Merchants Plan Inaugural St. Patrick's Day Parade," *Journal News*, February 2, 2012, http://www.lohud.com/apps/pbcs.dll/article?AID=2012302120052; "Newest St. Patrick's Day Parade in America a Huge Success," *Irish Voice*, March 26, 2012, http://www.irishcentral.com/news/Newest-St-Patricks-Day-Parade-in-America-a-huge-success-VIDEO-144194255.html.

ABOUT THE AUTHOR

Jennifer Nugent Duffy is Associate Professor of History at Western Connecticut State University in Danbury, Connecticut.